Themes in
Speculative Psychology

Themes in
Speculative Psychology

NEHEMIAH JORDAN

TAVISTOCK PUBLICATIONS
London . New York . Sydney . Toronto . Wellington

First published in 1968
by Tavistock Publications Limited
11 New Fetter Lane, London E.C.4
and printed in Great Britain
in 10pt Times, 2pt leaded
by Camelot Press, Southampton
© *Nehemiah Jordan 1968*

1·1
SBN 422 73020 3

Distributed in the USA
by Barnes & Noble Inc.

Science is rooted in the will to truth. With the will to truth it stands or falls. Lower the standard even slightly and science becomes diseased at the core. Not only science, but man. The will to truth, pure and unadulterated, is among the essential conditions of his existence; if the standard is compromised he easily becomes a kind of tragic caricature of himself.

MAX WERTHEIMER, On Truth
(*Social Research*, 1934, vol. 1, p. 135)

Contents

Acknowledgements

Thanks are due to the publishers concerned for permission to quote from the following works:

Cambridge University Press in respect of *What is Life?* by Erwin Schrödinger; Routledge & Kegan Paul in respect of *Ideology and Utopia* by Karl Mannheim; and G. & C. Merriam Company in respect of *Webster's New International Dictionary*, *Webster's New Collegiate Dictionary*, and *Webster's Dictionary of Synonyms*.

1

Overview

It can be said that American academic psychology, that is, scientific psychology, finds itself in a crisis. In almost whatever area it is applied, it doesn't seem to work too well.

Some months ago I was talking to two senior engineers who were responsible for a major project for the Government. The discussion devolved upon the role of psychologists, specifically human engineering, in contributing towards design and development. At this, one of the engineers announced somewhat heatedly that since Government contracts demand that human engineers be included in the design and development stages he hires them. Pausing, he relaxed and added that it's really not too bad – they ask for a laboratory and he gives them one and by the time they get through with whatever they do there, generally the design is over and development is so far ahead that they cannot do any damage.

This is obviously unfair to the human engineering profession as a profession, but it indicates an attitude or mood which is spreading, and the mood is not arbitrary but based upon hard and sad experience. The laboratory as a tool that leads to useful knowledge is not as successful as had been hoped. In other areas of academic psychology, clinical, social, and educational, the failure of the laboratory is even more pronounced. It is difficult to point to anything coming from laboratory research which has withstood the pragmatic test of real-life usage.

The blame for this situation does not lie with the laboratory *per se*; the laboratory is only a tool, and a tool cannot be blamed for its ineffectiveness – only the tool-user can be blamed for its ineffectiveness.

Until World War II there was comparatively little so-called 'applied psychology' in the United States. For close to fifty years, since Titchener's establishing himself as the 'dean' of scientific psychologists in the United States, almost all academic thinking and research in psychology was restricted to a university setting and concerned with abstract theorizing. Although the behaviourist revolution did successfully sweep most of Titchener's substantive research and thinking from the psychological scene, his depreciation of 'applied psychology' as against the 'pure science' of psychology came through unscathed. It is perhaps the only one of his ideas which had a lasting effect upon American academic psychological thinking and research. In order to justify and guide this thinking and research, a methodology based upon the statistical analysis of 'measurements' of the behaviour obtained in a psychological laboratory, and an epistemology based upon one or another form of philosophical positivism, developed with time.

With World War II, and especially in the period following it, psychology 'emerged' from the university and began to apply itself to real-life problems. Although the discipline at the outset did make some notable contributions, especially in human engineering and in testing, it soon seemed to fall into a rut and the contributions have become fewer and farther between. One major reason for its poor performance may be the rather uncritical carry-over of traditional methodology and epistemology as a guide for psychologists in their new work. At the outset, the limitations of this carry-over were not evident, the traditional methodology being adequate for investigating human behavioural abilities, the rather restricted area where 'applied psychology' made its initial notable contributions. But the tradition appears to be inadequate for coping with problems of motivation, cognition, and meaning – problems which were, on the whole, neglected by the academic investigators despite the fact that they may have used these words to denote some of their interests. And unfortunately for 'applied' psychology, more and more of the problems confronting it do involve problems in motivation, cognition, and meaning.

It is not that facts are lacking; if anything we are overwhelmed with facts, we have far too many facts at our disposal. What seems to be needed are new ways of processing the facts, new ways of *thinking* about the facts, perhaps in conjunction with a revival of some of the older, neglected ways of thinking about psychological facts as well. Indeed, it may be more correct to assert that what is needed is to *start* thinking about the facts, the hard stubborn facts which surround us daily and with which we all have to cope.

Academic psychology has defined the role of science to be the attainment of predictions, preferably in numbers, to be achieved by the application of the proper methodology consisting of sophisticated experimental design and sophisticated statistical analysis. With rare exceptions the professional journals in psychology have restricted themselves to the publication of 'substantive' contributions, i.e. experimental results devoted almost exclusively to methodological discussions. Somewhere in the shuffle a simple and straightforward discussion of psychological problems and psychological issues has been lost. Science has been equated to methodology while ideas about things as such have been relegated to the 'garbage heap' of metaphysics.

When one ceases to think about the phenomena one ostensibly studies and concentrates almost exclusively upon ersatz problems, be they methodology or anything else; one discovers difficulties in thinking clearly in general. How else can one explain the almost universal uncritical acceptance of the definition of science as prediction? It makes no sense. If there were any substance to this definition we would be unable to differentiate science from magic – successful magic predicts. The argument that magic cannot predict is not well taken. Even though we may not believe in magic, i.e. when we accept the proposition: *magic cannot predict*, to be true, we still properly use the word 'magic' to characterize aspects of empirical situations, whereas to denote those same aspects by the word 'science' would be improper. Are wrong scientific theories, i.e. those that do not predict, indistinguishable from magic? It follows that, at the very least, science is prediction plus something else.

An even stronger case can be made against the role of prediction for science. It can be demonstrated in a psychologically convincing manner that science can exist and thrive in the absence of all need for prediction. For this, imagination must be used.

Imagine the green man from Mars coming in his space-ship and giving us the gift we have all been looking for – the perfect computer. The computer is an unopenable black box with two slots, one for inputting the questions and the other for outputting empirical pre-dictions of observable events. Perfect prediction is achieved. Does this toll the death knell for science? Not at all. The scientists of the existing disciplines will be compelled to try to figure out why the predictions are correct. And a new science will undoubtedly develop to try to answer the most burning question of them all. The name of this science will be a Graeco-Latin neologism which will mean: 'How the hell does this damn black box work?'

4 · *Themes in speculative psychology*

Prediction is a very useful outcome of contemporary science and a very useful means for checking and verifying scientific thinking; it also gives man a fantastic control over his environment, but it is not *the* essential aspect, nor even *an* essential aspect of science. Science is an attempt to order the world, to make sense of the world, to explain the world. Prediction and control that make no sense are magic, not science. There are quite a few disciplines with little if any predictive value that are considered to be sciences, e.g. philosophy, evolution, history, etc. Actually the queen of sciences, mathematics, is really not predictive either.

The core meaning of the word 'science' refers to its essence, its role in explaining the connection between two or more events which leads to understanding. By virtue of speaking English we have internalized this core meaning and we intuit it even though we may not be explicitly aware of it. Therefore, it makes no intuitive sense when 'science' is defined 'wrongly' in terms of prediction rather than of understanding. As a result of this 'senseless' definition of science, we have become slaves to our methodology without being able to check whether it itself makes sense or not. And we therefore find ourselves confronted with a science of psychology that really doesn't make much sense either, which explains very little, and which devotes most of its effort to discovering 'magical' formulas which predict. Shades of the philosopher's stone.

Sense must be brought back into psychology!

2

The need, above all, to make sense to myself struck me very strongly several years ago. I had, for some time, been working for a corporation which 'applied' psychological knowledge to the training of large and complex military man–machine systems. Hundreds of professionals, the majority of them being psychologists with advanced degrees, were engaged in this training programme. Literally hundreds of professional man-years of effort were invested in overcoming the difficulties and solving the many problems which were met with in implementing the training programme. The result of this effort was quite an effective training technique plus a rich experience in the implementation of this technique. Much that was valuable was learned from this both for training in general and for psychology.

Yet almost nothing was published in the literature to impart to the professional world at large, as well as to others who might have been interested in the subject, the lessons to be learned from this vast pool of experience and accomplishment. It wasn't that the people involved were not interested in sharing their knowledge with the professional world; on the contrary, this was one of their most sincere desires – most of them were trained academic psychologists and had accepted the values and aspirations of academic psychology of which publication is central. Perhaps the most single frustrating aspect of the job for a large number of these professionals was their inability to get something down on paper of which they could be proud and which would reflect the many unique things they had to contribute as a result of their experience. But when it came to writing they acted as if they were paralysed.

I remember arguing, both in writing and orally, that this should not be tolerated, that we had much to contribute, not only from a practical standpoint, but from a theoretical standpoint as well. It was inconceivable that the thinking-through of the rich experience available to that body of professionals would not yield to theoretical insights. But I was not successful. Two somewhat contradicting arguments, often enunciated by the same person, generally emerged, blocking movement in this direction. The first argument was that it is not possible to write for professional publications unless the paper consists of results couched in an accepted theoretical framework, results which were the product of laboratory experimentation or, at a lower level of respectability, the product of carefully planned and administered field research. There is much truth in this argument as anyone who has interacted with the editors of the very great majority of professional psychological publications well knows. But what is relevant in the present context is that the people who invoked this argument accepted this state of affairs as being proper – they did not question it. The second argument was that the theory and research techniques taught in the graduate schools and practised by academic psychology did not apply to the work being done in the corporation. This argument is sort of belated vindication of an acid critique levelled against academic psychology years earlier by Karl Mannheim, a critique claiming that its conceptual categories are of such a nature that they do not enable the psychologist to think through the simplest life processes. What seemed to elude everybody's notice is that if the second argument is correct then the state of affairs underlying the first argument is unjustified; a situation perpetuating the divorce of scientific theory from reality is not proper.

The whole thing didn't make sense. When man is confronted with a situation that does not make sense, spontaneous and voluntary behaviour is greatly inhibited; people find it difficult to act when confronted with nonsense. With this realization the paralysis mentioned earlier began to make sense – the professionals in the corporation could not really write under these conditions. The professional in the corporation could act either as an intelligent practitioner or as a scientist – given the accepted academic definition of science – but he could not act, simultaneously, as both. Even worse, in good conscience he could not consciously transfer that which he learned as a practitioner to science and vice versa; but neither could he do otherwise. Hence, the paralysing inner conflict.

Sense can only be obtained by thinking issues through. All the experience in the world, be it in a laboratory, controlled field research, or that too neglected area of what happens to us during our waking day, cannot make sense unless it is thought through, unless it is submitted to speculation, to reflection, and again to speculation. This the professionals in the corporation just could not do, neither in writing for external or internal corporate publications, nor in the privacy of their own mind as it exhibited itself in informal discussions, bull-sessions, or brainstorming. It was fascinating to listen to the internal informal discussions of these professionals. Here were highly trained and able persons who were almost continuously confronted with serious problems of training and administration, who successfully solved many of them and learned much from their experiences, both successes and failures, yet who couldn't make the jump to speculate what all this has to do with the science of psychology, the science of human behaviour.

It is true that unbridled speculation has had its excesses and that thought, running wild, is not much better than anything else that runs wild. Along with much of the rest of science, psychology has reacted strongly to the empirically undisciplined thinking that characterized sophistic and scholastic studies of days gone by. But observing the difficulties which professionals have in thinking through even the most simple issues, observing the sloppy logic, the lack of logic, yes, even the illogic which passes for theoretical thinking in contemporary psychological publications, one cannot but suspect that the baby has been thrown out with the bathwater.

It was while wrangling with such thoughts that a paragraph flashed through my mind. I took the liberty of writing it down and it fits the present context:

When man was primitive he often cut off his hand when it sinned, all the good deeds accomplished and accomplishable by the hand to the contrary. Something similar seems to take place nowadays. Thought has at times led man into blind alleys, so we tend to punish it, to exile it. One aspect of the training meted out in contemporary modern education is a trained incapacity to think freely. Rather, our students are trained to apply well-tried, scientifically approved techniques and to rely more and more upon mechanical gadgets for problem-solving. Despite the dissimilarities in external accoutrements, is there really that much difference between us and primitive man?

3

With this realization, the need to think freely struck me quite strongly. A decision, rather long in developing, crystallized suddenly. Henceforth, were I to be confronted with a conflict between science, as currently defined and practised, and sense, I would choose the latter. Henceforth, I would not formally assert anything or write anything unless it made sense to me. This did not mean that I was rejecting science *a priori*; it did mean that I would reject those aspects of science that did not make sense to me. And there was much in scientific psychology that was found to be senseless and I had to reject, but much came through with flying colours.

The decision yielded an immediate pay-off; I found that I could think issues through and reach conclusions which were really experienced as a personal advance forward. This was very satisfying. I found that when confronted with problems the corporation groped with, I did come up with solutions which worked when applied, even though the more rigorous research that followed the academic scheme yielded little. But what was most exciting, I found that I could write. After thinking, wrangling, and speculating about a problem or issue and coming up with a subjectively satisfying solution, I found that in addition to the solution I had an outline for a short paper or essay in my mind as well. All that remained was to write it down. Generally, the outline was quite detailed so that all I had to do was write it out, but it was also often the case that the outline was sparse and I did not, at the outset, know what I had specifically to say; I did know, however, or to be more precise, I felt that once I started to write, the essay would write itself. And this was the rule. There was no problem concerning problems. I was surrounded with them and the task was to choose among them. This I left to intuition, assuming that the problem I would end up with, without

B

explicitly choosing, would be the one that is actually the most important for my purposes and inner development.*

This is how I found myself writing these various essays. In a way they are dialogues with myself. They are not finished expositions of an explicated point of view, neither are they a simple record of the process of my attempts to make sense by thinking issues through. Rather they are more like an attempt to verify a thinking-through process to see whether the sense achieved stands up to scrutiny. As I just noted, a more or less detailed outline of an essay would emerge into my consciousness as a result of prior thinking, wrangling, and speculating; each outline being a rounded-out treatment of the problem in question. I felt that the outline made sense and in order to prove to myself that it did, I had to write it out. If it could be written out, and then stood up when being reread, closure and sense were achieved and I lost interest in the specific problem. Not all that was written withstood this test; obviously I feel that all the essays included in this collection did.

As the essays were turned out they were privately printed by the RAND Corporation and distributed among friends and colleagues. I was pleasantly surprised to find that these rather personal 'dialogues' found a responsive audience. With the wisdom of hindsight one wonders why the surprise; after all, what makes sense to any man should make sense to every man – but that is the weakness of the wisdom of hindsight, it projects the clarity and simplicity achieved through the solution, to the problem itself, thereby obscuring what was accomplished by the solution. The fact that colleagues, including many who disagreed and still disagree with the opinions expressed in the papers they read, found them to be interesting and often exciting, has encouraged me to hope that a wider audience will also find them so.

4

As was just mentioned, these essays were all written as a terminal stage of a process whereby I sought to make personal sense of problems that forced themselves to my attention. They were written during a period of two years. Upon rereading them I find that, although each essay was written independently as a result of my pre-

* In working for the RAND Corporation I found myself in the enviable position of not only being permitted to write these essays when I felt ready to do so, but rather encouraged to do so.

occupation with a specific problem, they nevertheless form a coherent whole. Underlying them I find a consistent thought model that is applied to the various problems – I was tempted to write 'theoretical model' instead of 'thought model' but rejected the phrase because the word 'theory' has too many pretentious nuances to its meaning.

I suppose that basically the model is theoretical, but it is a 'low-level' theory to be spelled with a very small 't'. It is theoretical because it involves a relatively small set of concepts that are found to apply to a rather wide array of psychological problems; ultimately theoretical analysis is such a conceptual analysis. The theory is low-level theory because all concepts are, at least so it seems to me, anchored immediately to common sense, or to the phenomenal world (I consider these two terms to be psychologically equivalent). Theories become 'high-level' to the extent that it takes at least more than one step to get back from them to common sense. The theory is spelled with a very small 't' because no attempt is made either to explain everything or to predict anything. And no attempt whatsoever is made to become hypothetico-deductive – although it seems that at present no social scientist can 'arrive' unless he formulates his own little hypothetico-deductive theory that has been demonstrated to hold statistically in a selected set of experiments conducted by him.

It isn't that I am against hypothetico-deductive theories. In principle I am all for them, though I do have my doubts whether I would like to live to see one formulated that is applicable to human beings. It is a crowning achievement of a science when it develops a hypothetico-deductive theory to account for the phenomena in which it is interested. The theory then serves as a magnificent pent-house for it to reside in. But a pent-house is on top of a high building which contains many humbler dwellings on the lower floors and hopefully rests upon a solid foundation.

What I rebel against is this mad rush for formulating theories. The humbler dwellings and the foundations for the pent-house theory are built by hundreds of researchers who seek solutions that make sense to 'limited' problems which interest them. Given enough of this effort some one researcher, somewhat luckier and, perhaps, somewhat more intelligent than the average, is vouchsafed the insight of a general pattern underlying this work – and a significant theory is born. We really ought not expect more than one or two theories a generation. Theories seems to have qualities reminiscent of Maeterlinck's bluebird – the more strenuously they are sought for, the more difficult they become to find.* The dictum attributed to Lao-Tze that he who walks last comes first seems to apply to this context quite well.

I have not sought to spell this model out explicitly in all its details (this is often a euphemism for inability and may very well be so in the present case). It is nice to think that there are positive reasons for not spelling the model out. Were I to do so, and were I successful, it would become the focus of attention, whether worthy of it or not, and would change into the kind of theory I am trying to avoid. People would accept it or reject it and worst of all, from my viewpoint, they would get busy setting up crucial experiments to demonstrate the correctness of their viewpoints, before bothering to think it through. There is another reason for not trying to spell out the model. I have already pointed out that too many of our academically trained psychologists find it difficult to indulge in untrammelled speculation and in thinking issues through. This difficulty is not due to inability but rather to fear of violating social strictures and of trying out 'something new'. I have found the process to be stimulating, exciting, and intellectually rewarding. To the extent that I managed to 'capture' these emotions in the papers, it may induce others to do the same. It would therefore be self-defeating to spell the model out. I am convinced that psychology as a discipline cannot but benefit from such a development.

5

One final comment. It was necessary to edit the essays for this volume for several reasons. First, redundancies had to be eliminated and there were quite a few. Since most of the papers were basically first drafts, the language had to be sharpened in quite a few places. And finally, some had to be expanded since they presumed certain knowledge which was commonplace among the professionals to which they were addressed but is not well known to the public at large. There was no polishing up or rounding out for its own sake. Every effort was made to retain the spontaneity, personal involvement, fervour, or – if you wish – crudity, of the original drafts.

* I do not consider the so-called scientific theories which are really theologies in scientific garb.

2

On the nature of simplicity

Nothing is objectively simple or complex except that man makes it so. This is the reason that philosophers and scientists who seek an objective denotation for 'simplicity' are bound to fail. There isn't any.

Simplicity is intimately related to understanding. Whenever a person cries out in relief: 'Aha! now I understand what is going on', it indicates that what he previously experienced as a complex mess has suddenly made at least one quantum jump towards simplicity.* The fact that often, upon reflection, the person may later find that he was wrong, that his solution does not hold, is irrelevant in this context.

Perhaps the best example of the close connection between simplicity and understanding is that butt of so much humour directed at mathematicians, the concept of 'mathematical obviousness'. When a mathematician asserts, after hours of hard thinking and after filling pages with mathematical expressions, that the transformation of one statement to another statement is obvious, he isn't kidding. All his labour led him to understand how the transformation is effected; once he understood the transformation it became obvious; and 'obvious' is a pretty close synonym to 'simple'. For him to assert, after all this work, that the transformation is not obvious would be psychologically false.

Mathematics offers us another interesting example to ponder over as to the complexity of 'simple' when we consider the concept of 'mathematical elegance'. When there are several distinct but equivalent mathematical proofs, that proof which has less steps and/or utilizes less theorems is considered to be the more elegant. Some philosophers have used this as an argument to equate simplicity with

* The term 'quantum jump' is used deliberately. The 'aha' is experienced as an instantaneous change of state; as an emergence from darkness to more light.

less numbers or entities. But as Wertheimer [1] points out, quite convincingly, in his penetrating discussion of the discovery of the Gaussian theorem on the summation of a series, an elegant mathematical proof can be quite complex and difficult to understand, albeit easy to follow. And, for the student at any rate, when this is the case, it is the less elegant proof, when all is said and done, which is really simpler.

It follows, therefore, and this holds for planning for research as well as for any other human activity, that simplicity *as such* cannot be a goal, or better still, is a chimerical goal with all the characteristics of the end of a rainbow. The goal of planning is to find a solution to a clearly formulated problem. To the extent that the solution is adequate and meaningful, i.e. the problem-solver understands why it is adequate, it necessarily becomes simple.

REFERENCE

[1] WERTHEIMER, MAX, *Productive Thinking*. Revised edition, Harper, New York, 1959; Tavistock Publications, London, 1961.

3

On looking at the obvious

Several days after the publication of an internal note by B.T.J., 'Some Crew Development Ideas', I was shown the following critique via internal corporation mail. It is a rather novel form of professional critique in two ways. First, it is unsigned. Secondly, although it is obviously aimed at professional readers at large, it is a hand-typed and written copy and there is reason to doubt that anyone but the anonymous writer, B.T.J., and the few people B.T.J. showed it to, have seen it. But since the problem posed in the critique is important, I think it is worth while to present the critique to the professional body within the corporation* for their consideration and then attempt to answer it to some extent.

The critique bears no title and is reproduced below verbatim:

> We were perusing some 'incunabula' a few days back when we came accross (sic) a fine specimen by a Mr. J.
>
> Mr. J. had gone to a great deal of trouble to tell us that when a group of people has to do something, the personalities of the individuals within the group will interact and affect the solution that the group will use to do the 'something'. Since there are so many 'personalities' that the combinations of such approach infinity, the number of solutions is limited only by the environment and some of the previous experience that the individuals might have with it. Even when such a large number of solutions occur, it is possible to rank them according to any criteria we might set up such as efficiency or speed of performance of the task to be accomplished. We will find then that, according to these criteria, some solutions are preferable to others. The factors that lead to the development of each solution are such that when it becomes desirable to lead the group into changing the solution, we find it a difficult task. So difficult, in fact, that we as yet have not been able to even analyse what factors there are. However, Mr. J. feels that one

* Not the RAND Corporation.

of them seems to be that the group's solution is that one that takes least effort for the group, regardless of how inefficient it may seem to an outsider, and therefore, the group thinks it impossible to improve upon it.

Now, if all this seems to be a major breakthrough to you, you should go pat Mr. J's back, or at least shake hands with him, since he thinks so too. We will sit here, busy, as we are keeping up with our medieval manuscript readings.

There are several specific and one general professional issue raised by this critique. The specific issues relate to the adequacy of this critique of B.T.J.'s paper. I do not care to go into this. Those of the readers who are interested in this can read the paper and judge for themselves. I would, however, like to question some of the implications of the last paragraph of the critique. Must everything a professional writes be interpreted as having to be a major breakthrough, and then be judged as to whether it is so or not? Shouldn't there be room for professionals to write down their ideas on a subject just by virtue of the fact that the ideas interest the writers at the time and, as such, they may be of interest to other colleagues? I, for one, have often found the free association of a colleague just as exciting as his most reasoned presentation, and sometimes even more so. Only those who have something to hide are afraid to let themselves or others think out loud, figuratively to parade their nakedness.

The general professional issue is a very important one. It refers to the fact that the epithet 'obvious' all too often acts as a 'kiss of death' for promising research and thought. To a certain degree almost anything we can know about human relations is obvious. Every competent group leader or educator must know it – either implicitly or explicitly. Otherwise, how could he be successful? But it does not follow that the student of human behaviour should, therefore, neglect the obvious, refuse to study it, and/or be afraid to write about it, be afraid to point it out.

Many arguments have been raised in defence of thinking about the obvious. Inherently, one of the least important, though socially often a most effective argument that can be raised is that this procedure has been OK'd by recognized authorities in the social sciences and philosophy of science.*

---

* In *Science and the Modern World* [1] Whitehead says that one who recognizes the importance of investigating the obvious is a rare intelligence. In his review of Kurt Lewin's book, *Field Theory in Social Science* [2], Isidor Chein writes [3]: 'Ever since my first contacts with Lewin's writings and, toward the end of his life, with Lewin himself, I have been deeply impressed with three interlocking facets of his extraordinary genius any one of which would have been sufficient to number him among the immortals of

But I propose to defend it in a more substantive manner.

One argument against investigating the obvious does not deny the importance of the obvious. It is based on the success of the physical sciences that followed their breaking away from the Aristotelian focus on the phenomenal given and their concentrating on 'pure' or ideal cases which lead to the formulation of concepts whose conceptual properties are known and whose systematic relations with other concepts are explicit. In physics one does not speak of *weight*, one speaks of *mass*. Weight is a variant, contingent property of physical objects – things weigh less in water than they do in the air – while mass is an invariant systematic property of these identical objects. Of course, *weight* is intimately connected to *mass*, it having served as the phenomenal datum that led to the formulation of systematic concept. To use the clearer language of symbolic logic, it can be asserted that 'weight' is the explicandum of 'mass'. The argument then proceeds that scientific language should consist of systematic concepts rather than of the unsystematic names of phenomenal entities. In other words, to be of any scientific use, the obvious must be reformulated into a conceptual system.

I accept this argument wholeheartedly and only wish that I could do it. If only there were an adequate conceptual system available for such a reformulation. Unfortunately, in the field of social psychology such a conceptual system is simply not available. The use of so-called scientific terms is generally an act of *renaming*, rather than an act of explication. It is reminiscent of primitive renaming to avoid an evil eye. The sentence, 'He is motivated to achieve X.', carries no more meaning that the sentence, 'He wishes to do X.', because the word 'motivation' is not any more conceptually clear than is the word 'wish'.

The use of scientific cant, under these conditions, is ego-gratifying. It hides ignorance from the laity and plays the role that the academic gown played in the Middle Ages, i.e. it is a sign that the user has had a higher education. But it also cloaks the obvious, and therein lies its danger. By cloaking the obvious it also tends to blind us to the obvious. When all is said and done, science is ultimately a special kind of explanation of the obvious, of the phenomenal given. Hence, by blinding ourselves to the obvious, we effectively retard the progress of science. Let us, by all means, strive to use concepts instead of mere words, but let us not delude ourselves that just because we *call* a word a concept, it is so.

social science. First, there was his singular talent for discerning the significant obvious – obvious and obviously significant, that is, once people like Lewin have pointed it out.'

A second argument against the investigation of the obvious is far more prevalent in psychology, either tacitly or explicitly, and is far more pernicious. Its clearest enunciation is in unimaginative orthodox Freudian theory in terms of manifest and latent context. The manifest content of a behaviour event, i.e. the obvious, is proscribed *ex cathedra*. It is of importance only to the extent that it leads one to the latent context, the 'real' reality. Hence, we find that so much of the data presented in clinical literature comes from the couch. It is only in this setting that the blinding effects of the manifest seem to be overcome. One is reminded of classical psychology's distinction between *Kundgabe* and *Beschreibung*.

Learning psychology, the mainstay of American academia, despite its vigorous verbal opposition to Freudianism in its many forms shares this basic attitude. The manifold appearance of the obvious is not true. It but hides and obscures the real process which underlies all behaviour, the process of reinforcement. Most respectable textbooks in introductory psychology warn the beginning student that in matters of psychology, the obvious is to be eschewed.

But if our thoughts on psychology cannot be based on the obvious, on the phenomenal given, upon what can they be based? Upon prediction? But we have no prediction. The significant correlations which abound in our literature are worthless as predictive indices. How are we to judge the substantiality of our theories and arguments? Isn't it possible that they are as substantial as that classic problem which involved the church fathers, the substantiality of angels and how many of them could dance on the point of a needle? This is the pernicious effect of the rejection of the obvious. Perhaps Freudian theory and/or learning theory are more substantial, but, excluding personal faith, on what basis can we know this?

Hence, let us not eschew the obvious, but accept it wholeheartedly and study it carefully to see whereto it leads. We may not know where we will end up, but we can reasonably be sure that it can be a worthwhile attempt.

At this point, a warning can be levelled at us. All you will end up with will be a set of platitudes, truisms, and/or trivialities. In other words, how do you know that what you will come up with is relevant to significant problems of social science? The essence of creative scientific research is relevance. It seems to us that in this argument we are forewarned not to be stupid. We will certainly try our best not to be stupid. And if it turns out that we were not successful in this attempt, we will have the satisfaction of knowing that we do not hide our stupidity behind a mess of cant but expose it honestly and openly for all to see, and to criticize productively. The behavioural sciences will be 'saved' when their knowledge and theories are organically related to the obvious.

REFERENCES

[1] WHITEHEAD, A. N., *Science and the Modern World*. Cambridge University Press, Cambridge, 1953.
[2] LEWIN, KURT, *Field Theory in Social Science*. Harper, New York; Tavistock Publications, London, 1951.
[3] CHEIN, ISIDOR, Review of [2] in *Int. J. Opn. Att. Res.*, 1951–52, **5**, 562–3.

4

Perception, cognition, and science*

1. INTRODUCTION

It is to Brunswik's credit to have formulated the most articulate description of what must take place in the perceptual process. That this description is veridical seems to be indicated by the fact that it is independent of existing psychological theories and of epistemological postulates as to how man knows what he knows or as to what science is. It seems difficult to conceive that this description will be found to be incorrect in the future, though, of course, it is to be expected that with the increase of factual knowledge and conceptual sophistication many additional details may be added to it. The power of this description is such that it can be used to develop a chain of thought that is in many ways in opposition to Brunswik's assumptions concerning knowledge and science. Such a development will be attempted in this paper.

The paper is frankly discursive and speculative, and does not pretend to be either operationally or logically rigorous. Although much of the tone of contemporary psychology is still determined by the revolt against the sterile, unbridled speculation which was so characteristic of much thinking called 'psychological' in the years gone by, too much of a good thing also is undesirable. Bridled speculation and casual discourse can play a desirable role on the contemporary scene.

2. THE BRUNSWIK PERCEPTUAL MODEL AS APPLIED TO 'SIMPLE' PERCEPTION

Brunswik asserts that the perceptual process entails five discriminable

* The extent to which I am indebted to Heider rather than to Brunswik for much of what I have to say here about perception is inestimable. But because both Brunswik

aspects. First, an object which, following Heider, I call: 'the distal stimulus', must exist in physical space. The necessity for the existence of a distal stimulus can easily be demonstrated at the risk of sounding trite or trivial; when the distal stimulus is removed the perceiver does not see it any more. Perception starts with a distal stimulus as a first step.

The light reflected from the object through space proceeds until it hits the eye, the sense organ. This is a mechanical mediating process in a physical environment, i.e. a form of physical mediation, and constitutes the second aspect of the process. The necessity of this aspect can also be tritely demonstrated – when an opaque screen that blocks the movement of light is placed between the object and the eye, the object is no longer seen.

The physical mediation then impinges upon the sensorium in a definite pattern; in the case of seeing, this pattern is primarily spatial; in the case of hearing, it is temporal. This pattern, transformed by the sense organ into a physiological nerve process constitutes the third aspect in the process; again following Heider, I call it 'the proximal stimulus'. As Ames, among others, has strikingly demonstrated, by controlling the proximal stimulus it is possible to get people to see literal absurdities.

Once the process 'enters' the person, it becomes much more speculative. Nevertheless, two additional aspects seem to be logical necessities before an object can be perceived. First, a nerve process must be set off by the proximal stimulus and proceed up to the brain – a process which can be called physiological mediation. And finally, there must be some quasi-stationary neural state which we experience as the perceived object. This end state will be denoted by the term: 'phenomenal object'. The bulk of the empirical evidence for these two inner steps rests upon pathological phenomena. Damage to the optic tract, such as hemiamblyopia, creates a blind spot in the visual field very similar to the effect of an opaque screen hiding part of the light streaming to the eye; it is as if the mediation of the nerve process is interfered with. Finally, as Werner, Lehtinen, and Strauss, among others, have demonstrated [13], certain types of brain injury lead to difficulty in segregating a figure from a ground, i.e. the quasi-stationary neural state, the phenomenal object, cannot be firmly established.

The five aspects of the Brunswik model are consequently:

and Heider acknowledged and acknowledge their mutual debt to each other, I feel less ill at ease at not attempting to disentangle and identify what I got from whom.

(1) The distal stimulus,
(2) The physical mediation,
(3) The proximal stimulus,
(4) The physiological mediation,
(5) The quasi-stationary physiological state in the brain.

Since these aspects are sequential, they can also be called steps or stages.

If only a short span of time is taken into account, the process exhibits three stationary aspects and two dynamic aspects, the latter being the two mediating processes. However, if the span of time is increased and either the perceiver or the object is moved, the proximal stimulus, as well as the mediating processes, undergoes noticeable changes. Within broad limits, however, the perceived object does not undergo a change for the adult perceiver. This is the phenomenon of constancy. Under these conditions therefore, only the initial and terminal steps of the perceptual process remain relatively unchanged and the three intermediary steps become dynamic.

Brunswik calls this coupling between the physical object and the quasi-stationary physiological brain state, the phenomenal object – 'the wide-arched dependency'. He calls the initial and terminal steps, the foci of the perceptual process. The three intervening steps become, consequently, the process which mediates between the two foci; hence they are called the mediating processes. In addition, as the constancy phenomena show, many different specific mediating processes result in our perception of the same object, each one being as good as any other one in mediating this perception, i.e. they are interchangeable without noticeable effects. Hence, Brunswik calls them 'vicarious'. Perception can therefore be characterized as a stable relationship between the physical object and the phenomenal object, the foci of the perceptual process, and a vicariously mediating process which connects the two. Brunswik calls the perception of an object: the attainment of the object.*

3. AN ATTEMPT AT SOME EXPLANATION OF 'DISTAL STIMULUS' AND 'VICARIOUS MEDIATION'

What is the distal stimulus? It is the object which we look at. But is this so simple? A person enters a strange room. He notices that it is

---

* Needless to say, this is a simplified presentation of the model. It suffices for the purpose of this paper. The initial schematic formulation of this model is given in Brunswik, 1952, p. 678. An articulated formulation of the model is given in Brunswik, 1956, p. 51 [2, 3].

large, that it is furnished, that it is painted a certain colour, that it has three chairs and one sofa, that one of the chairs has a plastic upholstery, and finally that there is a stain on the upholstery. Of course, he could have noticed many other objects. Another example. A person sees a beautiful house, then he sees that its roof is made of slate, that it has a large picture window and two small windows, and finally that one of the small windows has a cracked pane. Again he could have noticed many different things about the house in many different kinds of order. Everything noticed by this hypothetical person was, in its turn, a distal stimulus, yet at the same time, the stimulus manifold impinging upon the person remained relatively constant.

The fact that the stimulus manifold impinging upon the organism contains no object in itself has long been recognized by perception psychologists. Koffka [10], for instance, in discussing the proximal stimulus, talks about a local stimulus and the total stimulus – the total stimulus referring to the entire energy process acting upon the retina; the local stimulus referring to that part of the energy process which serves as the mediation for the phenomenal object. Rubin's classical research [12] has established the fact that it is improper to speak about an object *per se* in perception, rather one should speak in terms of a figure–ground organization of the total stimulus impinging upon the organism's sensorium, the figure being the object perceived.

It is, however, correct to say that perception psychologists both of the Gestalt and post-Gestalt orientations have neglected the implications of this ability 'voluntarily' to see many different figures. They have concentrated upon the question of how a figure is organized, but not on the fact that the human organism can organize a given proximal stimulus manifold in many different ways. The specific object attended to is not a function of the object only or the external world only, rather it is also determined by an act of the organism in segregating the proximal stimulus manifold in a certain way; had it wanted to, it could have segregated the manifold in different ways. Of course, in the laboratory we psychologists can set up situations where people lose almost all freedom in this respect. When a subject is asked to fixate upon a simple geometrical figure with a homogeneous ground, he generally has little choice. Were we to sample the ecological environment* of the organism, we would be sure to find that many physical objects whose mediational processes

* Brunswik calls the everyday world in which an organism lives, its ecological environment.

impinge upon the sensorium are never perceived as such whereas many phenomenal events that are perceived as objects have no simple physical reality at all, i.e. the dirty lower left corner of a wall.

If the proximal stimulus manifold were considered to be a pie, we would have to admit that the human demonstrates considerable freedom in cutting this pie up. He can cut it up into physical entities of various sizes, he can fuse together several physical entities to see a group, or to complete a figure such as seeing a square when only two parallel sides are given, etc. At the same time, it would also have to be admitted that children and certain brain injured patients, among others, do not show equal facility; they are described as being more or less stimulus bound. For them the pie is much less cut-upable. Their perception is, to a greater degree, bound to macroscopic physical objects and they cannot reorganize the proximal stimulus manifold with the freedom that a normal adult possesses. This ability to cut up the pie in different ways will be called the ability to 'shift figure–ground relations', the phenomenon itself, 'shifting figure–ground relations'.

We summarize therefore that:

(1) Although the distal stimulus has an objective existence, the mere fact that the mediating processes stemming from it impinge upon the sensorium does not mean that it will be perceived as a phenomenal object. In a literal sense, the organism generally determines what it selects to see as a phenomenal object within limits set by the stimulus manifold.

(2) The distal stimulus need not be – although it often is – a physical object that is extended in Locke's sense.

The concept of 'vicarious mediation' has annoyed many and generated opposition, at least verbal, if not in print. One reason for this probably stems from a connotation attached to this word in the most prevalent English usage, vicarious experience, i.e. not a *real* experience but an *ersatz* experience, it being correctly felt that ersatz has no place in science. But the core meaning of 'vicarious' refers to the concept of substitution and as such the word is correctly used in light of Brunswik's definition of the function of perception. As already mentioned, for Brunswik perception is the process whereby the organism attains 'a given distal variable' [3, p. 140]. The organism's 'perfection' in this attainment is measured by a correlation between the objective measurements of the distal variable and either verbal or behavioural actions of the organism specifying those same measurements. Perceptual constancy shows that this correlation remains relatively the same over a wide range of mediating processes; hence, as far as the attainment of the given distal variable is concerned, the perfection of perception is not changed when any of these processes is substituted for any other. Each process can serve as a substitute for each other process without any effect on the attainment. Hence, in the light of the strict meaning of the word, they are vicarious.

Another reason for opposition to the concept can be reduced to a matter of definition. By 'perception' we commonly understand more than the mere attainment of the object; we understand it to include the relation of this object either to the perceiver or to a frame of reference related to the perceiver. In the light of this meaning, the term 'vicarious' becomes improper. Every specific mediational process becomes unique since, in addition to enabling the perceiver to attain the object, it also enables him to attain the distance of the object, its position in a plane relative to the perceiver's body, whether it is under bright or dim illumination, etc. To avoid confusion one should always keep Brunswik's definition of perception in mind when thinking of 'vicarious mediation'.

4. THE RECESSION OF THE DISTAL STIMULUS

The discussion up to now concerned 'simple' perception – the perception of a physical object or state of affairs. The term 'simple' was used because for this type of perception the mediating processes are not perceivable in the same manner as the distal stimulus; in fact, from a naïve, uncritical standpoint, they are invisible. It is this characteristic that underlies the current distinction between perception and inference. Perception is said to take place when the mediating processes are not perceivable; when, to anticipate the argument to be developed immediately, the mediating processes are perceivable, the distal stimulus is no longer said to be perceived but to be inferred. But the matter is not that simple.

Take the example of seeing written words. All English words are constructed by distribution of elements taken from the set of twenty-six letters which constitute the English alphabet. 'Simple' visual perception is constructed by distributions of elements taken from the set of photons. Letters mediate the perception of words just as photons mediate the perception of things. Although the perceiver can see the letters *per se* if he so wishes, he cannot simply see the photons. Nevertheless, the perceiver does not first see the letters and then infer the word.

C

Two arguments can be brought to bear denying the status of mediators for letters. The first can pick up an argument expounded earlier in this paper and say that the relationship between letters and words is similar to the relationship between houses and windows, that it is merely an analogous case of shifting figure–ground relationships. The second can point out that vicariousness is missing in this case, that since there is an univocal connection between a distribution of letters and a given word, it is a simpler matter of learning, that children who have yet to learn to read fluently do in fact spell out each word laboriously.

There is one significant difference between the relationship of houses to windows and words to letters. A window cannot 'mis-spell' a house. This difference is essential. What is mis-spelling? Misspelling seems to be a case of faulty mediation. When one drives along a highway on a hot day one sees the houses, trees, etc., shimmering in front of him. This shimmer is not seen as residing in the distal stimuli, but is attributed to faulty mediation, the photon distribution being affected by the heat waves rising from the roadbed. Brunswik recognizes this in the terms of 'stray effects', and 'stray causes'. Heider [7], in what is probably one of the most interesting papers on the subject, 'Thing and Medium', points out that some media are inherently more faulty than others. Water distorts sound because water particles have poorer mediating properties for sound than do air particles.

The second argument cannot be answered as simply. The relationship of learning and/or meaning to perception will be discussed below. As far as vicariousness is concerned, it is true that letters do not exhibit a kind of substitutability exhibited by the physical mediation processes. But then the argument has just been presented that vicariousness results from a specific definition of the nature of perception and that it disappears when another more commonly accepted definition is substituted. In other words, vicariousness is not a necessary condition for perception. However, it is possible to give examples of perception where parts of the mediating processes are perceivable, yet they exhibit as much substitutability as do the physical processes in 'simple' perception.

A person sits in an office in one of those air-conditioned relatively soundproofed buildings and looks out the window. He turns to a fellow worker and says 'It's quite gusty outside'. The fellow worker is busy writing. Having finished writing, the fellow worker asks 'What did you say?' The person repeats, 'It's quite gusty outside'. Episodes of this nature occur quite frequently and are generally terminated at this point. Were the fellow worker a psychologist or an epistemological philosopher, however, and were he lacking a feeling for the sensibility of the other, he might have asked, 'How do you know?' This question would have been quite confusing. Actually, it makes no sense at its initial impact. The person would feel that his sanity was being doubted and somewhat self-righteously might say 'I looked out the window and saw the wind blowing'. The psychologist/philosopher would now ask with a condescending air of incredibility, 'You can see wind?' This confuses the person no end – for the love of him he cannot recollect what it is he actually saw that mediated the perception of a gusty wind. And it is quite irrelevant, the point to be taken into account is that there was a gusty wind outside.

When the wind is perceived as not having changed since the last time it was seen, the situation is one of phenomenal constancy. The two mediating processes taking place at different temporal instants leading to the perception of an unchanged thing could not have been identical. Examples of this sort can be multiplied at will; many can be found in literature. Brunswik, Heider, and Ichheiser [3 ,6, 9] point out that in almost all, if not all, social perception, part of the mediating process is perceivable *per se*.

Brunswik himself recognized that there are foci within foci within foci. In a different context, he characterizes psychoanalysis as a form of molar behaviourism studying phenomena, which has its initial focus in the early years of childhood and its terminal focus in adolescence or much later [2, p. 679]. The term, 'the recession of the distal stimulus', will be used to denote the case where part of the mediation process becomes perceivable. It should be understood that there can be several 'layers' of perceivable mediation processes; it need not be restricted to one 'layer', as in the example of wind given above. At the proper time of the year, the perception of a gusty wind may mediate the perception that wintry weather has arrived.

Until now the recession of the stimulus has been discussed for cases where the perceivable mediatory processes need not be attended. But there are other cases where the recessed distal stimulus is literally seen through the stimulus, where it cannot be seen unless the mediatory stimulus is attended to. When Robinson Crusoe saw the footprint on the beach, he literally saw that there was a man on the island with an identical, if not greater, clarity than had he been on top of his mountain hideout at dusk and seen a small figure on the beach. In fact, in the latter case he might have told himself that his eyes were playing tricks on him, something which was almost impossible in the former. Trackers see the path of their quarry by being able to attend to traces which mediate this path not perceivable by the tenderfoot. The significance of being able to see through a stimulus lies in that it serves as a palpable instant of a phenomenon characteristic to all mediation – embedded in the medium a pattern can be found which is independent of the causal properties of the medium and which points to another event as its cause. One broken twig is not perceived as anything in particular beyond itself; a succession of broken twigs in a given distribution is perceived as a path. To use Heider's terminology [6, 7], a process is mediated by a pattern of offshoots in the medium which points back to it as the initiating cause. To the extent that we can contrive such a pattern, we can get the perceiver to see anything we wish him to see. This is what was essentially done by Ames.

One final comment before we proceed. It was argued above that the perception of a word is not equivalent to the shifting figure–ground relationships involved in first perceiving a house and then a window. Nevertheless, the recession of the distal stimulus is in many ways a homologous process to shifting figure–ground relationships. The ability to perceive to various 'levels' of depth for the distal stimulus seems to be as much perceiver determined as the ability to cut the pie up in different ways. Both processes exhibit many dynamic similarities.

5. PERCEPTION, A TEMPORAL ORGANISMIC PROCESS

In Brunswik's classical experiment which serves as a model for his ideas on representative ecological sampling, he had an observer following a subject in her daily routine, systematically asking her for the size of objects that were prominent in her visual field. In this Brunswik was following a standard psychological conception of considering perception as a relatively instantaneous event, sort of modelled after a camera. Had he taken an ecological sampling of perceptual acts, he would have found that perception is rarely, if ever, instantaneous; that people just do not look at things, that when people look at things they also generally examine them.

What happens when a person perceives an object for the first time? He looks at it carefully, studies it, his attention shifting from its shape to its bulk to its texture; and as he looks a twitching feeling emerges at his finger-tips, a twitching feeling that is more and more overpowering the younger the perceiver, which makes him want to touch the object, to manipulate it. He moves about to look at it from different vantage points, perspectives. And then suddenly he has seen enough and loses interest – the object has been attained.* Once the object is attained, a cursory glance is generally sufficient to establish whether the object is there or not there. It is this type of cursory glance that has been subjected to the burden of perceptual research, but, to emphasize by repetition, a cursory glance is not adequate for attaining objects, it is adequate for attained objects only.

An object in the real world has depth and richness and its perception is bound to be diminished when restricted solely to one modality. In discussing the perception of physical objects, the tendency to desire to touch that which is being seen has already been mentioned. In the perception of animate objects, the modalities of sound and smell also enter and assume an important role. Laboratory experimentation strips perception of this depth and richness. Sensory modalities are isolated and studied one at a time. Distal objects are restricted to still photographs or, more prevalently, black and white line drawings. Tachistoscopes restrict time, fixation restricts vantage points. This emphasis is both a result of and, in turn, a determinant of the scientific thinking about the subject. It is fair to say that the overwhelming amount of research to date has focused upon restricted modalities and restricted aspects of those modalities rather than upon perception as an organismic art. In addition, as Brunswik recognizes, the major emphasis has been placed upon aspects of the mediating process of perception, upon what have been called the autochthonous factors of perception. There is much to be learned from this research and much has already been learned, but a legitimate question can be raised as to whether it is, in itself, adequate for understanding ecological perception. The point of view taken in this paper is that it is insufficient. Brunswik's experiment suffers from some of the same limitations of the more restrictive laboratory approaches, and he recognized this.

6. THE PROBLEM OF VERIDICAL PERCEPTION

The problem of veridical perception has, for various reasons, assumed an importance in scientific research to which it is not at all entitled. For the science of ballistics, it is irrelevant whether the

---

* The meaning of 'attained' in this context goes beyond Brunswik's meaning since it also includes some understanding of what the object is, as well as an incorporation of the new object into the perceiver's frame of reference or cognitive map.

projectile hits the target or not; what is relevant is the explication of factors which determine the path the projectile takes with firing. To the extent that these factors are explicated, targets are hit more often. Veridical and non-veridical perception are both resultants of the same causal nexus. To the extent that we get to understand this nexus, we will be able more efficiently to set up situations leading to veridical perception as well as to recognize and correct for situations which lead to non-veridical perception.

Nevertheless, since veridicality of perception is of such intrinsic importance to us as human beings, it is worth while to pause and discuss some of the problems inherent in it.

Only the uncritically naïve expect veridical perception to be a true attainment of the object in all its aspects. Veridicality is therefore relative to a given criterion, to a desired degree of object attainment. If the person wishes to know whether he is confronted with a man or a horse, then the perception of a silhouette of a biped with hands is veridical for the purpose. If, however, the person goes on to conclude that it is the silhouette of John Doe, whereas it happens to be the silhouette of Joe Doaks, the perception is non-veridical. Given a manifold of mediated stimuli it is, by its very nature, adequate for some degree of veridicality and inadequate for others. For example, the normal light patterns hitting the retina are adequate for the veridical perception of the form of a small object, but they are inadequate for the veridical perception of its microscopic texture while the light patterns flowing through a microscope are adequate for the latter but not for the former.

Bowing to the primal biological relevance of perceiving molar objects in our ecological environment, the discussion will focus on the misperception of such things; the points to be brought out hold for all other kinds of perception as well. At least some of the causes of veridicality or non-veridicality will be explored.

In order to establish non-veridicality of perception we must compare an observer's report or action to some accepted standard. To the extent that the observer's report or action deviates from the standard, his perception is said to be non-veridical; i.e. we ask an observer to point to the longer of two sticks and then compare his choice with a numerical measurement of the sticks; we ask an observer to tell us the colour of an object under controlled illumination and compare his answer to our perception of the object under white light, etc. Man learned early in the game to construct instruments that could discriminate differences between objects far more finely than could his perceptual apparatus. The growing gap between what is discriminable by man's instruments and what is discriminable by his sensorium without the aid of instruments points to the first cause of non-veridicality. The perceptual apparatus has limitations beyond which veridicality breaks down; in order to achieve veridicality beyond these limitations we must use the instruments that we have invented for this purpose. This source of non-veridicality has been well explored by psycho-physics and is relatively trivial at present.

A more interesting source of misperception is the fact of inadequate information within the mediating manifold; when this occurs, a person is said to jump to conclusions on the basis of inadequate evidence, inadequate information. The perception given above of perceiving a silhouette as being John Doe is a case in point; had the person waited until he could see the silhouette's face and had got more information, he would have perceived Joe Doaks. Ames's illusions, among others, are also examples of the effect of restricted information. They break down as soon as the restriction of fixation is eliminated and the person is permitted to look normally, to change his vantage point, in order to get additional necessary information. Poor lighting, faulty media, stray effects, all can make the information in the mediating process inadequate to a greater or lesser degree. It makes sense to assume that the time needed by the organism in normal ecological perception has as its purpose, among other things, a check on the adequacy of information in the mediating processes – the organism seeks additional information if there is a paucity of information, seeks to separate that information which is a result of faulty mediation or stray effects from the information which consists of the mediating offshoots from the distal object, etc. This all takes time.

Finally, the non-veridicality due to faulty organization of the information in the mediating process should be mentioned. Here the information necessary for the veridical perception of an object is all available, the perceiver, however, cannot organize it correctly, if at all. When a subject is presented with a Street Gestalt figure, he will generally first perceive a chaotic distribution of black, nondescript geometrical figures, and only after 'struggling' with this distribution will the depicted object emerge. Since the stimulus manifold impinging upon the retina has not changed in this case, the change must be attributed to some reorganization of the proximal stimulus somewhere in the brain. Camouflage, both natural and man-made, is predicated upon this ability to create a mediating stimulus pattern that resists organization into a relatively stable neutral state that yields veridical perception. The effects of camouflage can be negated by gaining additional or different information such as by using light filters or infra-red sensors rather than white light sensors, etc.

7. PERCEPTION AND COGNITION

Perception and cognition are accepted as being different things: the difference is based upon the phenomenal difference of seeing things out there and thinking about things in here. With rare exceptions this bifurcation has been accepted rather uncritically by almost all.* If, as will be argued below, the bifurcation is unwarranted, its predication is bound to affect deleteriously our understanding of both perception and cognition. Let us develop the argument.

Brunswik talks about 'ecological validity', which refers to the correspondence between the phenomenal objects and the objective world. Unless an organism can discriminate effectively between those aspects of the external world which are a threat to its continued existence, and avoid them, and those aspects which are beneficial to the continued existence, and approach them, death would come soon. Organisms, in order to live, must be in contact with those aspects of the environment that affect them and must be in the position to take the proper action when it is called for. The organism must know the state of the world in which it finds itself and the action possibilities that this world admits to – these action possibilities consist of those things which the world can do to the organism and those things the organism can do with the world. This essentially is the meaning of the world for the organism.

Both perception and cognition play a significant role for man in getting to know the state of the world – cognition and its role for lower phyla is, at present, a mystery the less discussed the better. The terminal focus of both these modalities takes place in the brain. The above-mentioned bifurcation implies that the terminal foci of these two processes are discrete.

In the preceding sections of this paper, many aspects of perception were pointed out. Every one of these aspects has its counterpart in cognition. This is interesting and suggestive.

* Brunswik is not one of these. He recognized the close affinities between perception and thinking [3, Chapter XIV] although he stressed the measurable differences between the two at, what might be called, 'a lower level of abstraction' than the treatment in this paper.

The aspects of perception discussed in this paper will be listed in the order of their presentation, and their cognitive counterpart identified and discussed briefly.

(1) In perception we see things; in directed thinking we think about things.* There is no language that does not contain an adequate literal translation for the English word 'idea'. Man everywhere perceives that ideas come to his mind when he thinks. Ideas refer to things that exist in the world, or are believed to exist, or can be brought about by virtue of proper actions, and they also have thing qualities *per se*. They are basic unities and exhibit an invariance which makes them appropriate for many changing situations.

(2) Perception exhibits shifting figure–ground relationships; in thought recentring and reorganization (Wertheimer's 'recentring') play a prominent role. Just as in perception shifting involves a different cutting up of the stimulus manifold pie, so in thought we link ideas together differently or fuse ideas so that they become a new idea, etc.

(3) In perception, the ground affects the perception of the figure; in thought the frame of reference – what Bartlett calls the schema – influences the meaning of the idea. The meaning of words is an excellent and neglected example of this dependency of an idea upon a frame of reference. Philosophical positivists and the scientists influenced by them, knowingly or unknowingly, tend to complain that words are very poor media for meaning because they cannot be univocally correlated *per se* to an objective state of affairs. This is like arguing that perception is a very poor medium for seeing things because the figure is influenced by the ground which, by definition, is not part of the thing. A word has a core meaning which cannot become specific until it becomes embedded in a context which serves as a ground. When a word is embedded in a sentence its meaning becomes more restricted and more precise. The meaning of the sentence, in turn, is made more precise by the paragraph in which it is embedded, and the meaning of the paragraph depends upon the article of which it is a part. Finally, as Whitehead pointed out, the meaning of words used at a specific time is based upon metaphysical assumptions that are tacitly assumed by both the speaker and writer. These metaphysical assumptions serve as the fundamental ground for all meaning during a specific historical era.

(4) The recession of the stimulus – going up the abstraction ladder.

* Directed thinking is taken from the title of Humphrey's book [8]; it concisely delineates the difference between thinking and awareness.

Korzybski and his followers have made a great to-do about the abstraction ladder, about the fact that when we think about a cow, we do not think about the many distinct unique cows that exist at the time of the thought. They tend to attribute almost all the ills and woes that beset man to this neglect. More responsible thinkers do not go this far, but still think that there is something bad about having to disregard details when 'abstracting'. What these people disregard is that the cognition of a cow is just as real, tangible, and meaningful as the cognition of a specific cow doing a specific thing at a specific point in space–time. Or, equivalently, the latter is as much an abstraction as the former. The process is identical with the perception of a house without attending to the windows, doors, bricks, etc., the constituent things that go into the house which is in the visual field of the perceiver.

(5) The convergence of offshoots into a distal stimulus; the convergence of discrete ideas until they are 'unified' by a 'general' idea.* This process underlies much of problem-solving or creative organization of the cognitive field. Just as broken twigs converge to be perceived as a path and recede from perception as things *per se*, so does an aggregation of ideas suddenly change to be cognized as a 'general' idea and the individual ideas recede from cognition. When the original aggregation of ideas troubled the person, that is, constituted a problem for him, this seeing through the pattern to another idea is called problem-solving. If the original idea did not trouble the person, the new cognition is called pure insight.

(6) Perception is a temporal process; thinking is a temporal process. Just as perception generally takes some time until a closure is reached and the perceiver shifts his attention to other things, so in thinking one mulls over the relevant ideas that are kept in the mind's eye until a closure is reached.

(7) The counterpart of veridical perception is true, or logically consistent, thinking. The sensorium has limitation; man's thinking apparatus has limitations. Man invented instruments to compensate for his sensory limitations. Man invented instruments to compensate for his conceptual limitations, e.g. writing implements and script, calculators, etc. Misperception can stem from an inadequate offshoot pattern in the proximal stimulus manifold; faulty thinking

---

* Quotation marks are used because it is implicit in the schema being developed here that in shifting figure–ground in perception or cognition, there really is no unification or going from a more specific to a more general level. Any figure–ground organization is as real and as tangible as any other.

can stem from not enough facts. And finally, misperception can stem from faulty organization of the stimulus manifold and faulty thinking can stem from poor, illogical thinking.

8. THE PERCEPTUO–CONCEPTUO ACT

Based upon the fact that the terminal foci of both perception and cognition are found in the brain, taking into consideration the rather long list of similarities presented in the preceding section, and noting that problems of organismic functioning are at present forcing themselves upon us in many other areas both physical and physiological, it seems reasonable to assert that the bifurcation between perception and cognition is unwarranted. The process whereby an organism becomes aware of the state of the world in which it finds itself and the action possibilities which this world admits to is a unitary, organismic, perceptuo–conceptuo act. As is characteristic with many organismic acts, one is confronted in this instance with many discrete inputs, determinants, and/or forces which result in one unitary behaviour, the perception of the state of the world in which the organism finds itself, a perception differentiated into a figure and a ground.

Although the input has been dichotomized into major modes, perception and cognition, these modes themselves are not unitary. Perception has been broken down into various sensory modalities, perspectives, and points of view. Cognition too may exhibit a similar breakdown. The contribution of cognition to the perceptuo–conceptuo act is the assignment of meaning to the phenomenal object. In doing this the phenomenal object has to be figuratively viewed from many perspectives and points of view.

In the previous section a correlation was established between perceptual and cognitive phenomena. This correlation omitted one important characteristic of cognition – that of intelligence. If there is a perceptuo–conceptuo unit then there must be a perceptual counterpart to intelligence. And indeed there seems to be one. The degree and ease with which people can shift figure–ground relationships as well as their ability to increase the depth of the recession of the distal stimulus are the perceptual counterparts to intelligence; unintelligent people do both with much greater difficulty than do intelligent people.

As in other organismic acts that are the resolution of many inputs, not all the possible inputs to a perceptuo–conceptuo act need be present for the act to occur, neither need there be a preset relationship for the importance or magnitude for these inputs. For one act one modality can play the dominant role while for another, another modality. One can hear without seeing, or see without hearing, or think without seeing, but it seems that seeing without thinking is impossible. And this is an important point to be next discussed.

9. THE PRIMACY OF COGNITION IN THE PERCEPTUO–CONCEPTUO ACT

Can a person perceive a meaningless object? Obviously yes. A person perceives a meaningless object when he perceives it as being meaningless. But with such a perception the object ceases to be meaningless since it is given meaning by being classified as a member of a meaningful class. This piece of verbal sophistry seems to constitute a logical proof that perception implies meaning. However, it is reminiscent of St Anselm's ontological proof of God and one can be, or at least the author is, as ill at ease with this proof as he is with the other. Fortunately, additional material can be brought to bear which sheds light on this point.

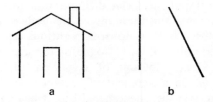

FIGURE 1 – Distal objects presented to brain-injured patient

Imagine behaviour demonstrated by a brain-injured patient who has an impaired ability to think abstractedly; abstract ideas are meaningless to him. The patient would be given pencil and paper and set down before a blackboard. *Figure 1, a* would then be drawn on the blackboard and the patient would be requested to copy it. The patient would copy it without any difficulty. Then *Figure 1, b* would be drawn and again the patient would be asked to copy. The patient would show a desire to comply, but he could not copy anything down. He would exhibit what amounts to a catastrophic reaction. For the normal person *Figure 1, b*, which consists of two lines only, is simpler than *Figure 1, a*, which consists of many more lines complexly related. The fact that *Figure 1, b* is literally meaningless is irrelevant since, as indicated in the 'proof' above, literal meaninglessness is always given meaning at a higher level of abstract thought. For this brain-injured person who has an impaired ability to think abstractly, literal meaninglessness cannot be given meaning. Does he see the distal object which he cannot draw?

Based on the performance with *Figure 1, a*, it must be concluded that the patient understands what he has to do and that he has an unimpaired eye and an adequate proximal stimulus. In addition, he must be able to attain a quasi-stationary neural state, the terminal focus of the perceptual process, which until now was equated to the phenomenal object. All the above must hold for the patient to be able to reproduce *Figure 1, a*. All the above must hold also when the patient is confronted with *Figure 1, b*. Yet he cannot reproduce it. It must be assumed that the patient under these conditions has not attained a phenomenal object. The quasi-stationary neural state resulting from the perceptual process cannot be resolved into a phenomenal object because it cannot be imbued with meaning; the only meaning it can be imbued with is abstract meaning, and this, by virtue of his injury, the patient is incapable of. It follows that there can be no phenomenal object unless it has some meaning.*

The argument that a phenomenal object exists, but that the patient cannot reproduce it begs the question. The only way to know that a phenomenal object exists for another is through the other's behaviour. If the patient cannot copy the object or indicate in any other behavioural manner that he sees the object, he has no phenomenal object.

Cassirer [4, p. 33] cites the example of Helen Keller which is relevant to the issue. First, he quotes in full the section which describes how Helen Keller discovered that water has a name and the tremendous effect this discovery had upon her development. Before this event, the child was a functional idiot; with this event she soon turned into a relatively normal child. Finding that a thing has a name does not mean much in itself. What is the significance of this discovery? What was the transformation that took place in Helen Keller's life when she suddenly understood that things have names?

Things cannot be given names until they are perceived as such. For the normal child this is not difficult. For Helen Keller, restricted to the sense of touch, this ability took a long time to come. In order

---

* This imaginary example is based upon material presented in Goldstein and Scheerer's monograph on abstract and concrete behaviour [5, pp. 131–48].

for her to have been able to discriminate things from the tactual stimulus manifold which was her only channel open to the world, she had to discriminate, to segregate specific aspects of that manifold. As soon as she could do that, as soon as she could cognize that a specific part of the stimulus manifold has, for example, the properties of being cool, flowing through the fingers, and leaving a noticeable residue which later dries up, she could segregate that part and cognize it as a thing – and then she could give it a name. But what is the meaning of a thing if not this process? Helen Keller was exposed to water many times before she could segregate water as a thing and name it. Nothing in the perceptual process altered with the discovery of names, except the ability to imbue a quasi-stationary neural process with meaning.

The case of Helen Keller indicates something else which is very important. Cognition of the world is relatively independent of the sensory mode though, of course, at least one channel to the world must be open. No person could know from reading her writings, unless explicitly told, that these were written by a person whose only contact with the world is through her fingertips. The world presented in her writings is as articulate, rich and veridical as the world of the rest of us. This is so because of her intelligence; her cognitive functions are unimpaired.

An interesting confirmation to the significance of cognition comes from another, unexpected source. In a rather dramatic departure from what is generally understood as being the position of the Vienna circle of logical positivism, Carnap has asserted, at a graduate seminar, that he is convinced that it is impossible to construct a logic upon denotation alone, but that it is possible to construct a logic upon connotation alone. Denotation refers to perception; connotation refers to meaning, thinking, cognition.

And finally, let us not forget that we can all think without perceiving – it is said of a person that he can be so enmeshed in thoughts that he is dead to the world – but none can experience perception without thinking.

Cognition is primary to, is a necessary condition for, perception.

10. SCIENCE, CONSTRUCTS, AND OPERATIONAL MEANING

The contemporary *Zeitgeist* in psychology, as well as in many other sciences, accepts two ideas as cornerstones of thought: the concept of a construct and the operational definition of meaning.

The connotation of 'construct' in its naked simplicity, is the postulation of a non-existent entity which enables either an ordering of a set of existing facts or the prediction of future facts. Great care is taken to emphasize that constructs do not exist, that they are really arbitrary, that the only criterion to decide whether to use a specific construct or not is the extent to which it orders or predicts facts. The job of science is consequently seen as being the postulation of a set of constructs which, in conjunction with their logical consequences, order and predict all known facts.

Operational meaning, or operationalism, has been concisely summarized by Brunswik as being 'the view that scientific statements have meaning only by virtue of the concrete operations that enter into the definition of the concepts employed'. Brunswik stresses that these operations must be physical, objective: 'Care must be taken that the concept of "operation" be sufficiently specified in the sense of methodological physicalism lest relatively casual testing procedures, including introspection, be placed on an equal footing with objective methods' [2, p. 671]. Operational meaning reinforces the non-existency of a construct because it asserts that whatever meaning a construct can have does not reside in it, but in a set of operations which are not it. And in fact, there are operationalists who do assert that a construct is nothing more than a shorthand name for a set of operations.

These two ideas are acceptable because of a basic attitude underlying much of scientific thought, an attitude of suspicion of common sense. This attitude expresses itself in other ways, such as a mistrust of perception, a mistrust of language, etc., Descartes' clinching argument against the reliability of perception is still met with: 'How can one discriminate between perception, hallucinations, and dreams?' Those bringing this argument forth forget that were man not able to discriminate between these states he would have had one name for them instead of three. Similarly, the complaint is commonplace that spoken language is too ambiguous and conceptually fuzzy to serve as an efficient instrument of communication, that it should be replaced by a scientific language. Yet, the people who make this assertion use this language to communicate to others. All scientific treatises, from the nebulous social sciences through the physical sciences to work in symbolic logic, where attempts are made to construct a rigorous scientific language, contain many more terms from the spoken language than from the specialized scientific language which is supposed to be more precise. In short, science is presented as being in opposition to common sense and what is good for one is bad for the other. To say the least, this is annoying.

The analysis of perception and cognition developed in this paper points to another, more satisfying way to understand science. It was just said that a set of facts are ordered by a construct. In what way is this different from the ordering of a subset of elements in the stimulus manifold to constitute a figure? Is the lady or train which appears suddenly after a prolonged inspection of a Street Gestalt figure a construct, while reality is but a set of geometrical black spots? The ordering of a set of facts by means of a construct is a *refined* cognitive counterpart of the perceptual ability to segregate part of the stimulus manifold so as to generate a desired phenomenal object, of the ability to shift figure–ground relationships.

When perception is veridical, a change in the point of view does not result in a corresponding change in the phenomenal object, e.g. perceptual constancy; when the construct is correct, the addition of new facts – which amounts dynamically to a change in point of view – does not present a problem. They too are orderable by the construct; this can be called construct constancy. The meaning that an object must have in order to be perceived entails at least some ways how that object will behave in an altered situation, i.e. leads to prediction. The meaning a construct must have in order to be formulated implies how it will behave in altered circumstances.

Both the ordering and predicting properties of a construct can therefore be perceived as being *refined* cognitive counterparts of perception. What about operationalism? Are the phenomena at present denoted by the term 'operationalism' in principle different from the phenomena denoted by the term 'the recession of the distal stimulus'? Operations are nothing more than mediating processes for the perception of the construct which happen to be visible in themselves. Scientific operations demonstrate both types of recession that were found in the perception of a wind and the perception of a path. We do not attend to the mediating properties when we see the electron moving in a Wilson cloud chamber; we see through the mediating stimuli when we see the path of an electron by reading a meter in a cyclotron. Operational determination of a construct is therefore a *refined* cognitive counterpart to the perceptual recession of the distal stimulus.

A construct thereby becomes nothing else but a *refined* phenomenal object. And since the meaning must be imbued in the phenomenal object, it is independent of the operations. In fact, the shoe is on the other foot. The meaning of the operations is determined by the meaning of the construct. This solves a problem which has confronted many when trying to understand operationalism in the literal sense. There is an infinity of operations, an infinity of possible measurements. If there were no meaning beyond the operations we would be in the position of Huxley's* monkeys pecking away at a typewriter. We should be measuring away like mad and occasionally find something that is useful, that is not gibberish. As far as is known, no scientist has ever initiated an operation which yielded gibberish. This is so because the meaning of the construct dictates what operations are called for, for it to be perceived. If it is not perceived there is something wrong, a problem to solve. This has its counterpart in sensory perception. We see an opaque object in a diffuse light. An opaque object should cast a shadow when light is shone upon it from a given angle. We shine a light. If no shadow appears then something is wrong somewhere.

The term 'refined' (emphasized) has been used several times in the preceding paragraphs. In a way this qualification was necessary since the simple cognitive counterparts to the various perceptual aspects discussed have already been given in Section 7, and the scientific counterpart had to be distinguished from them. But the term is not arbitrary. Science *is* a very refined form of the perceptuo–conceptuo act – it is a refined attainment of objects and nothing more.

Our instruments and operations are mere tools which specialize and increase our abilities to see; our conceptual schemes are mere tools which enable us to think more efficiently. Creative science is an integral outgrowth and sophistication of common sense. There is no more conflict between science and common sense than there is between Einsteinian physics and Newtonian physics. The so-called contradictions between the former are resolvable in a manner identical to the resolution of the 'contradictions' between the latter. Here again a point is reached that is stressed by Whitehead in many of his later writings.

One final comment. Is 'construct' then nonsense? It should be obvious that a meaningful word cannot be nonsense; only gibberish is nonsense. A meaningful word is always based upon a discriminable phenomenal event or a discriminable aspect of a phenomenal event, and the distal object which is the correlate of the phenomenon is always attainable by the person who understands the word. 'Construct' is based upon a discriminable cognitive state which has a very

* I think?

D

simple and common counterpart in perception. And, as such, when correctly used, it denotes an important condition in science.

Let us return to the example given in Section 6 which discussed veridical perception. Upon perceiving a silhouette of a biped with hands, the perceiver knew that he was seeing a man and not a horse, but he did not have enough information to determine whether he was seeing John Doe or Joe Doaks. In order to make the latter discrimination, he needed more information such as a closer look under light, or calling out a name, etc. In science it is generally the case that facts available do not mediate a clear perception of a distal object. The essence of scientific endeavour is the attainment of distal objects. Hence scientists are often in the position in which they figuratively have to decide whether they are seeing John Doe or Joe Doaks. They are aware of the uniqueness of the event in which they are saying: 'Based upon the information available to me I may be seeing John Doe'. This event is denoted by the term: 'John Doe is a construct'. Once John Doe is seen clearly, 'John Doe' ceases to be a construct but becomes a name of an object. Once this object has been attained, the scientist may shift his figure–ground relationships and ask a new question: 'Is the spot on John Doe's nose a temporary pimple or a permanent wart?' Until he can distinctly see what is actually the case, 'pimple' and 'wart' are constructs.

11. SO WHAT?

The road has been covered, the discussion has reached its goal. At this point a well-meaning critic may shrug his shoulders and ask: 'So what? Epistemologists and philosophers of science may be interested in the nature of constructs, but of what importance can this be to an empirical scientist who attempts to give an explanation of observed phenomena? Metaphysics are irrelevant as long as such an explanation can be given'. May it be suggested that what a scientist thinks he does, affects what he actually does.

In the late twenties Karl Mannheim found the necessity to write:

> The uncertainty which arises from relying upon scientific psychology in practical life becomes recurrently obvious as soon as the pedagogue or the political leader turns to it for guidance. The impression which he gets upon such an occasion is that psychology exists in another world and records its observations for citizens living in some society other than our own. This form of modern man's experience, which because of a highly

differentiated division of labour tends towards directionlessness, finds its counterpart in the rootlessness of a psychology with those categories not even the simplest life-process can be thought through. That this psychology actually constitutes a trained incapacity to deal with the problems of the mind accounts for the fact that it offers no foothold to living human beings in their daily life [11, p. 21].

If we drop our cognitive defences in order honestly to look at the state of our science today, we will be forced to admit, somewhat shamefully, that much of Mannheim's critique is still pertinent. Why is this so?

Man differentiates between real life and games. Real life is a serious matter, not to be played around with. Games, on the other hand, deal with make-believe, with non-existent entities. Up to and including the nineteenth century, science considered itself as seeking to unlock the secrets of nature, as seeking a clearer view of the world, as seeking the truth. Could it be that when a scientist redefines this job from the quest for truth to the formulation of mythical entities which yield some sort of order, he willy-nilly degrades his activity from the status of a most serious matter, not to be played around with, to that of a game?

There is a very important lesson, perhaps the most important lesson, to be learned from Asch's experiments on the perception of the equality of lines [1], but a lesson largely unremarked. Literally hundreds of subjects were confronted in these experiments with confederates of the experimenter, whom they thought to be unbiased peers, who publicly asserted, falsely, that they perceived two lines as being equal while in reality the two lines were not equal. Every one of the subjects perceived the two lines as not being equal. Regardless of whether the subjects yielded to the group or not, each and every one of them experienced a severe traumatic shock at this discrepancy. One cannot play around with the real world.

This shock in turn led the subjects to a most serious soul-searching, question-positing, and a quest for answers that really satisfy. Had they not been enlightened after the experiment, many of them would have persisted in this quest. They would have persisted doggedly until a satisfying answer had been obtained. This is the motivation and the inspiration that leads to creative science, that leads to a science which is relevant to the problems of man.

Had these same subjects been confronted with a similar situation, but where the group judgement would not be about a matter of concrete fact but about an arbitrary, non-existing entity, a construct as currently understood, would they have experienced as intense a traumatic shock? One need not conduct an experiment to know that the answer is in the negative. The more intellectually inquisitive among them might have speculated with interest about the strange thinking properties of the group, but the drive, the intensity, the inspiration would by and large be missing.

Were the correlation between the attended-to aspects of the distal object that make up the phenomenal object of a magnitude of 0·40 with the real aspects, we would be functionally blind. We would then scale heaven and earth to achieve the magnitude of correlation which enables us to walk with confidence, a correlation of 1·00. Yet a correlation of 0·40 is eminently respectable in our science. It seems to be a terminal goal for almost all published experimental work. For many investigators it becomes, perforce, a life goal since they cannot break through beyond it.

We accept this functional blindness with surprising docility; scaling heaven and earth is considered to be a rash act not befitting a sober and responsible scientist. And after all, how can one get excited about a truth which consists of a correlation of 0·40; it is just inappropriate. And perforce we slide into a philosophy so beautifully expressed by Pish Tush in *The Mikado* that: 'I am right, and you are right, and he is right, and all is right as right can be!'

May it be suggested that were we to accept a redefinition of our responsibilities as scientists as seeking to see the world more clearly, as seeking to know the world better, as seekers after truth, truth now meaning what it means to every man, including the scientist and philosopher when he leaves the office and is with his family, then we would less and less exhibit that behaviour which has been perceived by at least one very astute observer of the human scene as 'a trained incapacity to deal with problems of the mind'.

REFERENCES

[1] ASCH, S. E., Studies of Independence and Conformity: A Minority of One Against a Unanimous Majority. *Psychol. Monogr.*, 1956, **70** (9).

[2] BRUNSWIK, E., The Conceptual Framework of Psychology. *International Encyclopedia of Unified Sci.*, 1952, **1** (10), 656–760.

[3] BRUNSWIK, E., *Perception and the Representative Design of Psychological Experiments*. University of California, Berkeley, California, 1956.

[4] CASSIRER, E., *An Essay on Man*. Yale University Press, New Haven, Conn., 1944.

[5] GOLDSTEIN, K., and SCHEERER, M., Abstract and Concrete Behavior. *Psychol. Monogr.*, 1941, **53** (2).

[6] HEIDER, F., *The Psychology of Interpersonal Relations*. Wiley, New York, 1958.

[7] HEIDER, F., Thing and Medium. *Psychol. Issues*, **1** (3), 1959, 1–34.

[8] HUMPHREY, G., *Directed Thinking*. Dodd, Mead, New York, 1958.

[9] ICHHEISER, G., Misunderstandings in Human Relations. *Amer. J. Sociol.*, 1949, **55** (2), Part 2.

[10] KOFFKA, K., *Principles of Gestalt Psychology*. Harcourt, Brace, New York, 1935.

[11] MANNHEIM, K., *Ideology and Utopia*. Kegan Paul, Trench, Trubner, London, 1936. (Originally published in German, 1929.)

[12] RUBIN, E., *Visuall Wahrgenommene Figuren*. Syldendalsche Book-handel, Copenhagen, 1921.

[13] STRAUSS, A. A., and LEHTINEN, L. E., *Psychopathology and Education of the Brain-Injured Child*, Vol. 1, Fundamentals and Treatment. Grune and Stratton, New York, 1949.

5

Some thinking about 'system'

sys'tem (sĭs'tĕm; -tĭm), *n.* [LL. *systema*, fr. Gr. *systēma*, fr. *synistanai* to place together, fr. *syn* with + *histanai* to place; cf. F. *système*. See STAND.]

1. An aggregation or assemblage of objects united by some form of regular interaction or interdependence; a group of diverse units so combined by nature or art as to form an integral whole, and to function, operate, or move in unison and, often, in obedience to some form of control; an organic or organized whole; as, to view the universe as a *system;* the solar *system;* a new telegraph *system.*

   Knotted *systems* of steep small hills.   *Owen Wister.*

2. Specif.: **a** The universe; the entire known world;—often qualified by *this;* as, to regard this *system* with wonder. **b** The body considered as a functional unit; as, malaria pervades his *system.* **c** *Colloq.* One's whole affective being, body, mind, or spirit; as, his insinuation finally got into my *system.*

3. An organized or methodically arranged set of ideas; a complete exhibition of essential principles or facts, arranged in a rational dependence or connection; as, to reduce the dogmas to a *system;* also, a complex of ideas, principles, doctrines, laws, etc., forming a coherent whole and recognized as the intellectual content of a particular philosophy, religion, form of government, or the like; as, the theological *system* of Augustine; the American *system* of government; hence, a particular philosophy, religion, etc.

   Our little *systems* have their day.   *Tennyson.*

4. Hence: **a** A hypothesis; a formulated theory. **b** Theory, as opposed to practice. **c** A systematic exposition of a subject; a treatise. *All Now Rare.*

5. A formal scheme or method governing organization, arrangement, etc., of objects or material, or a mode of procedure; a definite or set plan of ordering, operating, or proceeding; a method of classification, codification, etc.; as, the Dewey decimal *system* of classifying books; the Bertillon *system* of fingerprinting; the Belgian *system* of tunneling; according to the Linnaean *system;* seeking a *system* by which to win at roulette.

6. Regular method or order; formal arrangement; orderliness; as, to have *system* in one's business.

7. (Usually with *the.*) The combination of a political machine with big financial or industrial interests for the purpose of corruptly influencing a government. *U.S.*

8. *Biol.* Those organs collectively which especially contribute toward one of the more important and complex vital functions; as, the alimentary or nervous *system.*

9. *Eng. Law.* Method or design as shown by other acts of a defendant similar to that charged, evidence of which is admissible to rebut or negative a defense of accident, mistake, or ignorance, or to prove a course of conduct.

10. *Geol.* A division of rocks usually larger than a series and smaller than a group, and deposited during a period; as, the Silurian *system.*

11. *Gr. & Lat. Pros.* A group of two or more periods. Also, a group of verses in the same measure.

12. *Music.* (1) An interval regarded as a compound of two lesser ones;—so used in Byzantine music. (2) A classified series of tones, as a mode or scale. (3) The collection of staffs which form a full *score* (which see).

13. *Physical Chem.* An assemblage of substances in, or tending toward, equilibrium. Systems are classed as two-component, or binary; three-component, or ternary; etc.; and also as univariant, bivariant, etc. See PHASE RULE.

14. *Transportation.* A large group of lines, usually of somewhat diverse character, under common ownership or permanent common control; as, the New York Central *system.*

15. *Zool.* In many compound ascidians, a group of zooids arranged about a cloacal cavity serving for them in common, and into which the atrial orifices of all open.

Syn. and Ant.—See ORDER.

SOME THINKING ABOUT 'SYSTEM'

1. *Introduction*

Recently I experienced something that struck me as being quite strange. It was my good fortune to be able to attend an interdisciplinary meeting devoted to the study of, and discussion on, 'self-organizing systems'. The participants at the meeting represented a gamut of disciplines ranging from the physical and engineering sciences through the physiological and medical sciences to the psychological and sociological sciences. Eighteen people addressed the meeting, and many others participated in subsequent discussions. Every one of the people who spoke found it difficult, either explicitly or implicitly, to define 'system' in general and 'self-organizing system' in particular. In fact, one very senior and influential scientist in this area asserted that there is no such thing as a 'self-organizing system'; then he asserted that he would continue to use the term, and did so.

Nevertheless, the meetings were quite successful, as these things go. The papers were well thought out and, by and large, challenging. The animated discussion that followed showed that the papers had generated serious thinking on the part of many of the audience. This is paradoxical. For how can we speak intelligently and interestingly about something which we cannot define, about which we cannot think clearly?

Since then I have on various occasions heard many people speak about problems concerning systems. Forewarned, I was on the alert. It is a fact that many who speak about systems are uneasy with 'system'. They assert that they will not try to define it, that it is vague, ambiguous, fuzzy, and even meaningless. And yet, since both the speakers and the audience do have a concrete system in mind, the subsequent discourse using this undefinable term generally proves to be valuable and rewarding. 'System' is, of course, now defined as the concrete system under discussion. This permits the ensuing discussion to be fruitful, but it also has some undesirable side effects.

We cannot use words cavalierly, as Humpty-Dumpty recommends, without reaping some crop of confusion, be it in communication with others, or in communication with ourselves. All of us are aware of most, if not all, the definitions of 'system' given in the dictionary – the definitions reproduced as the frontispiece to this paper. What's more, intuitively, willy-nilly, we accept all of them; after all, we have no alternative – the word is actually used in these ways in intelligent, meaningful discourse. Asserting that what we mean by 'system' is just a concrete concatenation of elements, the topic of the discussion, does not help us in the ensuing dilemma which makes every other definition of 'system' either wrong, arbitrary, or meaningless. We cannot use words arbitrarily without, concomitantly, sapping the foundations of the organized, meaningful, stable world in which we live; in which we must necessarily perceive ourselves to live in order to function effectively. The all-too-often heard apology that 'system' cannot be defined is a symptom of the disquiet, the ill-at-easeness that such a sapping generates.

Man cannot function too effectively when he is ill at ease; neither can he think too clearly. Ill-at-easeness generated by semantic confusion is generally unnecessary. This paper will attempt to dispel at least some of this confusion involving 'system'. It will attempt to show that 'system' is semantically legitimate *per se*, despite its many specific meanings by:

(*a*) reviewing some obvious but neglected facts of perception and cognition;

(*b*) explicating an implication of these facts – the 'core meaning' of a word;

(*c*) trying to show that the many definitions of 'system' are correct applications of the core meaning of 'system' to concrete cases;

(*d*) formulating a possible taxonomy of these applications.

2. *Some Obvious but Neglected Facts of Perception and Cognition*

In attempting to unravel the complexities that underlie the obvious, insights may be reached, so that something else which appeared to be complex and subtle thereby becomes simple and obvious. The obvious upon which I wish to focus attention is the nature of a thing, the nature of a stimulus, the nature of an idea. In what follows I will restrict myself to vision, but the points to be made are relevant to perception in general and are independent of the specific sensory modality mediating the perception.

In vision the lens in the eye focuses a projected picture of the environment upon the retina. The retina itself is basically a two-dimensional plane of points, each point being a light-sensitive terminus of an individual neuron. Hence, in the visual perceptual process, there is a stage where the non-homogeneous pattern of light rays mediating the picture of the environment is transformed to a non-homogeneous stimulation of a set of points that constitute the retina. As a result of this stimulation, each neuron that has a terminal point in the retina undergoes an electro-chemical change that starts a process which goes 'upward' into the central nervous system. As an end result of the process, the person sees the environment.

Somehow, and at the present mysteriously, the organism manages to partition this set of discrete point stimulations into two sets, one set becoming the visual figure being looked at and attended to, the other set becoming the background to the figure. The figure looked at is experienced as being 'a thing'; whereas, the background is just sort of there, and may consist of 'nothingness' or some combination of 'nothingness' and things unattended to.

The problems entailed in how the nervous system functions for man to see a figure are well known to psychologists and physiologists, and much work is current in a quest for solutions. There is, in addition, a closely related problem which is not attended to – the ability of man to see many different things in the environment confronting him. In other words, man can and does partition the set of discrete point stimulations relatively freely. This enables him to see that the figure has discriminable parts or that the background has discriminable parts. Even more important, this ability enables him to shift from one figure to another figure without a corresponding change in the distal stimulus field. Man, therefore, has the ability to organize the punctiform neural stimulation pattern and to reorganize it. Both the organization and the reorganization are to a great extent a function of what is of interest to a person at the time of perception, of what is relevant to him.

The world appears to us to be as it is because we have a sensorium that responds to certain physical stimuli and a central nervous system that can process these responses and organize them in determinate ways. It so happens, and not by chance, that these ways are biologically relevant, and this facilitates man's existence on the earth. The above analysis may point to a solution of a vexing metaphysical problem which plagues and has plagued many philosophers as to what things really are. The 'elementary' things that populate the world we live in are those aspects of the world which can generate upon our sensorium punctiform stimulation patterns which are organizable into visual figures.

Since the same visual field can be organized and reorganized in a variety of ways depending upon vagaries within the perceiver, it seems proper to speak about *modes of visual organization.*

Something similar seems to hold for cognition, by cognition I mean what is generally denoted by 'thinking'. The information stored in the 'memory banks' of a person's brain is analogous to the punctiform stimulus pattern impinging upon the peripheral sense organs. The idea we think about or the thought we are considering is analogous to the visual figure.

In olden days people liked to think that for each idea there corresponds a physical-thing-like engram which is sort of plucked out into consciousness when needed. Even slight consideration in a restricted mode of thinking, the use of words, shows that this is not feasible. Consider a person speaking or writing. Meaningful sentences emerge full blown. These sentences are combinations of words. Many of these sentences are unique in that they have never been used before. A sentence, by definition, expresses an idea. Yet the sentence *per se* could not have existed as an engram as such before its formulation. Words, of course, do and did exist; in this example, words are analogous to the punctiform stimuli. The sentence which expresses the idea is an organization of words. And this organization is determined by what is of interest to the person at the time of expression, of what is relevant to him.

It is difficult for me to grasp how an idea expressible by a sentence can exist as a determinate engram while the sentence expressing it must be organized from the unit words in the person's 'memory banks' at the time of expression. It seems simpler, and probably more correct, to look upon the process of organizing the words as at least one aspect of the basic underlying process of organizing the idea to be expressed. It is possible to bring additional arguments to buttress the contention that cognition exhibits rules of figure–ground organization and shifting figure–ground relationships similar to those found in perception, but I feel the above example to be sufficient.* Hence, consistent with the perceptual analogue, it seems proper to speak about *modes of cognitive organization.*

Perceptual figure–ground organization and its shifting relationships seem to point to a clarification of the metaphysical problem of

---

* 'Figure–ground organization' and 'shifting figure–ground relationships' are technical names for the two perceptual phenomena discussed above: (1) the ability of the organism to segregate the punctiform stimulus manifold on the retina into a visual figure and a background, and (2) The organism's ability to segregate the manifold into various different figures and backgrounds depending upon, among other things, its interests.

what a thing is; conceptual figure–ground organization and its shifting relationships seems to point to a clarification as to what creativity is. Given a set of punctiform elements of some sort dwelling somewhere in the brain it is relatively easy to conceive of creativity as being a novel organization of a subset of these elements which, in turn, may lead to the creation of a new element. It is much more difficult to conceive of creativity as the emergence of a new engram from, from . . . from where?

3. *On Words and Substantives in General and on 'System' in Particular*

It is the vogue among some philosophers and scientists to assert that the spoken language is a poor conveyer of meaning, that words have fuzzy meanings, ambiguous meanings, and sometimes even self-contradictory meanings. For evidence in support of this assertion they can point to many instances where people use words in a fuzzy, ambiguous, or self-contradictory way. At this the intelligent man-in-the-street will indignantly rise and 'frumiously' exclaim that in these instances people misuse words, and that words should not be blamed for being misused. And he is right. One should not blame words for the unfortunate fact that some people, even though they may be scientists, cannot use them correctly.

But, as is often the case, the philosophers and scientists are right too. Common language is a poor conveyer of what they have postulated meaning *ought* to be. They have postulated that the world ought to consist of some given set of irreducible unit things and that all perceivable and conceivable phenomena must be a result of lawful combinations of these unit things. A rigorous language should then be of a nature such that a sentence constructed in that language which denotes a phenomenon should clearly indicate the unit things and the lawful combinations that go into generating that phenomenon.

It so happens that regardless of whether these postulates are correct or not, man does not go about seeing and thinking in such a manner. The spoken language is a most subtle general instrument to express the things man does see and the ideas he does think about. It is a necessary truth that a word or a proper grouping of words expresses either a discriminable perceptual figure–ground organization or a discriminable conceptual figure–ground organization. This is what distinguishes meaningful word groupings from gibberish. When a person understands a word and/or a word grouping he either perceives or conceives the figure–ground organization it expresses. If he does not understand he cannot perceive or conceive of a figure–ground organization that is being expressed, if any is being expressed at all. If he misunderstands the word, the figure–ground organization he thinks it expresses is different from that which the user thinks it expresses. It is literally inconceivable for a person to communicate meaningfully, to make sense, unless he, and his audience, know the figure–ground organizations that his words express. Hence the paradox experienced by all when we agree that we cannot define 'x' and then proceed to use 'x' in our discussions. Every substantive term or word in any spoken language is a name for a discriminable figure or discriminable part of a figure – the part, of course, can, with the proper shift in figure–ground relationships, become a figure in its own right.

Now, I have argued that figures are anything but the irreducible, unique, unit things that some philosophy seems to consider to be necessary. They are flexible and changing. However, though they admit to being perceived or conceived as having parts or being part of a more inclusive figure, they nevertheless maintain a unit irreducible quality about them as long as they are figures. Substantive words or terms denote this quality. Perceptual figures exhibit the phenomenon of constancy. By this is meant the simple fact that a figure is seen as such despite many noticeable changes in its relationship to the perceiver or conceiver. A white sheet is seen as white whether it be under bright sunlight or dim electric light. Similarly a word maintains a constancy of meaning regardless of the many distinct and different contexts in which it can be meaningfully used. This constancy of meaning, which exists throughout the many different contexts or different specific meanings for which the word can be properly used, I call the 'core meaning' of the word. When we read a dictionary carefully and critically, we see that for words with many specific definitions a common core meaning can easily be identified that differentiates this group of definitions from another group found for another word. Admittedly it is sometimes the case that the core meaning is overlaid and hidden by historical accretions and must be uncovered through etymological analysis.*

It follows that 'system' has a core meaning, and that that core

* There are also cases where through a contingent, historical misuse of words the core meaning is lost in the shuffle. One finds this today predominantly within the scientific universes of discourse. This is a unique form of conceptual pathology which will be considered in some detail in some of the subsequent essays.

meaning expresses a perceptual or conceptual figure, a discriminable, distinguishable invariant that can be identified despite a host of different conditions and circumstances. What is this figure? The difficulty people have in identifying the figure is that they have looked for it in the wrong place; they have looked for it in the objective, simply perceived world, somehow equating the figure expressed by 'system' to be of the same nature as the figure expressed by 'dog', for example. Just as people could easily see the figural invariance of that thing called 'dog', they expected to find a similar figural invariance, 'out there' for that thing called 'system'. But the figure expressed by 'system' is not simply 'out there' – obviously, otherwise there would be no trouble in defining it.

Earlier the terms 'modes of perceptual organization' and 'modes of cognitive organization' were introduced. The use of 'modes' implies that there is more than one mode of cognition and more than one mode of perception. It is my contention that a thing is called a system to identify the unique mode by means of which it is seen. We call a thing a system when we wish to express the fact that the thing is perceived/conceived as consisting of a set of elements, of parts, that are connected to each other by at least one discriminable, distinguishing principle. Every one of fifteen definitions of 'system' in the frontispiece is a concrete exemplification of this core meaning.

Whenever one person can point to, or explain, a set of elements, and the nature of the connectivity between these elements, to another person, then the other person will perceive/conceive of the set as an entity, a thing. The word 'system' will then spontaneously emerge as the adequate expression, as a proper name for this thing. A system is therefore an interaction between what is 'out there' and how we organize it 'in here'. 'System' denotes an interaction between the objective world and how it is looked at or thought about; it denotes a mode of perceptuo–cognito organization.

'System' is a name for a very general invariance that can admit to much variation in details. This does not make it fuzzy or ambiguous. The term, 'a solar system' is just as clear and unambiguous as the term, 'our solar system' although the latter case permits knowledge of many details that are in principle unknowable for the former. A general concept, no matter how clear and precisely formulated, tells us little about specific cases or sets of cases that are instances of this concept. 'A solar system' can tell us nothing about the specific number of planets, moons, comets, and their respective orbits, that will be found when we become able to see more clearly what goes on around other stars. 'A solar system' does, however, specify minimum conditions that an aggregate of astronomical entities will have to meet in order to be named 'solar system'. Within the bounds of these conditions there is room for indefinite variety.

The mode of perceptuo/cognito functioning which enables us to perceive/cognize systems itself admits to various and different types of more concrete exemplification. There are many different kinds of connectivity which enable man to group entities together to form a system. Hence the fifteen definitions to be found in the dictionary. A step in an attempt to classify and order different types and aspects of connectivity between entities will be made in the remainder of this paper.

4. *A Classification into Bipolar Types that are somewhat similar to Dimensions – A possible Taxonomy*

(a) Structural–functional/static–dynamic

Phenomena can be seen or thought about in two ways. We can attend to those aspects of phenomena which do not change within a defined and delimited time span, and those that do. When the former serve as the perceptuo–cognito figure, we speak of structure or of a static state; when the latter are attended to, we speak of function or of a dynamic state. What emerges as a structural figure and what emerges as a functional figure is determined by the time span under attention. If we consider an infinite time span nothing can be structure, as Heraclitus recognized long ago; everything changes in the fullness of time. On the other hand change disappears when we consider an infinitesimal instant of time, since change makes no sense except as a specified relationship between at least two distinct instances in time.

The principle underlying the connectivity of a system during a given time period is static if the connection between the entities comprising the system can be seen or understood from knowledge of the state of the system for any one instant within that time period. If at least two instances within the time period are necessary before the principle can be demonstrated, the principle is then dynamic.

Shifting figure–ground relationships apply to systems as to any other kind of figures, hence the same set of entities can be looked at both from a static and a dynamic standpoint during the same time period. For example: the set of space–time points that constitutes a sleeping person during the wee hours of a night can be considered statically – a living organism which is inactive because it is asleep or it can be considered dynamically – a physiological organism undergoing an anabolism for which sleep is a necessity.

(b) Purposive or non-purposive

So much nonsense has been written about purpose that scientists in general, and social scientists in particular, have had, in some sort of self-defence, to proscribe the use of the word in scientific discourse. With this, unfortunately, they threw the baby out with the bathwater, since purposiveness seems to be an essential characteristic of life. By refusing to face 'purpose' the study of life in general, and the study of systems involving life – both physiological and ecological – has become much more difficult.

Like every other meaningful word, 'purpose' is a name for a discriminable perceptuo/cognito figure. It denotes a distinguishable pattern of action. What characterizes this pattern is convergence to a terminal state which is called 'its goal'. This convergence seems, to a considerable degree, to be independent of the vicissitudes of the external environment. It is this independence which enables us to assert that living organisms often exhibit great tenacity in achieving their goals, despite the great difficulties with which the environment confronts them. In addition, the goal is independent, at least as far as we know, of a point of maximum entropy. Goal-directed action generally decreases entropy rather than the opposite.

The often strange and generally unpredictable shape that the branches of a tree take in a crowded forest is seen/thought-of as the tree's quest for sun. The often equally strange and unpredictable shape the tree's root system will take is seen/thought-of as the tree's quest for water. (Note the word 'quest' which can be used properly in this context – look up its meaning in a dictionary.) The movement of billiard balls exhibits a pattern distinctively different from the movement of basketball players; the pattern of a rock flying through the air is distinctively different from the pattern of a bird. And finally, note how actors have to move in order to communicate to the audience that they are robots or zombies; the goal of the behaviour not being the goal of the behaving organism, but the goal of some external power which has the organism in thrall.

Purposive behaviour generally can take one of two forms; it can be directed either towards the environment, or towards the system itself. When behaviour is directed towards the environment it can either modify the environment so as to create a desired state, or it can overcome difficulties interposed between it and its desired state, or it can seek detours to circumvent and bypass these barriers. In all these cases the specific actions to be taken by the living organism are unpredictable unless one knows beforehand the vicissitudes with which the environment will confront it.

When a beaver builds a dam or a rabbit digs a burrow, we have instances where the environment is being modified. When a dog chews through his leash, he is overcoming difficulties interposed between himself and his goal, a state of free movement. When an animal seeks a path through a dense underbrush to reach a source of water which it senses to be on the other side, it is trying to circumvent barriers. It is easy to bring more complex examples of human behaviour for all these types of action directed towards the environment, but not necessary. These examples from animal life will suffice.

Action directed towards the system itself is omnipresent when a living organism is considered from a physiological standpoint. Cannon, who was the first to stress this aspect of living action, gave it the name of 'homeostasis'. Homeostasis is different from equilibrium. A point of equilibrium in a system is that point at which, given the constraints internal and external to the system, entropy is at a maximum. The homeostatic level is anything, as far as we know, but a point of maximum entropy; in fact the organism is almost continuously taking action to decrease its entropy in order to maintain its homeostatic levels.

Physiologically, a living organism can be characterized by constant endeavour to maintain homeostatic balance. Instances of homeostasis are the sugar level of the blood, the body temperature, the water content of the body, the hormonic balance, etc. With some generalization of the term, it is also possible to apply it to ecological communities and cultural configurations, since both seem able to initiate compensatory action as soon as certain entities that are part of them assume magnitudes above and/or below prescribed levels.

As man's knowledge of his world grew, he found it possible to contrive purposive systems of growing complexity. These systems are characterizable by (1) an input to the system, (2) a processing of the input by the system, and (3) a consequent output which consists of the input as modified by the system. The output of the system is the desired goal which man wished to achieve. In contriving this system man, therefore, had a definite intention in mind. Man-contrived systems are production systems and hence are purposive.

E

(c) Mechanistic–organismic

Since systems comprise a set of elements or entities, and the connection between elements or entities, it is possible to change, remove, or extirpate elements and/or the connections between elements within them. A system in which the remaining elements, and their connections, undergo no change with removal or extirpation is perceived as being intrinsically different from a system in which they do. In the former case I will call the system 'mechanical'; in the latter case I will call it 'organismic'.

Much of the nineteenth-century science shared the ideal that all phenomena is ultimately reducible to a mechanical system consisting of unit elements and a push–pull connectivity between them. With the formulation and development of concepts such as the space–time gravitational field, the sub-atomic electronic field, or chemical equilibrium, this idea has been found to be, most probably, wrong. Natural dynamic systems seem to be organismic. One must almost perforce go along with the conclusion reached by Whitehead that all natural dynamic physical phenomena are organismic. Whitehead, however, seeks a cosmological solution. The aim of this paper is far less ambitious. All that is sought for here is a clarification of how man perceives and thinks about what he calls 'system'.

Man sees many mechanical static systems. Geography abounds with them. Mountain systems, archipelagoes, are good examples. If we remove one mountain or connect two islands by a bridge, we in no way affect the remaining elements of the system. There are also mechanical dynamic systems. Most purposive production systems contrived by man are mechanical. When a machine in a production line breaks down, or a part of a machine breaks down, no change occurs in the other elements or among the relationships between them. When the broken part or the machine is replaced the system functions as before.

Not all static systems are mechanical. One cannot take a part of a soap bubble away nor a part of a suspension bridge without any effect upon the remaining parts. An electro-magnetic field can also be considered to be a static organic system.

One can also speak of a partially organic system such that the change, removal, or extirpation will affect a proper subset of the system. Damming a tributary to a major river will affect the tributary and the main river below the point of confluence. It will not affect the water flow in the other tributaries or in the main river above the point of confluence.

(d) The emerging taxonomy

The three bipolar 'dimensions' just discussed generate eight cells:

1. Structural, Purposive, Mechanical,
2. Structural, Purposive, Organismic,
3. Structural, Non-purposive, Mechanical,
4. Structural, Non-purposive, Organismic,
5. Functional, Purposive, Mechanical,
6. Functional, Purposive, Organismic,
7. Functional, Non-purposive, Mechanical,
8. Functional, Non-purposive, Organismic.

By permitting oneself to indulge in some mental elasticity* one can find at least one perceivable/conceivable system to fit each of the cells. Here goes.

A road network is easily a good example of a structural, purposive, mechanical system, cell 1. Road maps represent it adequately at a given instant in time, two instants being unnecessary; hence it is a structural system. It has an obvious purpose, that of connecting various communities and other desired geographical points to each other. It is mechanical because one can extirpate any part of it without introducing any change in the remaining parts.

As a structural, purposive, organismic system, cell 2, I will consider a suspension bridge. It is similar to a road network in the first two aspects, but no significant part can be taken from it without disturbing the forces acting upon every part of it. Hence it is an organismic system.

Many examples abound for a structural, non-purposive, mechanical system, cell 3. Let us look at a mountain range. We consider mountain ranges to be systems. They have no purposes, they are just there. If one levels any mountain in the system no conceivable change occurs in the rest of the system.

Any physical system characterized as being in a static equilibrium can serve as an example for a structural, non-purposive, organismic system, cell 4. Consider an electro-magnetic field, or better yet, consider a bubble. Both of these examples can be determined by

---

* Some, obviously unkind, souls would argue that 'elasticity' should be replaced by 'prestidigitation'.

knowledge of their state at one instant of time. They have no purpose; they just exist. And it is impossible to take any part out of them without changing the entire system, without changing the point of equilibrium.

Functional, purposive, mechanical systems, cell 5, abound around us. Men construct them all the time. A production line is a good example. It makes no sense to think of it except as a temporal succession of steps within which raw material is processed and changed into a desired finished product. It is eminently purposive. If any machine in the line breaks down, no change is undergone in any of the other machines in the line even though production may stop. Hence it is mechanical.

Living organisms, *qua* living organisms, are *the* examples of functional, purposive, organismic systems, cell 6. First, what is the meaning of a living organism at an instant in time, in contradistinction to static, structural anatomy? Unless we know its behaviour, both internal and external, we do not know it. Behaviour is a time-bound process; it is functional. Second, because I have no desire to get into metaphysical arguments as to what is really real and what is really scientific, I will assert dogmatically that the most parsimonious way to understand life at all its levels, from evolution, through physiological functioning, through overt behaviour, to cultural and ecological configurations, is by means of purpose. Let us not confuse the mechanisms by which this purpose is achieved and the purpose itself. Perhaps, in some future, purpose can be eliminated and shown to be some sensible function of physical causality. At present this is far from being the case and the stubborn phenomenal facts do show purpose. Third, and finally, an organism is an organism.

Mental elasticity is needed to find an example for cell 7, a functional, non-purposive, mechanical system. Consider the flowing water in a river stream. It is functional since 'flowing' makes no sense unless one takes at least two instances of time into account. Now consider the wild Missouri in its untamed state or that river of tears, the Hwang-ho. Both these rivers exhibit a tendency markedly to change their channels occasionally. These changes have been local as compared to the total system, and they have had no effect upon the rest of the system. And rivers, *per se*, have no purpose. Hence the changing flow of water as a result of a change in the river bed can be considered to be an example of a functional, non-purposive, mechanical system.

The last cell, cell 8, a functional non-purposive, organismic system, will become increasingly important if the physical sciences continue in the direction they have assumed since the formulation of Maxwell's field equations. More and more of the explanations given by the physical sciences to the observable facts of physical behaviour are of the nature of a dynamic interdependent field. The atom and the circular four-dimensional space–time continuum are both examples of such a system.

It is interesting to see how the fifteen definitions given in the dictionary fare with this taxonomy. Let us review them one by one.

Definition 1 is similar to the definition of 'system' as given in this paper. But this is hidden, implicit. It is also more limited than the definition presented here since it specifies only two of the six poles identified in this paper: organismic interdependence and function. It mentions four examples. The first two, the universe and the solar system, clearly belong to cell 8. The next example, a telegraph system, is, contextually, an example of cell 5. We can, however, consider it from a structural standpoint exclusively, and then it belongs to cell 1. The last example, a quote from literature, a system of hills, is clearly equivalent to my example for cell 1, a mountain range.

Definition 2 includes the universe again, which we have already treated. It also includes the body from a functional physiological standpoint, and from a psychological standpoint. Both of these fit into cell 6.

Definitions 3 and 4 both deal with the same class of things, systems of ideas connected to each other by some rational or coherent principle. These systems are structural and mechanical, and (somewhat elastically) I believe they are non-purposive, though, of course, the person who constructed them did have a purpose in mind. Hence they are examples of cell 3.

Definitions 5 and 6 deal with verbal instructions or formalized modes of procedures. They are structural, purposive – they exist in order to instruct a person what to do, and they are mechanical. Hence they belong in cell 3.

Definition 7 concerns 'the system'. It is colloquial American and concerns the interests and powers which control the Government to a greater and lesser extent. This system seems to be functional, since 'control' is time-bound, purposive, and mechanical; a denizen of cell 5.

Definition 8 is about physiological subsystems that contribute towards vital physiological functions of the organisms. It obviously belongs to cell 6.

Definition 9 is a very interesting usage of the word. It names a body of evidence submissible to a court which points to the intention of the defendant. Since 'pointing to' is one of the perceptuo–conceptuo criteria for purpose, this system is purposive. Since it exists at a given instant in time it is structural. It is also organismic and interdependent, as it is the *totality* of the evidence which points; its meaning can change with the exclusion of any specific bit of evidence. Hence it belongs to cell 2, the only definition that fits into this cell.

Definition 10 is about a division of rocks in geology. Such a division is structural. It just happens to be there and has no purpose. In addition, it is mechanical. Obviously a candidate for cell 3.

Definition 11 concerns an identified poetic form, structure. It is structural, non-purposive, mechanical and belongs to cell 3.

Definition 12 concerns the way 'system' is used in music and is conceptually very similar to definition 11. However, since music is time-bound, musical systems are functional. It is therefore a member of cell 7. The only definition to fit that cell.

Definition 13 concerns chemical systems in dynamic equilibrium. These have already been discussed as members of cell 8.

Definition 14 concerns a transportation system. It is discussed from a static standpoint, e.g. a large group of lines under common ownership. Since it is also purposive and mechanical it belongs to cell 1.

Definition 15 deals with physiological systems from a static, anatomical standpoint. As such it becomes static, non-purposive, and mechanical and belongs to cell 3.

Every one of the definitions seems to fit, without too much conceptual violence, into one of the cells. It is very interesting to note that not one of the systems defined in the dictionary fits into cell 5, a functional, purposive, mechanical system for which the example given was a production line. Other usages of 'system' that are common nowadays, like man–machine system, command–control system, and weapon system also seem basically to belong to this cell. The eight cells were generated through a systematic analysis of what the meaning of 'system' must be to make sense. Dictionary meanings are obtained through a thorough and assiduous 'nose-counting'. The fact that some of the best lexicographers in the country missed the specific meaning of 'system' in cell 5 seems to point, at least to me, to the superiority of even a simple intelligent analysis over the most elaborate and careful 'nose-counting' and classification of what was counted.

In addition, it is interesting to note the example of the use of 'system' quoted from Owen Wister: Knotted systems of steep small hills. This usage does not conform to the general definition given just above it. Hills do not interact nor are they interdependent. They do not form an integrated, organic, or organized whole. Nor do they function, operate, or move in unison. They are grouped together and perceived as a system on the basis of similarity and proximity. But the general definition cannot handle this. The systematic analysis can and does.

5. *Postscript: Some other Ways of Thinking about Systems – Not Dimensions*

(a) Self-organizing systems

The term 'self-organizing systems' is basically an instance of verbal magic that accompanies the changing of a name. In many primitive societies a person has a 'real' name by which he is never called, and a 'false' name which all members of the society use to call him. This magic was considered to be effective in protecting the person from the evil spirits which abounded. If the evil spirit never heard the 'real' name of the person, he could not know it; and if the spirit did not know the 'real' name, he could not identify the person to harm him. In Victorian England the changing of the name of an object from 'leg' to 'limb' was believed to reduce the salaciousness of that object. In our contemporary society 'passing away' is considered to be less tragic than 'dying'; being called a 'mortician' seems to be considered more ennobling than being called an 'undertaker'.

Horribile dictu, and not too surprising since scientists are also human, this form of verbal magic has also appeared in scientific thinking. Primitive psychological behaviourism asserted that man does not 'think', rather man has 'non-vocal laryngeal movements'. Now this would have been significant, had the early behaviourists been able to demonstrate that every time a person experienced himself to be thinking, one could find that his larynx moved non-vocally. But such non-vocal laryngeal movements have yet to be found. The behaviourists proscribed 'thinking' *ex cathedra*; 'thinking' like 'leg' was considered to be a dirty word. This because methodological positivism, which uncritically underlays so much of contemporary scientific thinking, asserts that only that which is physical is really real – in the case of life the really real is physiological, e.g. movements of the larynx. The fact that we perceive/cognize many discriminable life processes that are (*a*) only explainable by the concept of purpose, and (*b*) are just not reducible, at present, to physical processes, sticks like a bone in the throat of many. Like drowning men clutching at straws, they clutch at any physical phenomenon by the new physicalistic, 'scientific' name. They thereby exorcise the dirty words from their language.

As a result of exigencies of World War II, a technological breakthrough occurred in the design of control systems; simple control mechanisms having been known for centuries. The new control systems could sense subtle changes in the environment and could, as a result, modify the functional purposive system which they were designed to control. These modifications generally changed the function of the system in light of changes in the environment. With this 'feedback' entered the general vocabulary. Feedback was part of the electronic designer's vocabulary in the years prior to the war and, as already mentioned, was known for a longer period of time. What was radical in the new development was that now, for the first time, man developed a physical system which could 'see' the external world and change its behaviour in a manner appropriate to what was 'seen'. The analogy with life sprang forth immediately and was met with excitement and enthusiasm – at last a way was found to base living phenomena upon a physical substratum. The control systems were supposed to be analagous to the brain, and the systems they controlled, to the body. The total system was then given a name which was immediately, explicitly and/or implicitly, applied to living organisms. Hooray, a straw!

In the ensuing enthusiasm the very serious deficiencies of the analogy were not attended to. I can list many but will concentrate upon only one, since that is all that is necessary. It is an uncomfortable fact that man sees objects that are far away from him, that he sees at a distance. The sensa of the control system cannot; they can react only to the stimuli impinging upon their sense organs. Now it is true that man cannot see at a distance unless there are physical stimuli impinging upon his sensorium too, the proximal stimuli. But what he actually sees has a very tenuous relationship to the proximal stimuli. The only thing a control system can react to, however, is the proximal stimulus distribution. Brunswik denoted this by the term 'vicarious mediation'. Control systems do not exhibit any ability to respond to mediation vicariously. Hence the analogy is not well taken.

The conceptual confusion accompanying 'self-organizing system' results from the fact that explicitly and/or implicitly the scientists in defining this term wish to lump together both a certain set of physical systems and living organisms. This cannot be done, since the set of physical systems they have in mind is only superficially similar to living organisms and, although they may resist recognizing this, they feel it in their guts. Hence their difficulty at definition.

If we restrict ourselves to physical systems, the term offers no difficulty. Most machines contrived by man function unchangingly in a prescribed manner. To change their functioning the intervention of a human operator is generally needed. To the extent that we can construct control systems that can change the functioning of a machine or set of machines without human intervention, to that extent we have self-organizing systems. It's as simple as that.

(b) Central and peripheral properties and/or elements of organismic systems

In the preceding section it was noted that the self-organizing physical system was superficially similar to a human organism. In other words, the aspects in which it was similar to a living organism were not important aspects. The ability to react to physical stimuli is not, *per se*, an important aspect of living/functioning; it is the ability to react to a distant object over a wide range of mediating stimuli which is important and which differentiates life, at least many advanced forms of life, from sensory machines. This points to a problem that can be generalized, a problem which does not seem to exist for mechanical systems. The problem can be crudely formulated as 'When is a man a man?' or 'When is a solar system a solar system?'

Aristotle touched upon this problem when he asserted that a hand separated from a body is not a hand. I am not aware of him considering that a person without a hand is still a person. A hand, therefore, although itself it has no meaning, as such, unless attached to a person, is peripheral to the person as far as him being a person is concerned. In fact we can subtract all kinds of things from a person without him ceasing to be a person. Wars generally contribute to human progress in many scientific fields. Medicine has learned much in the last war. One of the things it learned is how, more efficiently, to keep people alive despite all kind of fantastic external dismemberment. Hence we now have a small number of quadruple amputees living among us. They are still perceived as men. Limbs therefore are peripheral characteristics of human beings. Surprising? No! Apes have four human-like limbs.

On the other hand, idiots, neonates, or psychotics are generally not perceived as persons even though their bodies are intact. Rational consciousness and the behaviour flowing from rational consciousness is a central property of man. We find something similar on a physiological level. The body can maintain relatively efficient life processes with many of its parts being subtracted from it. But there are other parts that are so essential to any ordered function that their slightest damage will cause death. Hence we have parts that are central for a physiological life and others that are peripheral. If we go to a solar system, we find something similar but far simpler. In order for a solar system to be perceived/cognized there must be a sun and at least one planet circling it. All other possible aspects and properties of a solar system are peripheral.

The most general definition, the core meaning, of an organismic system must be restricted to its central properties. The inclusion of peripheral properties will almost always exclude certain instances of this organismic system that lack this peripheral property, but are still seen as being the same as the defined system. This introduces confusion. A conceptual definition should be in accord with that which we see or think of spontaneously. I find it difficult to think through the problems entailed in how we perceive and discriminate centrality from peripherality in a systematic way. Nevertheless we do discriminate, and if we disregard these discriminations, we will run into conceptual difficulties. One can learn very little about an organismic system if he focuses his attention on its peripheral aspects.*

6. *Conclusion*

The difficulty in defining 'system' results from misusing a word that has a simple, clear meaning in a general context for a specific, concrete context. It is similar to the classical fallacy denoted by *pars pro toto* or that which was called by Whitehead 'the fallacy of misplaced concreteness'. 'System' is at a level of generality similar to 'phylum'. If we know the phylum to which an organism belongs and nothing else, we know very little about the organism. Ditto for system. The only things that need be common to all systems are identifiable entities and identifiable connections between them. In all other ways

---

* Since writing this I have 'discovered' Husserl. It seems clear that his 'essences' are what I call 'central properties'.

systems can vary unlimitedly. The quest for a more detailed, specified definition for 'system' is chimerical. The same holds for a quest for a general system analysis.

However, as I have attempted to show above, it is possible to group systems according to specifiable characteristics. The definitions for systems belonging to such groups become more detailed and specific. It is a fact that for many such groups, at present ill defined, if defined at all, certain analytic techniques are very appropriate. But it does not follow that they are appropriate for other groups of systems. By recognizing this we know better where we stand, the air gets clearer and we can see more clearly. And with this we can think better.

6

Why we cannot build 'thinking machines'

(At least at present)

1. INTRODUCTION

A vigorous controversy is going on at present. Computer engineers, programmers, and a select set of hard-headed social scientists are asserting, in faith and fervour, that we are at the verge of a significant scientific revolution, that we are at the verge, if not already beyond it, of building a machine that thinks. Humanists of all sorts, including the man-in-the-street, recoil at this prospect in horror, as if it were sacrilege – even if this could be done, it ought not be done. And the argument waxes – those opposing the machine being manœuvred into appearing to be mystical metaphysicians opposing the progress of science, into appearing to be 'reactionaries'.

If we step back somewhat, figuratively, and dispassionately attempt to survey the argument, we will find that both sides are wanting. Were we really in a position to construct thinking machines, then opposition to such construction would be futile. Those opposing it would be playing a role similar to the peasants who threw their sabots into the new-fangled weaving machines in an attempt to stop their use; and they would be just as effective. But, on the other hand, when we look at the arguments adduced by so many who believe that they are going to build, or are building, such a machine, we cannot but feel that they too have missed the boat somewhere, that they are not really talking about thinking.

And this is the contention of this paper. The present arguments on the thinking machine are a hopeless confusion of fact and fancy, of theories and data, of emotions and faiths. In our excitement we have lost sight of what thinking is, i.e. what the objective event pattern is, that we perceive as thinking; and we have lost sight of what the machine is as well. If we stop to consider the matter carefully and regain the proper perspective, we will clearly see that the present argument is irrelevant for thinking. We will be able to specify the necessary and sufficient conditions for the construction of a machine that can be accepted as a thinking machine. And we will also find that the construction of such a machine is, at present, inconceivable. In addition we will more clearly see what the currently so-called thinking machines really are.

First let us consider a simple* analogy: Can we build a walking machine?

2. THE WALKING MACHINE

With rare exceptions animal life which lives at least part of its life upon the land surface of the earth, locomotes by means of walking. Walking is a means for moving a mass from one point on the land surface to another. It always entails moving the mass of the organism *per se* and often the mass of other objects that the organism carries.

Man has built machines to do the same thing. They locomote from one point of the land surface to other points; they move their own mass and the mass of other objects they can carry. Were we to ask any man whether these machines, which we have constructed to move, actually walk, the answer would be invariably in the negative. It is easy to demonstrate that this must be the case. We take the sentential function: 'X walks', and try to substitute for X the name of any machine built by man for moving masses between points. For all substitutions the sentence will literally be false. It is therefore impossible for a man honestly or rationally to answer the question in the affirmative.

Were we, however, to ask the same person whether we *can* build a machine that walks, the answer most probably would be in the affirmative. We might then follow up by asking the respondent how he would build such a machine. He would probably find it easy to answer. Regardless of the specific words chosen, the answer would be of this general form: First I will have to construct a body or kind of box which will house the machinery which is being walked.

---

* The word simple is fraught with conceptual difficulties. I understand one thing to be simpler than another thing if it can be seen more clearly, if it be better understood than the other; in short, if it makes more sense. In this I follow Goldstein, who asserted that the behaviour of man is simpler than the behaviour of a protozoon because we understand it better [3, p. 3].

Then I will have to construct appendages from the body which will keep it off the ground and will move it by raising themselves in an ordered fashion off the ground and placing themselves on another point further along the ground in the direction of the desired movement. These latter two sentences are the conceptual definition of 'walking'. Any moving object for which these two sentences hold is perceived as walking.

Walking is a discriminable event pattern. With rare exceptions one can immediately discriminate whether a moving object is walking or not. The act of pointing to discriminable events that are clear instances of walking is called the ostensive definition of 'walking'. Walking is a mode of locomotion; there are other modes of locomtion denoted by the following words: rolling, crawling, swimming, sliding, sailing, flying, etc. Each one of these modes is easily discriminated from every other, i.e. each admits to relatively clear-cut definitions both ostensive and conceptual.

Machines accomplish the same things that men accomplish by walking; they move masses from one point to other points on the land surface. But although they locomote, they do not walk. Without exception machines are far more efficient in their locomotion for their specific purposes than are men, otherwise they would not be constructed. But they do not walk.

The reason we have no difficulty in deciding whether we have a walking machine or not is that we have both a clear ostensive definition and a clear conceptual definition for 'walking'. Were we to achieve a similar clarity for 'thinking', the difficulties in deciding whether a machine thinks or not would be no greater. Walking never intrigued the deep thinkers nor did it evoke philosophical speculation as to its true nature, its essence; thinking has and did. Once we peel off or disregard the encrusting and overencrusting of centuries of metaphysical speculation, we will find that the definitions of 'thinking', both ostensive and conceptual, are really not more complex than the definitions of 'walking'.

3. OSTENSIVE DEFINITIONS OF 'THINKING'

Upon approaching the problem of ostensive definitions of 'thinking' we are helped from an unexpected source, from the world of art. Most educated Westerners have seen, either in pictures or in a museum, a celebrated statue of a man by Rodin. No human observer, Westerner or otherwise, will fail to see that the man is thinking. I refer, of course, to the statue called, appropriately, 'The Thinker'.

Let us imagine ourselves in a museum watching a representative human being looking at the statue. Were we to ask him what the statue depicts, he would answer with ease that it depicts a man thinking. Were we to continue to ask him what the man is thinking about, we would most probably be answered that he is thinking about a profound problem. At this point the average person would desist from asking more questions since, intuitively, the topic has been exhausted. Not so the philosopher who distrusts intuition. He might proceed to prod and ask what specifically is the man thinking about. The wisdom of intuition would be vindicated by the response of the representative human being to such a question. He would probably blurt out in annoyance: 'How the devil should I know what he is thinking about?'*

Several interesting conclusions can be drawn from this example. First, we find that we can take a piece of stone, or any other solid substance for that matter, and so shape it that it is seeable as 'thinking'. Second it appears that men can visualize 'profound thinking' as a thing in itself without any necessary reference to what is being thought about. This is of relevance to philosophical ontology and will not be pursued further here. And finally we see that thinking can take place in connection with non-profound problems. Let us follow this last point up.

We have identified two types of thinking or two modes of thinking that are ostensively distinguishable: thinking about profound problems and thinking about non-profound problems. This raises the question: Are these the only modes of thinking or are there others?

Let us return to watch the representative human being looking at the statue. His head slightly cocked to the side he looks at the statue in deep thought. Without moving his body he slowly moves his head to change his perspective. He takes several steps to the side and resumes his previous looking. He steps forward and studies a detail carefully, examining several of its aspects. Then he steps back to where he originally stood, the entire statue being brought back to his visual field. Is he thinking? Obviously, yes. In describing his behaviour the term 'he looks at the statue in deep thought' emerged as an appropriate description. Is he solving a problem? This question is more difficult to answer. Upon some reflection, however, we will most probably feel that he really isn't.

* This is the typically human reaction to a phenomenally nonsensical question. Polite people suppress it.

What is he thinking about? He is taking the statue in, he is learning it, he is incorporating it, he is trying to get its full import. If we continue to watch him, we will eventually see that the intensity of his looking diminishes, and then rapidly disappears. With this we expect him to move on to another exhibit, and he soon does so. The statue has been attained.*

Here we are confronted with a new mode of thinking, the attainment of objects; a mode which does not simply seem to be a form of problem solving. We can of course assert, postulate, that whenever a person thinks, he is solving a problem. But this is an illusory solution. It does not account for the distinct differences between the pondering over profound problems, such as: 'What is the nature of man?'; the thinking about non-profound problems, such as 'What is the most scenic route between Los Angeles and San Francisco?'; or the studying of a thing until it is attained to the satisfaction of the person. Regardless of whether they are all really forms of problem-solving or not, they still are at least ostensively distinct forms of thinking.

We can proceed to identify additional ostensive forms of thinking by constructing more imaginary possible situations where thinking is perceived. But this would be a long drawn-out matter. Fortunately language comes to our help and renders this unnecessary. The ostensive definition of every meaningful word is a discriminable event pattern or a discriminable part or aspect of a discriminable event pattern. Hence, the tangible meaning of every true, proper sentence which contains the word 'think' is, at least in part, an ostensive definition of thinking. Better still, words synonymous and analogous to 'thinking', but which have enough different shades of meaning to justify their separate existence, probably have for their tangible meanings many, if not all, the discriminable event patterns which we see as thinking. Let us therefore turn to *Webster's Dictionary of Synonyms*.

The dictionary lists, on page 834, the following words as synonyms or analogues for 'think'; *synonyms* – conceive, imagine, fancy, realize, envisage, envision, cogitate, reflect, reason, speculate, deliberate; *analogues* – consider, weigh, revolve, study, contemplate, understand, comprehend, surmise, conjecture, guess, ponder, meditate, muse, ruminate, infer, deduce, conclude, judge.† Any objective

* I have taken the usage of the word 'attained' in this context from Egon Brunswik's theoretical model of perception. I use it, however, in a broader, more general way.

† To change these twenty-nine words into synonyms and analogues for 'thinking' simply add 'ing' to them appropriately. Note with interest that the word 'solve' is not listed among them.

pattern of events for which a sentence using any of these words holds, is, to some extent, an ostensive definition of what we perceive to be thinking, or one of the modes of thinking.

4. THE CONCEPTUAL DEFINITION OF THINKING

Our imaginary informant in Section 2 of this paper had no difficulty in answering the two questions we posed to him. It was clear to him that the machines we build do not walk and he could specify, with ease, how to build a machine that would walk. He would experience great difficulty were we to ask him to build a machine that thinks; in fact, upon some reflection he would probably say, without being able to justify it too well, that what we ask is a contradiction of terms.

What do we actually think of when we think of thinking? How does man actually think of man? Thinking is in many ways the essence of man. In order to answer these questions we must explicate the conceptual definition that underlies and is common to all the possible ostensive definitions mentioned in the preceding section; the core meaning of 'thinking'. This is not difficult to do if one only knows where to look.

Of all the literatures that record what man has learned about the world in which he lives, the literature on man himself is by far the oldest and the richest. The main burden of the world's literature, from prehistoric myths, through the ancient classics, until contemporary literature, throughout all cultures, is the study and understanding of man. And man early reached profundities in this area. Although still impressed by the intellectual brilliance of Aristotle, we cannot but smile condescendingly at the naïvete of his physics; his politics, however, are intrinsically interesting and still studied seriously; and his psychology, though currently neglected, merits serious study as well. We are still moved and stand in awe of the profound analysis of wrath and wisdom in the *Iliad* and the *Odyssey*. Moses and Aaron emerge from the Old Testament as human, all too human; as do the gods of Valhalla and Olympus.

And, despite the many differences between the oriental view of things and the occidental view of things, they fade to insignificance as far as their views of man are concerned. The *Kama Sutra** is quoted with approval in the work of contemporary scientists writing

---

* The *Kama Sutra* is a fascinating encyclopaedic treatment of the sex behaviour of humans written by an ascetic, celibate Hindu monk somewhere around the fifth or sixth century.

F

on the sex behaviour of men. The maxims of Confucius, laws of behaviour formulated about 2,500 years ago, can still be followed with profit by each and every one of us today.

Truly our picture of man emerged early in history and has well withstood the test of time and experience. The view is simple, clear, and known to all: Man consists of a body and a mind. Man exhibits bodily behaviour – physical behaviour; and he exhibits mental behaviour – . ? . behaviour. Walking is bodily behaviour, hence we have no difficulty imagining a physical machine walking. But this is also why we have difficulty in imagining a physical machine thinking – thinking is mental behaviour.

Most cultures accepted this body–mind dichotomy as a primitive and did not question it. Not so the Greeks, the sires of science. Among the many other significant problems formulated by them, the body–mind problem is also to be found. And it has not yet been solved.

Despite the fact that mind has, as yet, to be reduced to a physical causal nexus, man has a very clear tangible picture of what mind is. Had he not had a clear picture of mind, it would not have functioned as a primitive for so many millennia. The mind contains a picture or representation of the world; the picture is never complete and many parts of the picture are often wrong. The elements of this picture are called 'ideas' and the relationships between the ideas constitute the structure of the picture. Man has the ability to select an idea or small group of ideas and literally look at them with his mind's eye. This literal looking at ideas is the tangible act of thinking; it is as real as the typewriter upon which I am typing; it is as palpable as appendages which move a body by raising themselves off the ground in an ordered fashion. Just as a machine that effectively achieves the same effects as walking but does not exhibit a tangible pattern of walking cannot be called a walking machine, so a machine that achieves the same effects as thinking but does not exhibit the tangible pattern of thinking cannot be called a thinking machine.

And with this we gain insight into some of the impassioned arguments levelled against those claiming that thinking machines can be built. By making this assertion they deny the reality seen by all of us, they imply that what we clearly see is an hallucination. This threatenes a person's sanity, and a threat to sanity is the most traumatic, disturbing, fearful thing that can occur.* The vehement

---

* In conjunction with this the accounts about subjects' behaviour in a brilliant experiment conducted by Asch [1] are quite instructive. In this experiment individual

opposition, in days gone by, even by educated laymen to scientists' assertions that the earth is round, was also based upon this fear.

This example, the opposition to the assertion that the earth is round, was purposively chosen; it is the classic example brought forth by those who argue that science need not be tied to common sense, to that which we simply see. They then continue to assert that the task of science is to formulate explanations that predict future events, and it is irrelevant whether the explanation *per se* makes any sense. All cultures recognize that explanations believed to have predictive value and which make no sense do, in fact, exist; their languages all have a word for these types of explanations. But the word is not 'science,' it is 'magic'. Science never contradicts common sense. The same scientific thinking that led man to the conclusion that the earth is round also explained why man perceives it as being flat and why there is no contradiction between the two. Science must be irrevocably based upon and connected to common sense, else all kinds of metaphysics will rear their confusing heads.

A scientific theory of thinking must explain why thinking is perceived the way it is. To the extent that the theory cannot do this, then, despite any predictive abilities, it will be mere magic.

Let us return to our conceptual definition of thinking: the looking at ideas and/or their relationships with the mind's eye. Is it adequate? I suggest that every reader reflect upon the list of synonyms and analogues given above. He will find that for each of them he can construct a meaningful sentence whose ostensive definition will necessarily entail a person looking at his ideas for one purpose or another. The definition is therefore adequate.

Permit me to quote, with some omissions, the definition of 'think' to be found in the dictionary: '. . . the most general and least explicit word of this group [think], may imply nothing more than the entrance of an idea or notion into one'ᵥ mind . . . but usually it suggests some consideration or reflection . . . and often, it implies a conscious mental act such as a recalling . . . or a bringing of a definite picture or a clear idea into one's mind . . . or the framing of a purpose or intention. . . .'*

---

subjects were ostensibly members of a group of subjects in a psychophysical experiment aimed at determining the accuracy of estimating the length of lines. In reality, however, the other members of the group were confederates of the experimenter and were instructed, at appropriate times, to assert that two lines noticeably different in length were equal. Each and every one of the hundreds of individual subjects who were exposed to this situation was profoundly disturbed by this.

* By permission. From *Webster's Dictionary of Synonyms*, copyright 1951 by G. & C. Merriam Company, Publishers of Merriam-Webster Dictionaries.

With this the first part of the paper is concluded. The argument that at present we cannot construct a thinking machine (without doing violence to the meaning of 'thinking') rests. The conceptual definition of thinking refers to scanning ideas in a mind. Since we haven't the faintest idea as to the physical or physiological base underlying this scanning, we cannot construct a physical or physiological mechanism which can scan ideas. The best we can do is to construct machines which accomplish some of the same things that men accomplish by thinking. But they are as much thinking machines as trucks are walking machines.

Some may counter that the above is quibbling, is sterile semantics. A word is a symbol, they argue, and symbols can be defined with freedom in the quest for conceptual clarity. In fact, they often emphatically continue, this *is* the power of mathematics, the freedom one has in defining symbols; this it is that makes mathematics the queen of sciences.

But wait. They are overlooking several important things. First, to anticipate something to be emphasized soon in a slightly different context, there are significant differences between mathematical symbols and words; they are not the same thing. Second, the freedom in defining the meaning of mathematical symbols has one significant restriction: the definition must be rigorously adhered to within the same context; otherwise chaos will reign. This holds for words also; and the context for words is the phenomenal world which is the real world. It is not by accident that one of the earliest and surest signs of an impending psychosis is the idiosyncratic usage of words.

In the second part of this paper we will attempt to clarify what the so-called thinking machines actually do accomplish, what actually they are.

5. WHAT DO 'THINKING MACHINES' DO?

What do 'thinking machines' do? There is no difficulty in answering this question – they solve problems. But the term 'solve problems' is a slick answer which hides problems.

From a certain standpoint every machine solves problems. I am confronted with a problem: I have to dig a big hole in a short amount of time. I call in a power shovel and it solves my problem; it digs the big hole rapidly. So for every tool, instrument, and machine invented by man. Nevertheless, we use the term 'thinking machine' for but a small proper subset of machines. The members of this subset are characterized by a property lacking in all other machines, they solve problems by processing symbols. We will return to this point immediately.

How is problem-solving related to thinking? Logically problem-solving is independent of thinking, i.e. one can exist without the other. We have seen in the previous sections that there is a lot of thinking that just does not involve problem-solving; day-dreaming or free-associating are forms of thinking which, by their very meaning, preclude problem-solving. On the other hand, we perceive many people solving problems without thinking about them, either they guess luckily, or they are so expert in the problem area that they do not have to think about the specific problem in order to come up with a solution. It is not through oversight that, as remarked in a footnote earlier, 'solve' is not included as either a synonym or an analogue for 'think'.

It can, however, be argued that whenever a person thinks about a problem, i.e. scans and manipulates ideas, he is in reality processing symbols: hence, when the machine processes symbols it does essentially the same thing that man does when he thinks about solving a problem. I will concede the first part of this argument for the nonce, and show that the second part of the argument, introduced by 'hence', does not necessarily follow or, to be more precise, may follow only in special cases.

The machine cannot process any kind of symbol. It processes symbols of a restricted type. It can only process symbols of a formal systematical language, of a logico-mathematical language. Logico-mathematical languages are very powerful instruments for problem-solving. A scientific theory is fundamentally the construction of such a formal language to adequately represent the phenomena that the science studies.

But man uses many languages that are not systematic but merely descriptive. These are the languages of everyday communication and thinking. The elements of these latter languages are words or terms that are not systematically related to each other as are mathematical symbols; they are descriptive symbols, names. The machines cannot solve problems phrased in descriptive symbols. These problems have first to be rephrased, translated, into a systematic language. Since it is the job of science to construct theories, one can characterize the job of all sciences as attempts to effect such a translation.

Man can and does solve problems expressible only in descriptive symbols, in words. At the very best, therefore, a symbol-processing machine can solve only a subset of problems confronting man, those problems representable in a systematic language.

But *does* man process systematic symbols in his mind? The answer seems obviously to be in the affirmative – it emerges into conscious-ness immediately, without any necessity to think about it. Let me suggest that we do stop and think about it; before answering let us suspend our judgement and reflect carefully. Systematic evidence is meagre, but unsystematic evidence, both direct and indirect, abounds. Careful reflection seems to point to the conclusion that basically man cannot process systematic symbols in his mind, that all he can process in his mind is words.

In thinking about a problem expressible in words, be it an indi-vidual or a group, there seems to be no need to write the problem out physically. People effectively keep a verbally formulated problem in their mind's eye and think about it, analyse it, propose and weigh solutions, and finally reach conclusions and make decisions without having to *write down one word*. The entire symbolic processing takes place in the mind, and in the mind alone. But! Once the problem or parts of the problem can be represented in a systematic language, i.e. by means of a formula or geometrical figure, then paper and pencil, or their functional equivalents, immediately become a necessity. Although we obviously formulate systematic languages in our mind, we do not seem to be able to keep them in our mind's eye. In order to be able to use these languages we must write them out, we must process them outside our mind, on paper. What goes on in our mind while we process these systematic languages on paper? I assert that we think about what we are doing in words.

Now it is certain that experienced mathematicians and scientists do think about formulas and can solve them to a certain extent without the use of physical aids like a paper and pencil. Careful study of these processes will show, I believe, that in these cases the expressions of the systematic languages processed in the mind are used like words, i.e. they are processed and handled differently than when they are used in calculations spelled out on paper or its equivalent.

Hence, although I cannot claim that this is a proven fact, it still seems reasonable to assert that most probably the symbolic proces-sing done by contemporary machines is of a kind which man never could do anyway, for which he always had to resort to external aids: be they lines drawn with a stick in smooth sand, through an abacus, to pencil and paper and the blackboards in offices which are a sign of the research scientist.

6. ARE 'THINKING MACHINES' INTELLIGENT?

This is not as knotty a problem as some people wish to make it. Some reflection will show that 'Are machines intelligent?' is basically a meaningless question. It is a member of the class of meaningless questions that take the form of: 'Are machines phlegmatic?', 'Are machines immune to cancer?', etc.

Intelligence is a descriptive name of a discriminable pattern, an aspect of behaviour. It is most easily, though not exclusively, perceived in successful problem-solving and, although empirically intelligence is highly correlated to successful problem-solving, it is logically independent of this success, i.e. we can clearly perceive and describe an intelligent failure at reaching a solution as well as a stupid successful solution. This discussion has been definitively presented by Wolfgang Köhler in his book, *The Mentality of Apes* [2] and I need not repeat it here.

Despite the many flaws in the many intelligence tests constructed by psychologists, the tests nevertheless do have face validity, they do make sense. This sense is expressed by certain common principles that underlie both the construction of all intelligence tests and the interpretation of their results. These principles are common not only to the many tests constructed to measure human intelligence but also to those tests which measure the intelligence of animals at any phylogenetic level. I challenge anyone who speaks of the intelligence of machines to construct a test to measure that intelligence; a test that will be logically compatible to the principles underlying intelligence testing. I assert that this is an impossibility; if anyone can do this in one instance, I will be proved to be wrong.

And finally, let us consider the fact that once we can translate a problem into a systematic language and we do construct a program to solve the translated problem, the job of intelligence is finished and the solution can be ground out mechanically. Actual examples abound in which formulations originally conceived by men of rare genius are then understood by men of much lesser intelligence. Euclidean geometry is teachable to elementary school children, but it took a man of very high intelligence to formulate it. *Idiot-savants* can use the multiplication tables with a facility almost never found among men of high intelligence, but they are nevertheless imbeciles, morons, or men of borderline intelligence. The men who formulated these tables, however, were anything but stupid.

Let us look at the computer programs themselves. Once the

problem is formulated in the program language, how intelligent need a person be in order to be able to follow the program and solve the problem? *Idiot-savant* morons, i.e. those who can memorize and *blindly* follow an addition table, are, in principle, sufficient. In fact, such people would most probably have to be morons; any normal person would quit the job in disgust after the novelty wore off. This is a 'Turing test' in reverse.* The intelligence of a machine cannot be any higher than the minimum human intelligence needed to follow its program.†

Let us introduce a myth, in the manner of Plato – a man of no mean intelligence. In order to solve a problem expressed in descriptive symbols, a certain amount of intelligence must be invested. To the extent that we can formulate formulas and systematic languages we invest some of the necessary intelligence, and less intelligence is subsequently needed to solve the problems for which these are available. As a result, men of lower intelligence can then solve problems which earlier only men of higher intelligence could solve. Once we become wise enough to construct a machine, a program, and find out how to translate a problem into the program language, all the intelligence necessary for the solution to that problem has been invested and the machine can proceed to grind out the solution without an iota of intelligence.

7. ARE 'THINKING MACHINES' CREATIVE?

We all know that machines do many stupid things. However, there are those who argue that despite this, machines can grind out important novel findings, important novel proofs. Because of this ability, they continue, we should say that machines can be creative. Let us assume that machines can do this. What is the value of this kind of creativity?

Somewhere in his writings Whitehead comments that whenever we say that a certain genius formulated a brilliant idea, some historian of science is bound to rise and demonstrate that somebody

---

* A. M. Turing, a British mathematician, suggested that to the extent that a machine problem-solving protocol is indistinguishable from a human problem-solving protocol, the machine should be considered to be at least as intelligent as the human. This is called a 'Turing test' [5].

† Human beings may not even be needed for this purpose. If the Harvard professor Dr B. F. Skinner can follow through on his claims, given enough money for experimentation he should be able to teach a covey of quail to follow program directions and solve problems.

else expressed the same idea earlier. But Whitehead is not impressed by this. He points out correctly that the mark of genius rests not on the brow of the person who, for whatever reason, was merely the first to formulate the brilliant idea; it rests on the brow of the person who was first to see and to show to others its brilliance. Given machines as they exist, or as they will exist in the foreseeable future, it is difficult to conceive of the construction of a machine that will be able to discriminate between the garbage that it can produce and its brilliant findings; a machine produces whatever it produces. And of what use would this brilliant creativity be if men of equal creativity were not available to understand it? The machine will then be in the position of one of the most brilliant and ineffective scientists the world has known, Leonardo.

But the problem of creativity goes deeper than this. Creativity is not merely that which is new. A novelty is something new and it is not creative; it is a mere novel concatenation of known elements which, for unimportant reasons, nobody concatenated in that manner before. Let me attempt a conceptual definition that will differentiate a scientific novelty from the creatively scientific. It was mentioned above that man uses two types of symbol: descriptive symbols in non-systematic languages and formal symbols in systematic logico-mathematical languages. Let me suggest that within a scientific context, the novel is a novelty whenever it is merely a combination of symbols consistent with the syntactic and semantic rules of a systematic language which no one happened to have combined before, whereas the novel is creative when it shows how to translate phenomena previously expressible only in the descriptive language into an existing systematic language, or a new systematic language.

This definition fits the myth of intelligence. Intelligence is needed to give explanations, to find reasons. The present ultimate scientific explanation for human beings takes the form of a systematic language, a scientific theory. Once such an explanation is formulated, the creative act is accomplished, the job of intelligence is finished. And the computer can take over.

In terms of this definition the computer, since it is currently restricted to formal systematic languages, cannot be creative.

8. CAN THE MACHINE FORMULATE PROBLEMS?

This is another meaningless question. It is a member of the set of problems which includes the question 'Are machines intelligent?'

because, in order to be useful, it implies the question 'Are machines aware of problems?'

Problems arise from two sources; either a man or animal is blocked from getting to where he/it wants to go – the problem then becomes how to overcome the block – or, and this seems to be restricted to organisms at the higher phylogenetic levels, he/it is just cussedly curious.

As far as we can conceive at present, it is just inappropriate to speak of machines in this context. Machines cannot be blocked from goals and they certainly are not endowed with curiosity.

Machines cannot formulate problems.

9. DOES THE MACHINE SIMULATE MAN'S THINKING IN SOLVING PROBLEMS?

Enough evidence exists to enable us to answer this question in the categorical negative.

When the machine embarks upon a solution to a problem it follows the program, or the deductive steps inherent in the program – if the program is a heuristic program. At no time during this process does it or anybody else have any idea as to what the solution will be. At the end of its problem-solving process the solution emerges, full blown, as Athena emerged from Zeus's brow.

Men just do not think this way. When having to solve a problem, either in a descriptive language or a systematic language, they always first formulate a solution and only then seek a line of reasoning to see whether the solution is really a solution. In more technical terms, they always test unproven hypotheses.

The schema of the machine solution process is: problem–deduction–solution; the schema of a human solution process is: problem–solution–deduction. A human being cannot embark upon a deductive chain unless he has an idea where he wants to go to.

All serious investigators of thinking* converge to this point. I need not quote them since anyone can read the literature. Nevertheless, I cannot refrain from reproducing a quote with which Polya opens Chapter V of his book on *Induction and Analogy in Mathematics* [4, p. 76]: 'When you have satisfied yourself that the theorem

* This excludes behaviourists. They do not study thinking. They study the products of thinking, or the time it takes to think, or other irrelevant marginalia somehow associated with thinking; the main criterion that seems to underlie what they choose to study is that it be measurable. Whether the measurements make any sense or not they do not seem to consider.

is true, you start proving it. – The Traditional Mathematics Professor.'

Each and every one of us is a living proof of the basic truth underlying this assertion. All we have to do is to introspect while we are trying to solve a problem.

10. CAN THE MACHINE SIMULATE MAN'S THINKING IN SOLVING PROBLEMS?

Were we to restrict ourselves to the dictionary meaning of 'simulation' then some could assert facetiously that the machines are doing a pretty good job of it right now.* But this is unfair; those who use 'simulation' in this context do not mean simulation; they mean the construction of a machine that does the same thing that man does when he thinks, and as such, in addition to all the benefits to be obtained from such a machine, it will constitute a theory of thinking. Can this be done with present-day computers?

This question has already been tentatively answered in the negative when, in Section 5, it was proposed that man does not process systematic languages but words, whereas machines are restricted to the processing of systematic languages. Nevertheless, it pays to attend to this matter in somewhat more detail. Let us summarize and slightly reformulate what has been said about the role and function of creative scientific thinking.

Man lives in a world of things that have various aspects and are related to each other in discriminable ways. He gives these things, aspects, and relations names, which have here been called descriptive symbols. The body of these names constitutes a descriptive language which is used by man in everyday life. For various reasons man wonders why the things, aspects, and relationships are the way they are, have the properties he perceives them to have. He seeks explanations.

'Science' denotes a way of reaching explanations. Its explanations are different in two unique ways from all other kinds. They have given man greater control over the environment in which he lives than any other kind of explanation, if it can even be said that the

---

* Simulation: **1.** Act of simulating, or assuming an appearance which is feigned, or not true; pretense or profession meant to deceive. **2.** Assumption of a superficial semblance; a counterfeit display. **3.** *Civil Law.* A feigned or fictitious transaction, as one to effect a fraud, or one done as a matter of form. (By permission. From *Webster's New International Dictionary*, Second Edition, copyright 1959, by G. & C. Merriam Company, Publishers of the Merriam-Webster Dictionaries.)

other kinds of explanations have given man any control whatsoever. In addition, they constitute the only form of explanation that has met with universal acceptance in many areas by all those who have the necessary training and ability to understand the scientific languages.

Scientific explanations all follow the same pattern; they entail the formulation of scientific theories. Scientific theories are *the* scientific languages. A scientific theory is couched, as much as possible, in systematic, logico-mathematical symbols. An ultimate scientific theory should be couched entirely in such symbols. A scientific theory, therefore, constitutes an approach to a systematic language, a logico-mathematical system – an approach to a calculus. To the extent that man can represent a significant set of things, aspects, and their relations in a scientific language, he finds that he can now do two things with relative ease: First, he can calculate, deduce both the future and/or the past of that which is represented; this gives him control over his environment; and second, he sees that this complex concatenation of events is a necessary and ordered consequence of a small set of primitive notions; this is experienced as *the explanation.*

The main problem of creative thinking in science is to find ways to translate observable facts which have names in the descriptive language to systematic symbols in a scientific language and, concomitantly, to formulate a scientific theory, a calculus which explains these facts. In other words, we can say that the job of science is to formulate adequate calculi to explain observed facts. To date, calculators of all sorts, from the abacus to the IBM monstrosities, take over to the extent that such translations are available. This is the important meaning underlying the statement earlier in the chapter that calculators can process systematic symbols only.

In order to formulate a scientific theory of thinking, we have to be able to represent the process whereby man figures out how to translate from his descriptive language to a systematic language in its own systematic language. In other words we have to formulate a calculus such that when we apply a set of name-words to it, it will calculate a calculus adequate for these name-words or indicate that it is impossible to do so. Hence, we have to formulate a calculus which will calculate calculi. And herein lies a serious difficulty if we limit ourselves to present-day computers.

All present-day computing designs are based upon Boolean algebra, which in turn is a special case of the more general logical language developed in *Principia Mathematica.* In order to be able to use a contemporary calculator to deduce the consequences of a theory of thought, that theory will also have to be formulated in a principia language so that there is a univocal translation between it and the Boolean language used by the machine. In the light of this restriction, a calculus to calculate calculi becomes a contradiction in terms; it is logically impossible for a calculus in a principia language to generate another, independent calculus in the same language. All that a calculus in a principia language can do is to generate theorems, that is consequences of the primitives and axioms which underlay it.

Hence, as long as we are restricted to principia languages, and these are the only languages used by science today, we cannot formulate a scientific theory of scientific thinking, of scientific problem-solving. As a first step in being able to formulate a scientific theory of thinking, we will have to apprehend, to grasp a new type of logic, a new type of deduction schema which is independent of the principia and which can generate all kinds of principia languages. *And this is no mean task!*

The conclusion seems unavoidable. Despite the best of intention and effort on the part of investigators, contemporary calculators by their very mathematical nature seem to be restricted to the simulation of thought – in the dictionary meaning of the word.

CONCLUSIONS

There is no reason to get excited about the issue of 'thinking' machines. The existing machines cannot think; they will not replace man nor render him obsolete. There is nothing to worry about. Like all other machines, they are intelligent solutions to problems that have confronted man and, as such, they increase his range of possible actions and free his intelligence from the tedious labour entailed in grinding out the solutions to problems that have already been solved. The freed intelligence can therefore be applied to creative work. The more efficient these machines become, the greater their benefit will be to mankind.

To those who are actively pursuing the task of improving our present-day calculators one word of warning should be levelled. Words in the descriptive language are not the inherently meaningless symbols of the systematic languages. They are names of real entities of the world we live in. By using these names improperly, that is by using them to refer to things of which they are not the name, you introduce confusion not only in the minds of those you try to talk to, but also within yourself. This confusion will probably not be severe enough to vitiate your attempts to achieve the important goals, the forwarding of an exciting and revolutionary area of human knowledge and accomplishment, but it will most certainly slow down your rate of progress.

REFERENCES

[1] ASCH, S. E., Studies of Independence and Conformity: 1. A Minority of One Against a Unanimous Majority. *Psychol. Monogr.*, 1956, **70** (a).
[2] KÖHLER, W., *The Mentality of Apes*. Vintage Books, Random House, New York, 1960.
[3] GOLDSTEIN, K., *The Organism*. Amer. Book Co., New York, 1939.
[4] POLYA, G., *Induction and Analogy in Mathematics*. Princeton Univ. Press, Princeton, New Jersey, 1954.
[5] TURING, A. M., Computing Machinery and Intelligence. *Mind*, 1950, **59**, 433–60.

7

On goals and means

One of the more dubious accomplishments of the contemporary social sciences and of the attempts to apply science to social problems has been the sowing and reaping of semantic and conceptual confusion. This has been brought about by an uncritical acceptance of the dictum that common sense, i.e. sense, is not to be trusted, is misleading. One of the most distressing consequences of this acceptance is the attitude so many of us display towards the words in the language we speak; the more responsible among us assert that these words are ambiguous, the more irresponsible assert that many of them are literally nonsense.

All of us know, or should know, the myth of the tower of Babylon. Jehovah, by causing every member of its construction team to speak a different language, introduced such a babel, such confusion, that further construction became impossible. However, as is to be expected, Jehovah was merciful. By permitting every man to understand his own language he introduced confusion only between men, not within men. We are much more cruel to ourselves. By rejecting the language that serves as the structure for our thinking we find it difficult not only to communicate to others but to communicate to ourselves as well. Inner as well as outer confusion seems to be the norm in contemporary social science.

Some professional discussions involving the words 'goal', 'means', 'strategy', and 'tactic' are an excellent example of this confusion. In our quest for clarity we try to define the words rigorously, but by the time we get through rigorously defining them, either in terms of logico-mathematical schemata or operationalism, it becomes difficult to deny the impression that no one, including the speaker, really knows what's being talked about. We persevere in this activity only because, either explicitly or implicitly, we assert the credo that this is the necessary darkness preceding the light; a light which will be brighter and clearer than any of the lights we had had before. At least for some of us this credo is beginning to have a hollow sound. Whither the way?

I, for one, when recognizing my confusion, have found it very useful to return to the mother tongue, to return to the guidance of common sense. The return to the mother tongue was forced upon me when once, while struggling with a string of words that did not make sense to me, a question flashed before my mind's eye. What is the real meaning of these words? Going to a dictionary proved to be very fruitful; it became evident that the words in the string did not mean what the author intended them to mean. Hence the confusion. Common sense then stepped in to help. It facilitated the perception of a coherent relationship between real, intuitive, meanings which dispelled much of the existing confusion. This was useful in more ways than one. At the very least I found that I could communicate with myself, but I also found it easier to communicate to others.

For the purposes both of communication and as an example of the confusion that I have in mind I will discuss parts of a document before me in some detail. This document, a representative sample of much of the discussion on arms control and the resolution of inter-national conflict, has been chosen because it is a particularly clear example of what I have in mind. As such it is unimportant in and of itself and will therefore not be identified, although quoted.

The paper in question is an attempt to achieve clarity through a logical analysis. As a first step, in accordance with the basic pre-suppositions of logical analysis, it starts off with definitions of the terms to be used. And here we meet up with an initial and very significant source of confusion which may be called *irresponsible use of words* or *careless definition*.

Humpty-Dumpty asserted that when he used a word, it meant only that which he intended it to mean, and nothing else. It was a matter of personal pride with him and he phrased it in terms of who was to be the master, he or the word. But Charles Lutwidge Dodgson did not depict Humpty-Dumpty for emulation.

The practice of careless definition, ironically, stems from a very useful practice in mathematics and formal logic. Many of the intrinsically meaningless symbols used in these disciplines are defined to stand for the particular expressions or measurements that are of immediate interest to the investigator. This ability of arbitrary definition within a prescribed context gives the logico-mathematical sciences much of their power. But words from the mother tongue are not intrinsically meaningless. Contrariwise, man has yet to invent a more effective bearer of meaning. Exercising the right asserted by Humpty-Dumpty therefore wreaks havoc with communication, both inter- and intra-personal.

The paper in question starts out with a 'classic' example of careless definition. Three terms are defined: goal, policy, and strategy. I quote, with some omissions:

1. A goal is a happening (or set of happenings, or avoidance of happenings) with two distinguishing characteristics: It has value in itself, according to somebody's scheme of values. . . . A goal cannot be reached directly. . . .

2. A policy is an action (or intended action or action made possible) which is distinguished from a goal because: it has no value in itself, but derives its value only from the aid it provides in the achievement of a goal. . . .

3. A strategy is a set of policies considered as a whole.

The first definition is poor and will be discussed in some detail later. The second and third definitions do not correspond to the meaning of the words they define.

When a formal definition of a word does not correspond to its dictionary meaning, it messes up communication. Regardless of how rigorously we try to stick to the formal definition, the dictionary meaning of the word keeps intruding itself whether we are aware of it or not. This document offers an excellent example of this in-creeping of real meaning. On the same page with the definition of 'policy' the following is given as an example of a set of policies that can comprise a strategy: 'an active defence *policy* plus a passive defence *policy* might yield an air defence *strategy* designed to reach the *goal* of defending the United States against war damage' (italics in original). The fact that 'policy' is emphasized indicates that the sentence was given considerable thought, that we are not dealing with a slip of the tongue.

'Policy', in this sentence, does not conform to the formal definition just quoted. In this context 'defence policy', whether active or passive, does not involve a specific act or set of acts since nobody can know what specific acts will be called for. 'Policy' here refers to a principle or set of principles which should guide us to set up and allocate resources in order to be in a position to undertake many different

G

kinds of actions, depending upon what will confront us in the future. Were we to take the formal definition literally, we would be committing ourselves to a course of action(s) before the future event occurs which no person with responsibility would be willing to do; and rightly so. It is the precommitment to a prescribed course of action that makes the most wonderful machines appear so fantastically stupid when confronted with the least unexpected change.

Military policies determine domains of possible actions. Within each domain there should be optimally, a non-denumerable indefinite number of possible actions. This gives the man who ultimately has to take action the greatest flexibility to meet the contingencies of the future within the constraints imposed upon him by the policy. What is the dictionary definition of policy?

> **1.** *Now Rare.* Government; the science of government. **2.** Prudence, or wisdom in the management of affairs; sagacity; shrewdness. **3.** Management or procedure based primarily on material interest, rather than on higher principles; hence, worldly wisdom. **4.** A settled course adopted and followed by a government, institution, body, or individual.*

The first three definitions in the dictionary have nothing to do with acts or sets of acts. In these definitions 'policy' is characterized by words like 'science', 'prudence', 'wisdom', etc.; the policy behind the action refers to the science, prudence, wisdom, etc., which determined the choice of that action. The term 'a settled course' in definition 4 may be a prescribed set of acts however; military SOP (Standard Operating Procedures) are an excellent example of such a prescribed set. But the acts that go into this prescribed set are not just any acts. It is presupposed that they are the result of science, prudence, wisdom, etc. In addition, the prescribed course need not spell out any specific actions. It may be a principle of the general form: choose actions that will lead to a given set of outcomes and will avoid another set of outcomes. Some principles to aid in making the choice can also be spelled out, the specific action to be taken still being left up to the individual decision-maker.

It can be seen that the use of 'policy' in the sentence I am discussing fits the dictionary definition, hence it is a good example of the in-creeping of real meaning.

Let us turn to 'strategy'. *Webster's New Collegiate Dictionary* gives the following definition:*

---

* By permission. From *Webster's New Collegiate Dictionary*, copyright 1961 by G. & C. Merriam Company, Publishers of Merriam-Webster Dictionaries.

1. The science and art of employing the armed strength of a belligerent to secure the objects of a war, esp. the large-scale planning and directing of operations in adjustment to combat area, possible enemy action, political alignments, etc.; also, an instance of it. **2.** Use of stratagem or artifice; intrigue.

The key verbs in this definition are: 'employing', 'planning', and 'directing'. 'Armed strength' is the object of these verbs. A strategy is executed by the means of many specific actions. While it is true that strategies are affected by policies, in the real meaning of that word, any good policy will permit a choice from a range of strategies.

In addition, strategies are also affected by, to quote from the definition 1, 'adjustment to combat area, possible enemy action, political alignments, etc.' Since man considers strategies most successful when the opponent is led into a trap, and since leading into a trap means the use of ruses and artifices, we immediately see how definition 2 of 'strategy' evolved.

The first thing to note about the definition of 'strategy' is that it is applied in a restricted specific context, generally that of war. Or, as in the case of definition 2, some form of cold war where someone wants to get the better of another. 'Policy' is used in a much broader context, a context which includes war and conflict between people as a special case. It follows, therefore, that the set of events for which the 'strategy' can be meaningfully used is a *proper* subset of the set of events for which 'policy' can be meaningfully used. The formal definition of 'strategy' as a set of policies becomes a logical contradiction. It just doesn't make psychological sense and, therefore, because of the in-creeping of meaning, we find it difficult to keep it in mind.

Careless definitions are quite common in contemporary social science. People discuss games within the context of mathematical game theory; as if the latter has anything to do with people playing games; they discuss decision-making within the context of mathematical decision-making, ditto. Psychological 'learning theory' has very little to do with 'learning' as it is understood in common discourse where it is almost synonymous with education. Behaviourism in psychology does not study behaviour, rather it studies the outcomes of behaviour. The use of the word 'value' in much of economics specifically excludes those priceless things which in common discourse are considered to be the most important and significant values for man.

The misapplication of rigorous definition confuses communication in an additional way. Whenever a word is used meaningfully, it evokes a discriminable pattern event or a possible discriminable pattern event. This justifies the usage of this particular word in this specific context, and no other word. It is rarely, if ever, the case that language, when used sensitively to nuances of meaning, admits to an interchangeability of so-called synonyms as do a *definiens* and *definiendum* in formal logic. When a word is carelessly defined, the objectively discriminable events which should give it meaning tend either to disappear or to become obscure.

If we revert to the dictionary definition of strategy, we find a concept that is completely overlooked in the formal definition being criticized which makes all the difference in the world – the concept is 'planning'. A strategy is not just a collection of actions or policies, no matter how you define policy; it is a collection based upon a plan, which has an inner reason determining every major aspect of its formulation. When, in a military context, we see a series of actions that make sense in terms of an overall plan, we speak about strategies; if we cannot see the overall plan we do not speak about strategies.

Many social scientists are aware of this pitfall inherent in rigorous definitions and attempt to avoid it by specifying operational definition. Psychology, perhaps, has gone more in this direction than any of the other social sciences. Operationalism has its own pitfalls some of which have been discussed above in Chapter 4, 'Perception, Cognition, and Science'.

So much for strategy and policy – let us proceed to goals.

Let us refresh our memories by requoting the definition of 'goal':

1. A goal is a happening (or set of happenings, or avoidance of happenings) with two distinguishing characteristics: it has value in itself, according to somebody's scheme of values. . . . A goal cannot be reached directly. . . .

I have said above that this is a poor definition, and I will now attempt to justify this assertion.

The purpose of definitions is the clarification of thought. This is generally achieved in two ways. The definition can serve as a shorthand for a complex denotative statement, e.g. the term 'President of the United States' can define 'a person who meets the following qualifications specified in the American constitution . . . who is elected during a year whose number is divisible by four, by a majority of the electoral college and for the next four years has the responsibilities . . . as specified by the American constitution'. In the present context this type of clarification is rather trivial. The second type of definition, when used properly, leads to a more tangible conceptual clarification. It is employed when we reduce a concept that is cognitively fuzzy, i.e. difficult to discriminate in real life, to a unique, structured aggregate of elements where both the structure and the elements are cognitively clearer than the concept defined, i.e. both the structure and the elements are more easily discriminable. For example: 'libido' is the motive power behind behaviour where a person attempts either or both to master and to gain the love of an object in his environment. In the *definiens* of 'libido' the elements are a *person* and *objects* in his *environment*; the structure is a rather easily discriminable style of behaviour of the person in regard to these elements. Since every element in the *definiens* can be seen rather clearly, we thereby see more clearly what is meant by those people who use 'libido'.

In the present definition the reverse is done; the relatively simple is defined in terms of the fuzzy and no attempt is made even slightly to clarify the latter. A goal is defined in terms of values, but the concept of goal is and always has been clearer than the concept of value. It is precisely because of the latter's obscurity that so much thinking has been focused upon it, whereas little attention has been placed upon goals *per se*. Goals are easily seen. When a person acts, 'strives' is a better word, the pattern of actions which constitute this striving often clearly point to a terminal point, the goal. As a check, or if the pattern is ambiguous, we can ask the person what he is doing. His answer will be immediate: I wish to achieve x. If we continue to ask him why he wishes to achieve x, all too often he will not know what to say. A man is generally aware of the pay-off he expects from an action he undertakes; why he wishes that pay-off from among the host of all possible pay-offs is a difficult question.

The answer that he wishes that pay-off because he values that pay-off does not explain things, rather it is an act of verbal necromancy almost tantamount to double-talk. Subjectively, one may feel that the question has been answered, but has it really? If we return and focus upon the clearly visible, upon a person striving towards a goal, we find that the goal's value or, as it may be called, its valence, is a rather complex thing many of whose determinants are identifiable and manipulateable. There are a few good books written on the subject. But now we are defining values in terms of goal characteristics rather than vice versa.

In addition, restricting the use of 'goal' to situations that the person cannot reach directly does violence to a very common usage of the term. Consider a person's behaviour aimed at the creation of positions of strength in order to buttress his present position against possible threats. Under these conditions the person is where he wants to be, at his goal, yet at the same time he takes precautions so that if a threat to his position ever arises, he will be ready to meet it, to counter it and render it ineffective. Actually, this is the context within which the arms control discussion is taking place. The country is at peace, of sorts, and our primary interest is the maintaining of this peace, the planning for countering moves that may be a threat to this peace.

One of the most interesting aspects of this behaviour is that by its very nature it cannot be specific, it must be flexible, since it must be prepared to cope with a host of contingencies; the person is where he wants to be, but he must be prepared to cope with any and every contingency that threatens to push him out of there against his will.

To summarize why I judge the definition to be poor, to create confusion rather than clarification. First, it replaces clearer concepts by fuzzier concepts, and second, denies a very important aspect of goal behaviour, that of maintaining one's position rather than striving towards a new position.

If we continue to think about goals and how they affect behaviour, we almost immediately come upon another practice which generates confusion, a practice which seems to have been borrowed from Procrustes. As will be remembered, Procrustes had the habit of tailoring his guests to fit his bed; we tend to exhibit the habit of tailoring our facts to fit our methodology. Hence, I will call this the *procrustean approach* in science.

Mathematics does wonderful things. If we have a set of elements a_i and a set b_i, and if we have a set of probabilities such that given any element a_i there is a determinate probability for every element b_i that it will follow, then a specialized form of matrix algebra enables us to calculate a subset of a_i which will maximize the probability that a desired subset of b_i will follow. Now, if the elements a_i are available actions and the elements b_i desirable goals, mathematics seems to offer us a means whereby we can efficiently select a set of means to achieve a desired set of goals.

However, in order to be able to apply mathematics, the elements in the two sets must be discrete since a set consisting of non-discrete elements is not a set. In addition, for simplicity's sake, it is preferable that they be independent. And this is uncritically and naïvely done in the paper being discussed.

The author assumes, and probably properly, that the disagreements within the discussion of arms control, most specifically between 'pacifists' and 'warmongers' generally result from differences between discrete means, not goals. Now the most impassioned argument as to which of two sticks is longer will subside immediately when an *a priori* agreed-upon careful measurement will show that one stick is a quarter of an inch longer than the other. If something similar could be done for means, many arguments concerning means would cease. In Harmony with the *Zeitgeist*, the author of the paper criticized believes that the above-noted mathematical techniques can go a long way towards this goal. So he lists six goals and eight means (which he calls strategies) in order to construct a matrix.

In what follows I will discuss the goals only, but my criticism levelled at the treatment of the goals is also pertinent to the means. The author writes:

> . . . (We) can list six goals for the United States for which military policies are relevant. . . .
> 1. Avoid central war between US and Soviet Union (and perhaps China);
> 2. Win central war;
> 3. Limit damage done to US and to Americans;
> 4. Avoid limited war;
> 5a. Avoid enemy political gains in third countries which are involuntary on the part of the third countries;
> 5b. Avoid enemy political gains in third countries which are voluntary on the part of the third countries.

Since for the application of the mathematical schema these goals have to be discrete, and it is preferable that they be independent, the author assumes both. We find the following assertion: 'It is possible to hold any of the goals 1 through 5b and to reject any other one.'

Now anyone who has any feel for cognitive functioning, be he a professional cognitive psychologist or an intelligent sensitive layman, cannot but be repelled by such assumptions for these six specific goals. It just goes counter to common sense.

Cognitive psychology, the psychology of perception as well as the psychology of thinking, supports this rebellion of common sense. What are some of its main findings in this connection?

As we have seen, the psychology of perception has demonstrated that a person can never look at more than one thing at a time, a figure – whether it be a simple physical entity, a complex organized whole, or a clearly discriminable part of a physical entity like a crack of a mirror. It can be a vaguely discriminable part of a physical entity as in the perception that the upper third of a wall is clean. It can be a *lack of an entity* such as the very distinct figural qualities of silence which we all experience when moving from a setting with a high permanent noise level to a setting with a low noise level. We can perceive a group of people as a figure or several stones on the roadway. Despite all this variation, it is one thing we are looking at, and it has qualities that isolate it from the rest of the perceptual field.

A figure is always embedded within a ground which is not attended to. Cognitive psychology goes beyond common sense which disregards the ground; sophisticated perception theory talks about figure–ground relationships rather than of a simple perception of things.

Since both the figure and the ground are not homogeneous, perception psychology introduces a concept 'articulation'. Whatever serves as an articulation for a figure or a ground can also serve as a figure in its own right, by 'shifting figure–ground relationships'. To eliminate this shifting, perception psychologists, who were interested primarily in studying the determinants of figure formation, generally introduce a homogeneous ground and a simplified figure into their experiments which does not easily yield to articulation. In normal perception, called ecological perception, the figure and the ground are always articulated and shifting figure–ground is commonplace.

Does shifting figure–ground have a behavioural effect? It does. With each shift, with each reorganization of the perceptual field, every element in the field that goes into articulating the new figure–ground is seen from a new perspective. In addition some elements may disappear, whereas others which have played no role in the previous organization may appear. The weights of the elements, the relevance of their contributions to perception changes. The elements that articulate the perception of a person not feeling well are quite different from those elements that articulate the perception of a person being handsome, even when there is no formal shift in figure–ground relationships. The perception of *a woman with a rose in her hair* is quite different from the perception of *a rose in a woman's hair*. Meanings change, relationships between elements change, interdependencies change with each shift in figure–ground relationships.

The same holds for ideation, for thinking about possibilities. An idea is nothing more than a figure. As such what is thought about is affected by its inner articulation and the articulation of the 'frame of reference' which serves as its ground.

The frame of reference, to the extent that it is adequate and enables an individual to think effectively, must contain the significant ideas that are related to the idea being focused upon as the figure, and this is the reason that the five goals listed cannot be conceived as being discrete. The meaning of the idea focused upon is affected by the ideas which are in the ground, and the meaning of the ideas in the ground are affected by the idea being focused upon. This is the nature of figure–ground interdependence. One cannot arbitrarily hold any one of these goals while rejecting any of the others. As long as one of these goals is held in the mind's eye, the meaning of the other goals in the list is determined to a great extent, their range of variation and significance is thereby greatly limited. This is why common sense rebels at such an analytic approach – this is why the assumption of independence makes no sense.

None of these goals make sense *per se* unless viewed within a broader context which gives them a tangible meaning. One can always avoid central war by surrendering. This will also keep the damage to the country at a minimum. We will then not need to win the central war and the enemy's actions in neighbouring countries will become completely irrelevant.

It is impossible to focus upon a limited war or what should be done about a limited war unless the dangers of a general war are kept in sight. Look at how the US reacted in Korea in which the threat to the country was relatively intangible and its reaction to Cuba where the threat was, at least geographically, so much closer.

This list of five contains a confusion between goals and means. What do we really care what happens in a third country *per se* except to the extent that the enemy's action in the country affects the balance of power between us and the enemy. In fact, we would welcome enemy expansion were we to believe that he would be more harmed than helped by it. (See Aesop and the fable about the fox who swallowed the bone.)

Of course we would like to win, if we have to fight, but we would rather not fight. Even more so, many of us believe that no one can win the next war, that the best we can do is to emulate Samson in his destruction of the Philistines. This is a figure which is dominant in American national thinking; the Philistines will not attack the country as long as it is strong enough to destroy the temple. With such a fundamental conceptual figure all other talk seems to have illusory qualities, seems to be non-realistic. It is almost as difficult to cast this figure aside to consider other possible alternatives as it is to see a circle when a square is presented for inspection.

The five so-called goals listed, or discussed in conjunction with other so-called goals in other papers, are essentially a jumble of possible end-states, or articulations, of means, within the context of the one stable goal behind American policy – the goal of the nation peacefully existing as an independent entity that is a master of its own fate.

The problems of war and peace and the treacherous path that the country is forced to tread at present are an integrated whole and just cannot be considered each in splendid isolation even when we go through the motions of doing so. The sense of unreality of this type of discussion is an important contributor to confusion. No matter what conclusions it comes up with, we will *feel* them to be futile, and this confuses.

We have blinded ourselves as to the role goals really play in human behaviour, how they actually affect human behaviour, what a goal really is, and have redefined them to fit our mathematical matrix. This is the procrustean approach.

This paper will not be all critical; I will attempt to be constructive and delineate, as clearly as I can, a more meaningful conceptualization of what a goal is which will be harmonious with the findings of cognitive psychology and with common sense. But first I wish to touch briefly upon a third source of conceptual confusion to be found in the paper discussed. This source is the price we pay for disregarding the problems with which operationalism attempts to cope.

Having set up a goals and means matrix, the paper resorts to a commonly accepted technique. To show how a solution can be reached were the phenomena in question mensurable, fictitious numbers are plugged in and the calculations ground out. But are the phenomena mensurable? And if they are mensurable are they simply mensurable, or are exotic number fields necessary for their representation, number fields which are inappropriate for the mathematical analysis employed in the fictitious example.

My grandfather used to argue in the proper context that had *his* grandmother had wheels she would have been a trolley car. There is a profound scientific truth embedded in that comment. After all, his grandmother was dead at the time he said this and not available for study, whereas trolley cars abounded in the streets. But even better, one could always buy a construction toy and construct a simplified model of a trolley, remove its wheels, and then study it *ad libitum* and *ad nauseam* within the comfortable confines of one's own house. One can learn quite a lot about one's grandmother in comfort, ease, and elegance in this manner.

The problems of meaningful measurement, neglected in this area by so many who use numbers as examples, are neglected at the investigator's peril.

The question as to what number fields or domains are applicable to social phenomena does not admit of a simple answer. Several things seem to be obvious. Neither the infinitely large nor the infinitely small is applicable to social phenomena *hence the real number continuum is out*. In most psychological phenomena cardinal numbers are meaningless and only ordinal numbers may be tolerated. In many areas involving judgement a number field modulo 5 is sufficient for all purposes, and anything going beyond that amounts to the gilding of a lily – and gilding a lily kills it. In sensory psychology the progression is logarithmic. In other areas the most adequate mathematics is topological and admits no simple mensuration at all.

The use of probability in social science constitutes a special case. Mathematical statisticians agree that the mathematical concept of probability is meaningless unless it is related to a conceptually clear Sample Space (Feller) or Fundamental Probability Set (Neyman). To what extent are these sets explicated in theoretical work in the social sciences? Generally not at all, and for a simple reason. Were they explicated, we would all-too-often find that they make no sense in real life.

Using mathematics in this manner has the effect of mental dazzle (from David Katz who reports some fascinating experimental demonstrations of its effects). It yields an insubstantial aura of science while at the same time hampering us from attending to those gaps and discontinuities in our knowledge of the world that are the source of misunderstanding.

Before proceeding to the second part of this paper, a short summary is in order.

I have been criticizing an important segment of the contemporary discussion on arms control, asserting that it is in the wrong ball-park because of its misuse of words. The important words misused are: 'goal', 'means', 'value', 'policy', and 'strategy'. The misuse takes the form of arbitrary, careless definitions which do violence to the words' real meaning. The results are confusion since people stop knowing what they are talking about. And confusion compounds confusion.

I have used the term 'real meaning' because I believe that words have a real meaning – generally to be found either explicitly or implicitly in a good dictionary. The real meaning of the word is a perceptually or conceptually discriminable event or an articulated part of an event. Careless definition vitiates this simple discriminability. As a result of this we literally do not know what we are talking about.

In the second part of this paper I will take a hazardous leap and attempt to explicate the discriminable events which we all see – or can see when we strip ourselves of the methodological blinders imposed upon us by theological science – that are designated by the words 'goal', 'means', and 'value', i.e. what are the real meaning of these words.

2. ON GOALS AND MEANS

(*a*) What is a goal? Well, let's follow precedent and look it up in a dictionary: Goal: n. (ME. *gol*, of uncert. origin) 1. The mark set to bound a race; the end of a race or a journey. 2. The end to which a design tends; objective; aim. 3. In various games, one of the stations or bounds towards which the players strive to advance the ball, puck, etc., to score points; also, act of causing the ball, etc., to go through or into a goal, or the point or score thus made.

This definition is interesting. The core meaning of the word obviously refers to the end of a structured, generally complex, pattern of behaviour, a terminal point of action. This structure is generally designated by the word 'striving'. This is reinforced if we look up 'goal' in a thesaurus or a dictionary of synonyms and antonyms. If we return to our definition and study it carefully we find that in definitions 1 and 3 'goal' refers to a very concretely specified end state, operationally defined in terms of a game. 'The end of a journey' which is part of definition 1 and does not relate to a game can also be construed as being a concrete state of affairs – be it terminal city, country, or house. It is therefore not surprising that we find the word 'goal' when used in a context proper to definition 2 – the end to which a design tends; objective; aim – also interpreted as if a concretely *specified* end-state is meant. This may be the case for designs but is most certainly not generally the case for objectives, aims, purposes of behaviour. The dictionary definition is lacking.*

By and large, aims and purposes of behaviour, i.e. the goals of behaviour, are sketched in rather broad outlines leaving room for a great variety of specific detail. This is necessary in order to be able to achieve any goal. Even games with highly specified criteria for goal achievement exhibit great flexibility in what constitutes goal achievement. It makes no difference how you get the ball over the line, as long as you can get it over to the satisfaction of the referees. Were it not so, games would be deadeningly boring. The variation permitted in real life with respect to goals is far greater.

Take the example of the person who decides to dine out. Often the goal is not more detailed than that. He may go to the restaurant district to explore what is available. Upon arriving there he studies the menus that are hung out until something strikes his fancy. He enters that restaurant. The initial goal setting – going to dine out – was quite poorly defined as to concrete details. The initial steps taken to achieve this goal though concretely specific, were broadly defined – to get to the restaurant district. It is only after arriving at the district and surveying the situation that the person finally committed himself to a more specific goal, a specific restaurant. And even had he had a specific goal in mind, such as a specific restaurant, he would still not have had a specific table in mind, any of the tables available in the restaurant could have served as the terminal goal.

A newly graduated student goes out to look for a job. He has a specific purpose, goal in mind – to find a job. But must he know specifically what kind of a job he wants? No. He will generally survey the field to see the opportunities open to him and only then decide what job to apply for.

Buying an expensive product is a clear-cut form of goal-directed behaviour: by and large, the decision to buy a specific product should not be made before the prospective customer shops at least a little bit. In other words, it is foolish to commit oneself too early after having decided to buy a product; one must leave some indeterminancy open to see what the future or what the environment has to offer in the way of unexpected opportunities. Again, given the decision to buy a product, the specific product to be bought, the specific goal to be achieved, is often indeterminate for quite a while.

This does not mean that goals are always indeterminate. There are times when a goal is quite articulated and very little else will do.

* This is proof that I do not accept a dictionary definition indiscriminately.

For normal adults this is the exception rather than the rule. When this becomes the rule, rather than the exception, adults are then characterized as being compulsive and are considered to be good candidates for psychotherapy.

Some of the most fascinating investigations in psychology are a series of experiments conducted by Kurt Lewin and his students where a rough measurement of the tensions resulting from non-goal achievement was obtained. It was then shown that these tensions decreased markedly when substitute goals were achieved. Even more surprising is the fact that the subjects were not aware that the new goals achieved were substitutes for the old goals. Upon the success of achieving the new goals the old goals were literally forgotten.

To summarize what has been argued until now: When a person sets out to achieve a goal, there is always some degree of indeterminacy inherent in this quest. That is, the specific end-state that serves a termination for action, that amounts to goal achievement, can admit to many unexpected and acceptable variations, all of which are experienced as a successful conclusion to the expenditure of effort.

The fact that different specific end-states all generate the same feeling of success points to a theoretical model. Goal-directed behaviour is characterized by a striving towards an end-state. It can be considered to be an expression of an inner motive force, which in turn can be considered to have been generated by a state of tension within the person. Upon the achievement of the goal the tension is reduced and the goal-directed behaviour ceases. If, for whatever reason, the goal cannot be achieved the goal-directed behaviour may also disappear with the tension remaining; the remaining tension is experienced as frustration. It follows therefore that the satisfaction and pleasure experienced with goal achievement, the feeling of success, is related to the reduction of the tension with goal achievement. Of course, it may happen that a person's expectations are not met upon achieving a striven-for goal, and the tension is not reduced. This accounts for the feelings of disappointment, of being betrayed, which many experience upon reaching a long and hard-striven-for goal and finding that things have remained basically the same.

Various possible end-states can serve as an adequate goal because they all have the same effect, they all reduce the tension which initially instigated the goal-directed behaviour to the same degree. The interesting thing, however, is *that they need not be anticipated as being equivalent* when thought about in the abstract. To return to the example of the person who wishes to dine out. Were an attitude opinion investigator to confront him before he left his home and to ask him to rate restaurants in order of preference and kind of food in order of preference, the person would find this a relatively easy task to do. The investigator would then be able to construct a food–restaurant matrix which would yield an objective order of subjective preference of possible end-states of dining out. But this order would probably have little, if any, validity since, as the goal was *dining out*, any one of these possible end-states may objectively be as good a tension reducer as any other one, regardless of their initial rank ordering of preference.

This was brought home to me rather forcefully some time ago when I confronted a friend of mine who had just returned from a trip to Las Vegas. I asked him whether he had had a good time and he replied, beaming, that he had. I then asked him whether he had won money and he replied, matter-of-factly, that he had not. Finally I asked him whether he would have had a better time had he won rather than lost. He admitted that although he obviously preferred winning over losing, in this specific instance he did not think it would have affected the overall pleasure derived from the trip. And he was correct in his evaluation. The 'psychological tension' which instigated his trip to Las Vegas was satisfactorily reduced by what had happened to him; no other possible happenings could have yielded a greater feeling of success, a greater feeling of satisfaction.

There is an interesting difference between goal achievement and the failure to achieve a goal. Failures are not simply substitutable in their effect as are successes. Reactions to a failure range from a mild 'nothing ventured nothing gained' attitude, through the more serious state of 'I am lucky to get out of this unharmed', to a complete emotional collapse and a feeling of tragedy. There is also the nebulous area where neither or both successes and failure are experienced. What else can be the meaning of statements like: 'Well, I didn't get what I wanted but I didn't lose anything either', or 'Despite the fact that I didn't get what I wanted, it was a valuable experience nevertheless.'

The concept of tension seems to offer an explanation for these two states. When there is either no tension reduction or, as can happen, an increase in tension after the attempt to achieve the goal has been given up, one experiences lack of success. To the degree that tension increases, the greater will be the feelings of failure, of frustration. If there is no change in the tension level, the experience is one of 'nothing ventured, nothing gained'. If there is some reduction of tension there is a feeling of at least partial success. When all tension related to the goal disappears, one experiences success and the feelings of pleasure which accompany success.

(*b*) The specific goals discussed heretofore have all been of a restricted nature, they were of a class which permit man, upon having achieved them, to indulge in what can technically be called 'consummatory behaviour', they can be called 'immediate-need-reducing goals'. These states have properties which a person can and does enjoy *per se*; the aim of the goal-directed behaviour then becomes the tangible enjoyment of these properties. A person goes to a restaurant in order to eat; he goes to a beach in order to swim or bask in the sun; he goes to a theatre in order to be exposed to a stimulating play, etc. But there are many goals whose achievement, in itself, does not permit any consummatory behaviour. It is fair to say that the largest part of man's effort is spent in achieving goals which in and of themselves have little, if any, need-reducing properties, or where they are, as such, considered to be irrelevant.

Here another useful concept can be taken from Lewin. As man looks about him, he can discriminate many possible end-states that may serve as goals. These can be partitioned at any given time into two mutually exclusive sets. There is the set of goals achievable by a person were he to wish to achieve them, and the set of goals which are not achievable by the person, regardless of his wishes. The first set of goals is open to the person whereas the second set is closed to him. The first set constitutes a structured space of possible movements any one of which the person can undertake if he so wishes – hence it is called the *space of free movement*.

The space of free movement refers to the potential and not to the actual, and acts as a significant determinant of human behaviour. The frustration generated by social segregation or by any so-called irrevocable barrier to a possible goal has often little, if anything, to do with an immediate desire to achieve the need-reducing properties inherent in that unachievable goal. It is often generated by the choking feeling one experiences when he considers that were he ever to wish to achieve that goal, he would not be able to. This is the reason men climb high mountains; this is what drives man to explore the unknown. Much of man's behaviour, from infancy onwards, can only be understood as aiming at the expansion of his space of free movement, as increasing his potential, as a transcending of the actual. This is one of the striking differentia between human and animal life. Animals do not exhibit this quest for expansion; although they do exhibit a mild form of exploratory behaviour when put in a new environment.

Expansion of the space of free movement therefore becomes a goal in itself. The barrier that a person perceives as being interposed between himself and a possible goal often becomes a challenge in itself; its overcoming becomes the end-state of the behaviour striving rather than the specific state made achievable with its mastery. The prize gained by the victory loses its value, just as artists often lose interest in a work of art after they finish it. Here the barrier itself is the challenge; its overcoming leads nowhere. Often, however, the expansion of the space of free movement has a pragmatic purpose, the person being intrinsically interested in increasing the number of achievable goals. However, upon undertaking action that will lead to an expansion of the space of free movement as a goal, the new goals achievable once this goal has been achieved need not be specified, or, if specified, need not be actively sought.

The most obvious goal in our society, whose only virtue is the expansion of space of free movement, is money. Money has no intrinsic need-reductive properties; its importance lies in what goals it enables one to achieve once it is itself obtained. An automobile in many instances is a goal whose sole tangible purpose is a literal increase of rate, as well as space, of free movement. Even so prosaic a thing as a television set has no value *per se*; its function is to open one's house to the many programmes broadcast by the various television stations. In all these examples, as in the other examples of space of free movement, how we will specifically spend the money, where we will specifically drive to, which specific programmes we will choose to see, is relatively indeterminate at the time we are striving to achieve these end-states which expand this space.

Another set of goal-directed activity somewhat similar to the expansion of space of free movement is in the setting aside of resources, the achieving of positions of strength in order to meet future contingencies. The difference here is that the future contingencies are not known and may not occur. With the expansion of the space of free movement the new goals that become achievable are generally known beforehand. In the present case, however, the new goals are themselves indeterminate so that the present goal-directed activity may turn out to have been unnecessary. Keeping a cash reserve in the bank which is not earmarked for any particular

H

purpose is a good example of this. Keeping a gun in one's house as a protection against a possible burglar is another. One of the best examples of this kind of behaviour is rarely looked at in this context – it is the education of children. We try to give our children a good education so that they be well prepared to function in this world as adults – nothing could be more indeterminate than the kind of life our children will lead.

Two kinds of goal-directed behaviour aimed at setting up positions of strength to cope with future contingencies stand out. They can be called offensive and defensive. Offensive planning for the future is a higher type of expansion of space of free movement; it aims to set up the means so that if in the future the person wishes to expand his space of free movement, he will be in a better position to do so. Education is essentially of this nature. Defensive planning for the future aims at establishing means so that if a person's position be threatened in the future, he will be able to counter the threat. A good supply of tools enables a person to make minor repairs to his house before they become critical even though he cannot predict which specific repairs will have to be done. Defensive planning for the future is related to a type of goal-directed behaviour mentioned in the early part of the chapter and which is generally not considered in the various theoretical, not so theoretical, and experimental investigations of the subject. This is the behaviour where the person acts to retain his position, where his goal is not to be pushed out of the state wherein he finds himself.

How can offensive planning be characterized? As mentioned earlier, goal-directed behaviour exhibits a unique pattern called 'striving'. The goal is in a different part of the behavioural space than is the person and the person then moves through the behavioural space to achieve the goal. To the extent that this behaviour is articulated, the various elements of the articulation all point in harmony to a terminal region in the behavioural space; to the extent that barriers to his movement are met with, the person either overcomes or circumvents them where possible and resumes his movement in the direction to the terminal state. In these conditions actions are planned, the environment is surveyed; to the extent that the person is successful it is because he has mastered his environment and has established his control over it. By and large, then, the person is the initiator of the action while the environment is passive even though it presented barriers to the person. This holds to a great extent in competition too. The competitor who did not achieve the goal is now relatively impotent; he is perceived by the winner as just another barrier which had to be overcome.

The psychological situation when confronted with a defensive goal is quite different. The person is now being pushed out of the goal. He is now limited to reaction rather than to the initiation of action; he must plug up the leaks as they occur and is generally in a position where he cannot predict them. Planning becomes difficult. With each developing attack the person's feelings of mastery and control over the threatening environment undergo a shock. Efficient action becomes more and more difficult. This is the psychological ground underlying the military maxim that the best defence is an offence.

This seems to be the position in which the United States as a nation finds itself *vis-à-vis* the Russians. It is on the defensive. The only tangible goal which seems to characterize its behaviour is the maintaining of the *status quo* of non-violence. Its national policy since the implementation of the Marshall Plan exhibits a purposelessness, a flitting about in reaction to Russian initiative, but one which does not point in itself to any inherent tangible goal. There is no use in saying that it has tangible goals; its behaviour to date clearly indicates that it hasn't any.

The classes of goals just discussed above all have the common property that their achievement does not, in itself, enable consummatory behaviour. Nevertheless they are all intimately related to goals that enable such behaviour. The expansion of one's space of free movement enables the achievement of many additional goals having need-reductive properties in the present. Planning for the future facilitates such achievement in the future, and defensive actions protect actual achievements.

There is an additional class of determinants of striving which have nothing to do with any specific consummatory behaviour and yet are involved in all consummatory behaviour. This is the class whose elements are often called 'basic human values' and which I I prefer to call 'ought goals'. Kurt Lewin refused to consider values as goals because of methodological considerations. I feel, however, that in this he was mistaken. To put it crudely, all too often it is not what is being done but how it is being done that counts. As long as one behaves like a gentleman, as long as one behaves with finesse, society often lets him get away with stabbing his friend in the back. No matter what one is doing, one *ought* to observe certain standards. We will return to ought goals later.

(*c*) It can be, and has been, argued that the 'goal' should be used only in conjunction with end-states that have need-reductive properties, that enable consummatory behaviour. All other actions must then be seen as but means for the achievement of goals. This trend of thought dominates most of the 'scientific' models of man that are fashionable today, such as: the Freudian man; the learning-theory puppet for whom, despite the fact that everything he does is learned, insight and understanding are not achievable; the economic man, whether hedonistic or 'rational', etc.

This model works quite well with animals. If we observe animals carefully, we will often see the following sequence. The animal is quiescent (unless it is young and then, like all 'stupid' children, it 'wastes' a lot of energy playing); then it will suddenly, though very often after displaying signs of nervousness, embark upon a continuous stream of striving behaviour – such as seeking food. This stream of behaviour will stop with the attainment of food and a new pattern of behaviour will emerge, the eating-of-food consummatory behaviour. After the food has been eaten, we again find quiescence reappearing. This analysis is based upon the fact that we can easily discriminate behaviour segments that are relatively homogeneous within themselves but quite distinct one from another. These segments, which I call the natural units of behaviour, add up – in observations of animals, generally in captivity – to action, satisfaction, inaction. These, in turn, are reduced to need and need-reduction.

But, even for animals, the model soon breaks down. There is much animal action that does not lead to satisfaction, especially in the natural habitat. Upon killing her quarry, the lioness does not start consuming. Rather she guards the carcass for the entire tribe and, as a result, she does not even get the lion's share of the meat – the lion, who has been sunning himself all this time, does. Non-mammalian parents, such as birds, spend quite a lot of time and energy in feeding their young. Beavers engage in a complex co-ordinated activity in building a dam that contains many discriminable segments of behaviour that are non-need-reductive, etc. Biologists and naturalists use the adjective 'instinctual' specifically to denote this type of activity, but the word 'instinct' and its flexions are proscribed by positivism, so many scientists pretend not to see this and make as if it's not there.

The virtue of the 'action, satisfaction, inaction' schema is its conceptual simplicity; it differentiates very clearly between means and ends. It is very unfortunate, therefore, that its applicability, even for animal life, is so limited. As is to be expected, when attempting to apply this schema to human behaviour the limitations are multiplied geometrically. Every relatively sophisticated human culture and/or civilization judges the satisfaction of biological needs to be among the less important goals achievable by man. Most articulated cultures look upon the satisfaction of biological needs as constraints and barriers hampering the achievement of the really significant goals that man ought to achieve.

Is the means–end dichotomy therefore meaningless? No word that is meaningfully used in common discourse is meaningless. Every meaningful word used in common discourse denotes/connotes a discriminable phenomenon. So we are faced with the necessity of explicating the discriminable phenomena applicable to the dichotomy under discussion. How, when, and where do we perceive means and/or ends? We can try to be rigorous and restrict the usage of means/ends to phenomena that conform to the action, satisfaction, inaction schema where the events comprising the action are defined as means, and the events comprising the satisfaction are the goals. But since this immediately excludes much of animal behaviour and very much of human behaviour, it is not very useful to do so. A more serious objection to this solution is that it does violence to the actual usage of the terms. In most cases we clearly discriminate between means and ends when considering human behaviour. In order to shed light on this problem it pays to remind ourselves of some of the simple facts about perception mentioned earlier in a slightly different context.

We mentioned that, given a stimulus manifold impinging upon the human sensorium, the human brain can organize this manifold into various kinds of figure–ground configurations with a great degree of liberty, determined by the perceiver's interests and purposes, and that perception is a time-bound process. Behaviour is a discriminable organization of action through time. In order to be perceived, behaviour has to be discriminated as a figure; it has to have clear boundaries differentiating it from the surrounding ground; its boundaries include a temporal beginning and end; its body being in the middle. The body of behaviour is the smooth, continuous stream of action just mentioned. The perception of the movement is correlated to the beginning of this smooth stream; the perception of the end of the movement is correlated to the termination of the smooth stream. This enables one to perceive a person beginning to do a thing, doing it, and stopping it.

The perception of behaviour, of action, admits, as does all perception and cognition, to shifting figure–ground relationships. Hence, any stream of behaviour can be divided into many different kinds of discriminable segments, of 'natural' units, each unit consisting of a discriminable smoothness that has a beginning, a middle, and an end.

A most important determinant of what specific figure will be perceived is the time perspective of interest to the perceiver. And this can vary all over the place. On one hand, an action figure can be a short scratching of an itch. On the other hand, Robert A. Taft's political behaviour over decades could be, and is perceived by many political scientists and historians, as a constant striving to become president of the United States. This should not surprise anybody. The smoothest of all edges, that of a fine razor, looks like a series of jagged mountains when under a microscope whereas the rugged, jagged, mountains look like a smooth ridge from a perspective of fifty miles. What is really real?

We are now in the position to propose a solution to the problem of the perception of goals and means. Given a behaviour figure, the discriminable elements, the articulations, which are found in the smooth stream, are perceived as means; the end-state towards which this stream is pointed, towards which the articulations converge, is the goal. As in thing perception, articulations can become figures in their own rights, while figures can, in turn, become articulations for other figures.

When a goal changes to a mean, a relatively clear-cut change in meaning of the shifting figure is easily experienced. Whereas, as has already been argued, only the general characteristics of a goal region are important, its goal-satisfying properties remaining invariants despite many changes in specifics, when goals become means, the specific properties of the regions involved become important since it is by virtue of their utilization that movement towards the new goal is facilitated. Depending on the circumstances, the same entity can be perceived as being either a goal or a mean.

There is something disturbing about this; the relativity of goals and means has unpleasant overtones; if this is the world we live in, the ground underneath our feet begins to tremble, we lose a firm foundation upon which to walk. To regain our lost feelings of security, we can do one of three things: (a) we can reject the above analysis as being wrong, (b) we can accept it as being correct in its basic outlines and then, ostrich like, refuse to face it and formulate pleasing myths to take its place, and finally (c) accept the analysis as far as it goes, but decide that it is incomplete, that there is more to goals and means than presented up till now. I accept alternative (*c*) and will attempt to proceed with the analysis seeking a re-establishment of stability which will be consonant with the preceding arguments.

A goal has been characterized as the terminal point of a phenomenally smooth stream of striving behaviour. It has an additional phenomenal characteristic not stressed so far – when a person fails to reach a goal he exhibits behaviour indicating some degree of dissatisfaction or frustration. (The case where a person fails to reach a goal, because he loses interest in it midstream and turns to another goal, is obviously not relevant here.) To re-establish the desired stability, goals must be identified which meet these characteristics but which cannot shift in turn and be perceivable as means, i.e. which can never be perceived as being anything but goals and, as such, become 'ultimate' goals for human behaviour. These are such.

The time has come to return to the ought goals, to the basic human values.

(*d*) Ought goals have been characterized as not relating to any specific goals that lead to consummatory behaviour and as affecting all behaviour. One perceives the ought forces by seeing the effect they have on the means chosen and on how means are used for the achievement of *any* goal. Whether a person is considerate of others, whether a person is altruistic, is proud or humble, is honest or irresponsible, can probably be seen in every striving behaviour he exhibits if one looks long enough and understands what actually is going on.

If a person does not achieve his ought goals, he does not merely suffer dissatisfaction; he does not merely feel frustrated; he suffers pangs of conscience. He will not be able to free himself from them until and unless the ought be done.

The ought cannot be perceived as a means in any context. As soon as we perceive that behaviour, previously thought to have been an ought, was merely a means to achieve some goal, we see the earlier perception as false. There is only one way in which we can re-perceive acts of kindness; they are always seen as being disinterested. Were we later to find out that these acts were not disinterested, but motivated by a desire to be mentioned in a will, they would cease being perceived as acts of kindness.

Ought goals, basic human values, values in short, meet the

necessary characteristics for serving as the stable, fundamental goals which give order to, and make sense of, human existence. Means behaviour points to them; if they are not achieved, the person suffers a serious form of frustration; and they cannot, by their very nature, be means for anything beyond themselves.

Common sense is aware of this; all people are aware of this. The complex of oughts existing for a society at any given time is denoted by the term 'ethics'. Abnegation and martydom thereby become meaningful.

Words which move men move men because they touch upon profound truths. That truth I am struggling with here was expressed with power by the following words which moved many, many men: 'For what shall it profit a man, if he shall gain the whole world, and lose his own soul?'

(*e*) It is worth while to note that the concepts that are adequate for describing ought goals, such as honesty, doing a job well, consideration for others, etc., are also applicable and are often used to describe personality structure. This leads to an interesting speculation, an interesting tying together. The constellation of relatively invariant goals that are embedded within, and are mediated by, the behaviour leading to the achievement of tangible, need-reducing goals, serves as the basis for the perception of the personality, of the essence of a person. Hence ought forces are necessary for the perception of a person. This, at least partially, substantiates the feeling that a set of goals that cannot in themselves be means are necessary for the perception of a stable social universe.

Actually, it now becomes possible to restructure much of human behaviour so that it can be seen in a new way – actually, a very old way that has been recognized by wise men throughout man's history.

The action, satisfaction, inaction schema, although not applicable in the primitive simplicity hoped for by its formulators and adherents, is nevertheless a reasonably adequate characterization of animal life. Much of the animal behaviour can easily be seen as beginning with a literal appearance of a physiological need, a tissue tension and a restless behaviour emerging with the emerging need. As the need passes, some threshold action begins which is almost always terminated in consummatory behaviour. For all animals we also see a stable terminal goal which can never be a means – an animal lives to maintain life, its own and its offsprings' as long as they are too immature to assume the responsibility for maintaining their own life. As soon as animals lose the ability to bear young they soon die, at least in the feral state. The simple maintenance of life of individuals and of species is the ultimate goal towards which all animal behaviour points.

In their actions, i.e. interaction with their environment, all animals exhibit a fundamental style of behaviour which psychologists call stimulus-boundedness, and which consists of a certain type of stereotypy, *the lack of which* is a necessary condition for the perception of intelligence. They do not freely manipulate objects in the environment and they respond only to those physio-chemical properties inherent in the objects relevant to the maintenance of physiological life. And even this they do in an essentially blind, and, from a human point of view, stupid manner (blindness and stupidity being mediated by the same behavioural cues). In their ecological environment enough individuals manage to survive to guarantee the survival of the species, though the many extinct species show that this guarantee is not perfect.

Man, of course, is an evolutionary outgrowth of animal life. The perennial visitor from Mars, were he to be confronted with three skeletons, of a man, of an ape, and of a fish, would undoubtedly classify the first two as belonging together, as being quite different from the fish. Behaviourally, however, an ape is far more similar to a fish when the percentage of actions it undertakes that ends in physiological need-reductive behaviour is compared to similar actions on the part of man.

Man's behaviour differs from animal behaviour in many ways that are all interrelated and are often lumped together under the term of intelligence; man is called a thinking animal. This is not so simple. Animals too, especially the advanced mammals and birds, seem to exhibit acts of intelligence, seem to show that they can think. But a close scrutiny of the respective behaviour of animals and men shows significant differences. Animals exhibit the ability to think about concrete, simply physical, causal properties of the physical objects that exist in their environment here and now. In addition, this ability seems to be restricted in almost all cases to the objects that exist in the visual field of the animal. It is as if, almost literally, it is a case of 'out of sight, out of mind'. The question can even be raised whether they can see objects or things in any manner similar to man. Man's thinking, on the other hand, generally deals with the non-existent, be it from a geographical-temporal standpoint or a specific physical standpoint.

The essence of human thinking is the ability to deal with the possible, the ability to *construct* a possible, and the ability to recognize the *impossible*. This latter ability stops man from exhibiting stupidity in novel situations which is so common to animals and, in a different context, to computers said to be programmed to think. In short, to use a term common to many psychologists, man has the ability to think abstractly.

The emergence of the ability to think abstractly had important consequences that converged unto an important result – a reasonable guarantee that the physiological need-reduction necessary for the preservation of life can be met. Leisure enabled at least select groups of men in early human societies to contemplate the possible, and human communication then enabled others in these societies to acquire, in varying degrees, at least some of the fruits of this contemplation. There is no society that did and does not afford, at least for some of its members, some leisure time for contemplation. The contemplation of the possible has had the same effect upon all human societies, as far as we know, albeit again with various degrees of intensity and with manifold variation of content; transcendental goals emerged. The meaning of life changed. Whereas the ultimate goal of animal behaviour is the maintenance of physiological life, individual and species, for men, for every society of man at every level of culture, the maintenance of physical life *per se* has ceased to be the ultimate goal. Man lives in order to accomplish something else, a something else that is inherently irrelevant for the mere maintenance of physical life and is all too often inimical to it.

Examples abound all around us. One need not look at the obvious examples such as art, literature, philosophy, and religion. Let us just look at the way we eat, and what we eat, and the way we prepare our food. Eating is the paradigm of the need-reductive consummatory behaviour necessary for maintenance of physiological life. Animals 'know' this; they make no bones about it; they simply eat when they can, when they are hungry. But the act of eating for a man is overencrusted with ceremony and ritual. We do not merely eat food, we also spend much time in preparing it for eating. Cooking has become an art; the presentation of the food at the table has become an art; eating the food has become an art. We tend to lose much of our appetite when we are in a setting where food is either cooked, presented, or eaten in an artless manner. This has nothing to do with the physiological life-maintaining properties of the food *per se*. 'He eats like an animal' is a term of opprobrium.

Goals that are necessary to be achieved in order to maintain life, the simple animal goals, now become contingent barriers to the ahievement of the important goals of life, barriers which man feels he must overcome as he does the other barriers in his locomotion towards a goal; or they become contingent instrumentalities by means of which man does achieve transcendental goals, the basic values, the ought goals that give meaning to his life. An example of the former: a man works very hard to earn enough money so that he can retire early, the satisfaction of his physical needs being assured in order to do the things he really wants to do. An example of the latter is the case just discussed, the eating of food.

A conceptual closure is achieved. I experience a subjectively coherent conceptualization of the intricate interdependence of goals and means and how they relate to the stubbornly persistent phenomenal facts which it is the job of an empirical science to explain. What emerges is a complex organismic structure, a *gestaltung*, which retains its unity because of a basic principle, an ultimate goal irreducible to anything beyond itself; for animal life the goal is the maintenance of life; for human life the goal is the achievement of transcendental goals.

Given a finite time perspective, human behaviour can be portioned into figures and grounds by an observer as well as by the actor, which include both the ultimate goals and the specific relative means/goals relevant to the specific time segments; the specific means/goals being a resultant of the contingencies which the environment presents to the person within this specific time segment and his ultimate goals. In addition, all goals, beyond the immediate goal, are relatively non-specific, so that a set of possible specific end-states can serve as a terminus for behaviour.

(*f*) How does an individual function within this complex interdependency of relative tangible goals and means structure bounded by the more or less nebulous ultimate goals? It was noted above that a human observer can organize another's behaviour into a means/goal conceptual figure depending upon a specific time perspective. Well, every individual does the same for himself – he has no difficulty in discriminating long-range goals, shorter-range goals, short-range goals, and immediate goals – what he is actually trying to accomplish here and now.

It was argued above that many concrete situations can be of equal need-reductive properties and serve as a terminal goal. There is, however, a relationship between the indefiniteness of a future goal region and the time perspective – the longer the time perspective, the less specific the intended terminal goal need be, the greater the number of possible specific end-states which can serve as an adequate goal region.

The sequence of tangible, time-bound means/goals perceptions constitute a nested hierarchy which is bounded both on the bottom and on the top. The most inclusive tangible goal is what a person generally expects to achieve in his life (which may and does change with time but which is set at any given instant of time); it includes all possible relative goals for the person. The goal which does not include any sub-goals, the goal with a zero inclusiveness, is the unit goal which answers the question: 'What is the person doing here and now?' It is impossible to reduce a unit goal to something smaller without dealing with 'meaningless' muscle twitches that are, in themselves, inadequate to explain behaviour. As an example and analogy consider the problem of meaning. We can discuss the meaning of a word, a term (a group of words), a sentence, a paragraph, a chapter, a book, a group of works by an author, and finally the basic philosophy of an author as communicated by his life work, as well as the basic philosophy of an historical epoch as communicated by the collective social output of that epoch. The latter, the basic philosophies, are inclusive conceptual figures; the word with which this sequence begins is the unit conceptual figure. The individual letters that are used to spell the word out, that are used to build up the word, are no bearers of meaning in themselves.

Unit goals are the most clearly determined and admit of the least variability. They are also the goals with the shortest time perspective. As the time perspective increases, so does the acceptable variability of possible goal states. To return to the example of the restaurant given earlier. At the outset any restaurant will do, the time–space point that will serve as the final goal being pretty well indeterminate. With the decision to enter a specific restaurant the range of variations of time–space points narrows considerably, however the specific chair in which the person will sit still admits of quite a lot of variation. Once the person decides upon which chair to choose and starts to walk to it, a unit act, the set of time–space points defining the goal region is pretty well determined although it still admits to discriminable variation such as the exact position of the chair relative to the table.

At its most concrete level, goal-directed behaviour is then a sequence of unit goals whose meaning and order is a function of the superordinate goals within which they are embedded and the environmental contingencies which confront the person at the time of his behaviour. If perception is restricted solely to these unit goals, a patternless concatenation of acts will be observed yielding no meaningful order, making no sense.

If we use a mathematical analogy somewhat loosely, we can say that the ultimate goals are perceived to hold for an infinite time perspective. It follows therefore that they are completely indeterminate as far as specific concrete situations are concerned. And this holds. Ultimate goals, the ought goals, have to be achieved in every action of the individual. Hence they are to be achieved in any and every possible situation that can serve as a goal region. Hence no specific tangible situation can serve as a goal region for ultimate goals.

Man therefore perceived himself as striving to achieve many unit goals which in turn are either steps for the achievement of a hierarchy of superordinate goals or interludes in this process – such as a vacation, or taking a break to refresh oneself so that one can continue to work successfully, etc. As unit goals are achieved, superordinate goals change to unit goals and thereby become more determinate in character. With the achievement of each unit goal, man takes a step in his psychological space. With each step in psychological space, man's perspective changes. Hence he stops to assess his position. What is the nature of this assessment?

The order of this assessment is irrelevant but it usually consists of the following: The superordinate goal which turns into the new unit goal becomes much more determinate; the exact range of achievable concrete situations that can serve as goal regions becomes more delimited and specifiable. The person will therefore often re-evaluate the goal to see if it is still desirable. With the change of perspective the person gets to know more of the environment and/or can see the environment in the new context; hence he may often examine it to see whether new, more desirable goals, both unit or superordinate, are now achievable which, owing to the earlier, more limited perspective, he did not imagine achievable. In addition, he will survey the environment to see whether it conforms to his expectations, whether what he planned to do is feasible. He will also examine the environment to determine whether it has unanticipated windfalls or pitfalls. And finally he will look backward at the path he had just traversed to see how he handled himself and what of importance can be learned from the experience.

In short, he will exhibit that unique human talent for being intelligent and flexible. Emerson's dictum about foolish consistency being the hobgoblin of small minds is particularly cogent in this area of human endeavour. The art of the decision-maker and decision-implementer is the art of zigging and zagging, of changing tangible goals and means when appropriate, not too early and not too late.

(g) This then is the complex nexus which probably every man has in his mind, with a varying degree of clarity, when he uses the words 'goal', 'means', and 'value'. For any given time perspective man has in mind a set of possible, more or less abstractly defined, objective states that are partitioned into an articulated figure and an articulated ground, such that with every shift of figure–ground organization new meanings and new perspectives arise. In addition, each given time perspective is part of a temporal sequence consisting of a nesting hierarchy of means/goals – depending upon how you look at them. And this whole fluid, frightfully indeterminate relativism is given substance and sense through a set of absolute goals, of basic human values, which do not reside in any tangible goal *per se* but which use these tangible goals as means for their own actualization.

Men must have this complexity in mind when they use the words in order to make sense. When, as in the case of conformity to the dictates of an oversimplified positivism, they reject this complexity, they cease to make sense. The fact that the ensuing non-sense can be expressed mathematically does not help matters – one gets no more meaning out of mathematics than what one puts into it.

The positivists commit the sin of increasing confusion by acts of commission, advertently, by explicitly rejecting the fundamental basis of meaning and sense – common sense. Those who formulated the dictionary definition committed the sin of increasing confusion, inadvertently, by flanking definition 2 (page 98) – the only definition which yields a clue to the complexity here unravelled – with two definitions where goals are pretty-well-defined objective states within the context of a game. But then they too were probably affected by the spirit of positivism which, with rare exceptions, is the predominant tone of contemporary scientific thinking.

8

Decision-making under uncertainty and problem-solving

*A conceptual exploration from a Gestalt theoretical viewpoint**

1. INTRODUCTION

(a) *Gestalt Theory – How it Differs from Accepted Theoretical Approaches in Psychology*

Many different theories on thinking, problem-solving, and decision-making are to be found in contemporary psychology. It has been asserted [14] that, despite their varieties, most stem from two main traditional doctrines: the formal logical approach and association theory. Both these doctrines attempt to achieve a rigour of analysis modelled upon the Euclidean system hoping thereby to emulate the success of its application to physics. When having to choose between explaining a gamut of phenomenal events or the preservation of rigour, both doctrines choose the latter. Hence they are forced to select from among the phenomenal events those which exemplify the established rigour, or, when this is too difficult, set up experimental situations to serve as examples. Although the doctrines are aware of the phenomenal events which are unexplainable by their theories or seemingly contradict the theories, they argue that these will be explained in time as the theories are checked out and refined. The quest for rigour dictates the rejection of phenomenal perception and its replacement by operationally defined measurements yielding phenomenal 'pointer readings'. Cardinal numbers are the preferred readings; the state of the art, however, dictates ordinal numbers in

* Basically using concepts taken from Kurt Lewin, Kurt Goldstein, and Martin Scheerer.

most instances and the Boolean number system of Yes–No in many instances.

Gestalt theory, on the other hand, although not rejecting rigour where achievable, emphasizes the phenomenal given as a point of departure. An *a priori* set of basic elements, applicable to but a selected part of phenomenal experience, are almost certain to be inadequate and, in addition, will probably point to the wrong direction. The model underlying Gestalt theory seems, in broad methodological respects, to be Kepler's astronomy [12] rather than Newton's physics. Kepler sought to represent the phenomenal path of the planets. He sought circles but found elipses whose foci were related to characteristics of the planets. This was an empirical finding devoid of theory or, more properly, based on a primitive, unsystematic, non-rigorous theory. It was only after Galileo digested implications of this finding that Newton was able to formulate his rigorous theory.

Something similar preceded the Euclidean system. It is doubtful whether Pythagoras could have formulated his theorem had there not been a clear perception of certain empirical events showing that the square of the hypotenuse of some triangles is equal to the sum of the squares of the other two sides. And this in turn led, after additional centuries of thinking and development, to the formulation of the Euclidean system.

Gestalt psychology concentrates on the phenomenal given in its attempt to seek an understanding of psychological phenomena. Rigorous experimentation and operational measurement become less important in this scheme of things. The findings of the traditional doctrines are not rejected as findings. However, because they go counter to much that is phenomenally given, they are rejected as being insufficient to serve as adequate explanatory concepts. Of course, most Gestalt theoreticians go beyond this mild rejection. They feel that the elementaristic approach underlying the traditional doctrines is not only insufficient but wrong. They reject the proposition that behaviour events can be explained on the basis of elements and the combination of elements. They believe that the basic concepts that will ultimately emerge in the social sciences will entail part–whole interdependencies, holistic dynamic field interactions, etc. I share these beliefs, but it is certainly not proven. Although I consider it improbable, it is not impossible that the phenomena which buttress my beliefs will, in the fullness of time, be explained by the concepts of the traditional doctrines.

(b) *Outline and Purposes of this Chapter*

In what is to follow I will try to describe phenomena of thinking, problem-solving, and decision-making. I will assert that this is the way men behave in situations necessitating this behaviour. I will discuss these phenomena using some simple topological terms at a very low level of abstraction, knowing full well that the conceptual representation used is far from adequate. Nevertheless, the terms do help to clarify the issues and, because of this, I believe that the ultimate adequate conceptual representation will have to include them in some form or other.

The extent to which the ideas here are original is irrelevant. It is obvious that I am greatly in debt to the thinking of Kurt Lewin [8, 9, 10, 11]. It is not so obvious, but I am probably in even greater debt to the thinking of Fritz Heider [7]. The ideas about pyschological certainty are derived from Goldstein [4, 5]. My aim is not to be original but to try to make sense and thereby help in clarifying the issues.

(c) *Some Basic Concepts*

Man considers the world as consisting of entities that are related to each other in a lawful manner; he functions in this world on the basis of a partial mapping of the world. I call this mapping Frame of Reference.* Frame of reference is quite fuzzy for me at present but I know it is there. It seems to consist of meaning dimensions and specified values along each dimension. The frame of reference comprises all that a person knows about the world in terms of entities and the causal nexi within which they are embedded.

Language can be considered as simplified analogy. The total number of words available to a given person exist somehow in his brain. These words can be ordered along four meaning dimensions: names of entities, names of actions, modifiers of entities or actions, connectors of entities or actions. The specific value of each word is its specific meaning. This organized totality is the linguistic frame of reference. It is, in every individual case, a partial mapping of the objective language since no person knows all the words to be found in an unabridged dictionary.

The frame of reference is a function of the native integrating

* This concept is very similar to the concept of 'schema' as developed in British psychology and physiology by Head, Bartlett, and others [6, 1]. I prefer 'frame of reference' to 'schema' because it has connotations the latter lacks.

I

ability of the brain as it interacts with an individual history, a fusion of both nature and nurture. Since it constitutes the total knowledge of an individual, only a small part of its contents can play a role in any given behaviour event. To return to the linguistic analogy. Assume a bilingual person who speaks English and French. The total vocabulary of such a person is partitioned into two sets: English and French. When such a person is in an English-speaking group all the words along the French dimension are excluded from use. They do not emerge in the speaker's consciousness except in circumstances where unique meanings are expressible by them for which the speaker cannot find an English equivalent.

The frame of reference is like a storehouse of resources. Given a specific concrete situation, the person draws the relevant, available resources from it. This leads to a second basic concept: the Life-Space.

All ordered behaviour can be analysed as constituting three stages: (i) a person finds himself in a specific concrete situation; (ii) the person evaluates the situation, drawing upon the resources available to him in his frame of reference, and decides upon a course of action; and (iii) the person executes the decision. Stage (ii) is of primary interest in the present paper since it serves as the stage for thinking, problem-solving and decision-making. The situation in which a person finds himself at the onset of this stage is partitioned into various states. There is the state in which the person finds himself. There is (are) the state(s) of the goal(s) attainable in the situation. And there are the states of means available that may lead to the desired goal(s). As a result of the evaluation stage, the person decides upon which means to use to achieve the desired goal(s). The situation is an ordered manifold of states and, as such, it consti-tutes a space. Following Lewin, I call this space the Life-Space.

The life-space comprises various states. To repeat: There is the state where the person finds himself; there is (are) the goal state(s); and there are intermediate means states some of which may lead to the goal(s). It is in many ways similar to a topological space and hence topological terms can be used to name some of its elements. A state in the life-space will be called a *region* of the life-space. As a result of the evaluation stage the person decides upon a course of action through the means regions which he believes will lead him to the goal region(s). This course of action will be called a *distinguished path* that leads to the goal region(s). Behaviour, in turn, is called *locomotion* along a distinguished path towards the goal region(s).

The life-space can be represented by either an old-fashioned two-dimensional topological picture, *Figure 1, a*, or a more sophisticated point graph, *Figure 1, b*. Point graphs are preferable to pictures for various reasons but the latter are easier to understand at the outset. Hence they will be used in what follows.

If no restrictions are placed on the nature of the path, a topological analysis can yield an indefinite number of paths when the life-space consists of more than two regions. The person can locomote to region 2 and then back to region 1 and back to 2 indefinitely before reaching a goal region, $2 + n$. From a psychological standpoint a very reasonable restriction can be placed on the determination of a distinguished path; i.e. that no region can be entered into twice. This excludes endless cycling. Matters are thereby simplified considerably. In *Figure 1* the restriction immediately excludes regions 3, 4, 5, 9, 10, and 17 from any path since to get from them into any of the goal regions involves passing through a region which has already been entered. In addition the number of possible paths leading to the goal regions, although it still can be quite large, becomes finite and calculable. An added restriction that the number of regions in a path be a minimum settles the matter. In *Figure 1*, this determines two distinguished paths, one leading to the goal region, 15, and the other to the goal region, 20. The paths comprise regions 2, 14, and 15, 2, 19, and 20. This restriction makes pragmatic sense but not necessarily psychological sense. From a pragmatic standpoint people are often unreasonable.

It should be understood that the life-space changes as soon as the person locomotes into a new region since his position in the life-space has changed. This may or may not lead to changes in behaviour depending upon circumstances which cannot be represented adequately by the concepts used here.

It is very difficult, if not impossible, to define a region either conceptually or operationally. In many cases, however, it is possible to define locomotion into a new region ostensively, i.e. point it out, when looking at actual behaviour or upon a record of behaviour. 'Region', therefore, has to be treated as a primitive, self-evident concept. However, an attempt can be made to define the meaning of a region to an individual: the meaning of a region may be said to consist of the set of actions which a person thinks he can undertake when he enters it, i.e. what he can do in it, and the set of consequences that he thinks he will be subjected to, he will suffer, by being in it, or by what it can do to him. The meaning of a region are its

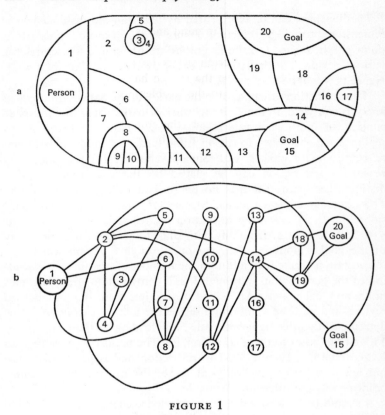

FIGURE 1

causal, its dispositional properties. It is determined by an interaction of the state of the real world and the frame of reference.

(d) *Thinking, Problem-solving, and Decision-making*

Thinking, problem-solving, and decision-making are names given to various aspects of behaviour to be found in stage (b) of ordered behaviour that constitutes the distinguished path. The generic meaning of thinking is the most general, and it includes the meanings of the other two terms as special cases. Decision-making, in turn, is a special case of problem-solving. The terms introduced in the preceding section enable us to circumscribe the meaning of these three terms in a manner that will clarify their usage in this paper. Thinking is used to denote the behaviour when the person is mentally exploring the regions in his life-space to determine their meaning. He does not necessarily have any goal in mind and is certainly not interested in determining a path. It refers to some sort of general region inventory so that when the occasion arises he will know what to do. Problem-solving occurs when the person has some goal(s) in mind but no path(s). A solution to the problem occurs when a distinguished path emerges which he believes will enable him to locomote to the goal. Sometimes, however, the solution takes one of two forms. Either several distinguished paths or several potential paths emerge. In both these cases the person must choose one of these paths. The mental activity involved in determining this choice is called decision-making.

2. DECISION-MAKING AND UNCERTAINTY

(a) *Logical Certainty and Psychological Certainty*

The word certainty was originally used to describe a psychological state in which a person had no doubt about the outcome of a given state of affairs. To the extent that he had doubts about the outcome he was said to be uncertain. Logic assumed such certainties unquestioningly for a long time and concentrated on deriving deductions on their basis which were equally certain. Given these certainties as premisses, logic showed men, in a convincing manner, that the deductions were also necessarily certain, that in no circumstances could they be false. This aspect of necessity, of necessary truth or necessary falsehood, was fused to the meaning of 'certainty' to devolve into the idea of logical certainty. The original psychological origin of the meaning of the term was lost sight of. The logical meaning of certainty became the impossibility of being wrong.

With the development of science, the problem of induction began to loom on the horizon. Cartesian philosophy raises the doubt as to whether premisses dealing with matters of fact can be logically certain. Philosophers disliked these implications and tried to salvage logical certainty in many ways, figuratively passing the ball from one to another when they were on the verge of fumbling. Finally Hume got the ball and settled the issue. Empirical statements cannot be certainly true or certainly false; only tautological statements can be certain. But tautological statements yield no information.

Meanwhile men, including Hume, behaved in blithe disregard to this crisis in philosophy. Their behaviour indicated certainty and uncertainty in many daily actions. If I am not mistaken, Hume was aware of this discrepancy in his own behaviour and he was disturbed by it.

It is a fact that psychological certainty, although probably corre-lated with logical certainty, is most certainly (logically speaking) not univocally co-ordinated with it. It is the case that men will experience psychological certainty even when aware of logical uncertainty. As I sit and write these words, I am completely certain that a meteor will not crash through the roof and tear my arm off. Logically, however, I am certain that this is a possible contingency. One can counter that the probability of such a contingency is so low that it may be disregarded. Yes, but this admits my basic argument with one modification – only if logical uncertainty is below a certain measure will it be disregarded by men.

I will whittle this modification down. I am writing these words in Southern California, a few miles from the San Andreas fault. The probability of an earthquake taking place today is far greater than the probability of being hit by a meteor. Yet I do not seem to worry about an earthquake any more than I do about being hit by a meteor. My psychological certainty that these events will not occur seems to be equal.

Against the contention that in both cases the probabilities are too small to be decisive I will bring forth a third, very common, example where most men are not only aware of the possibility that certain undesired events can occur but actually take steps to mitigate the effects of these events were they to occur, and then they act being sure that they will not occur. Every time we pay an insurance premium for a car we accept the logical analysis that there is a good probability that we will be involved in an accident – in most cases we accept this probability to the tune of several hundred dollars a year. Yet, we rarely if ever drive a car without being psychologically certain that the possible accident will not occur. I will argue below that this certainty is necessary before we can take confident control of the steering wheel.

At this point a contention may arise that I am discussing subjective intangibles that border upon sophistry and mysticism. This is not true. Psychological uncertainty is as objective a phenomenon, and can be seen clearly if one knows how and where to look, as is the curving path of starlight when it passes close to the sun. We all experience a difference when we are certain or uncertain. We can report this difference to others in words ranging from a simple declarative statement such as: 'I don't feel sure about this', through various picturesque and descriptive statements. Examples of the latter are: 'I feel ill at ease, my stomach is tight' – 'Things are running up and down my spine' – 'I feel ambivalent, I can't commit myself' – etc.

Psychological certainty and uncertainty can be defined ostensively, i.e. pointed to. We observe a white rat, a member of a class of creatures upon whose behaviour so much of our scientific psychological knowledge is predicated, running through a maze. He is running smoothly; his legs are in synchrony, his tail projecting behind him, and his conic head, whiskers stiff, is held parallel to the ground and points unwaveringly towards the end of the corridor. The entire action is a smooth harmony. Each instant of behaviour is an integral consequent of the preceding instant. All lead dynamically to the end of the corridor.

At the end of the corridor there is a choice point with several alternative paths available. When the rat reaches the choice point he stops and his behaviour starts to change. His body drops as his legs fold slightly, his whiskers start to quiver, and his tail starts to wriggle slowly. He points his nose into one path, then into another. He looks, he smells. One of his forefeet makes a tentative move in the direction of a path and then is jerked back. He 'thinks'. He is unsure of what to do. The smooth, integrated harmony of behaviour is broken. One instant is not an integral continuation of the preceding instant. The flow of behaviour is jerky, unpredictable. It is impossible not to see the striking difference between the behaviour exhibited while running through the corridor and the behaviour exhibited at the choice point.

Eventually the rat chooses a path. He takes a few tentative, hesitating steps into the new corridor, sniffs once or twice, and starts to run. The harmonious behaviour pattern reappears.

This then is an ostensive definition of psychological certainty. Men exhibit these differences too. In fact, when a difference exists between behavioural and verbal evidence as to psychological certainty, we give more weight to the former. When a person announces confidently, 'leave it to me, I can do it', and then proceeds to do the job in a jerky, hesitating manner, we tend to call him 'vain braggart' and do not believe that he knows what he is doing. If, despite this, he succeeds in his task we tend to attribute it to luck rather than to skill.

This is the reason that a driver should be psychologically certain that he will not have an accident while he drives. If he lacks certainty, his behaviour will not be smooth and co-ordinated enough to avoid an accident and most probably he will get into one. When I have had too much to drink at a party or am quite fatigued, my certainty in not having an automobile accident is undermined. I then hand the wheel to my wife.

Psychological certainty is closely related to psychological health. Clinical anxiety is considered by many psychotherapists to be nothing more than chronic uncertainty.

(b) *Game Theory, Structural Decision Theory, etc.*

Game theory, decision theory, etc., are proposed solutions to the problem of induction. Their formulation followed the development of mathematical probability and combinatorial analysis. At present there are logicians who are trying to develop logical probability to serve the same purpose [2, 3]. Despite many technical and theoretical differences between the mathematical and logical probability solutions to the problem of induction, they share a similar frame of reference, a frame of reference which stems from their uncritical acceptance of logical certainty as the only meaning of certainty.

Since logical certainty implies that man can never be certain of the outcome of any of his actions, the question poses itself: 'On what basis does he decide to act?' Given the premiss that man cannot decide on the basis of certainty the course of action he should take, and given the empirically true premiss that man does decide between alternate courses of action, two conclusions are derivable as answers.

The first conclusion asserts that man does not take the outcome of an action into account when deciding upon the action. This is the conclusion, underlying psychological association theory, that at a choice point the living organism will exhibit trial and error behaviour, i.e. decide upon a course of action randomly unless some sort of association or reflex bond exists between the stimulus situation and the repertoire of possible mechanized reflex chains stored, as it were, within it. The outcome of the decision will modify the repertoire and will therefore affect the behaviour of the organism at its next decision point; it can, however, have no effect upon the decision *per se*.

The second conclusion asserts that man can somehow evaluate the degree of certainty that an action will lead to a desired outcome, and then he will choose the action which has the highest degree of certainty, the greatest probability of success. This assertion is more consonant with common sense. Behaviour based on this conclusion is perceived to be rational; behaviour based on the first conclusion is perceived to be irrational. Game theory, decision theory, etc., are predicated upon this second conclusion.

The mathematical theory of probability and statistics enables man, given a certain mathematical model and set of adequate empirical data, to assign a number to this probability of success. A measure of the degree of logical certainty is thereby obtained. It can be argued that the potential utilization of this measure is simply analogous to a momentous discovery that must have taken place before man could erect reasonably large and stable structures. Man could always discriminate adequately enough between different lengths of logs. That one log is shorter than another or of almost the same length is easily seen. What cannot be seen is the *length* of the log, or whether it is one-third as long or three times as long as another log, or whether it is just right to fit a given gap. Until this knowledge is available, reasonably large and stable structures cannot be erected: man must be content with flimsy huts. Similarly, for complex human activity that is determined by decisions. Since our present complex organizations run on the basis of decisions that are made intuitively, that are based on the relatively crude and insensitive perception of the action that yields the greatest certainty of success, these organizations are like the flimsy huts built by primitive man. How much more efficient, large, and stable will these organizations be when man learns to measure the probability of success accurately?

Figure 2 is a simplified representation of the application of this

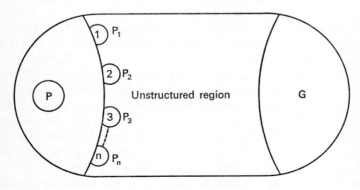

FIGURE 2

measure in a decision-making situation. The person p finds himself in one region whereas the goal G which he is trying to achieve is in another region. There is no distinguished path between the two hence, by definition, they are separated by an unstructured region. The person can take many specific actions, each of which may or may not be a first step of a distinguished path that will lead to the goal region. How is he to choose? Decision theory answers this question unequivocally. A mathematical analytic technique should be developed so that a number can be calculated for each possible alternate action available to p (or at least for each possible alternative action that it seems reasonable to take). This number will tell p which action has the greatest probability of success. Since p is rational, he seeks the action with the greatest probability. Because this number is rigorously calculated, rigorously measured, it is of necessity more accurate than human cerebral calculation just as the measurement of length with a yardstick is more accurate than a visual estimation of size. The cerebral calculation, the intuitive judgement which appears as a hunch, should therefore be rejected when it disagrees with the conclusion of the rigorous calculation, just as we reject the evidence of our senses in visual illusions. In *Figure 2* the alternate means of action available to p are represented by the small numbered regions. The probabilities of success associated with each possible action are represented by the p_1's.

The p_1's need not be a simple probability statement of success expectancy. They can be a weighted index or ordered n-tuple that estimate more than one effect of the possible action. For instance, it can be an ordered two-tuple, the first number giving an estimate of success, the second an estimate of costs. In a similar manner n-tuples of a larger magnitude can be calculated.

It should be noted that implicit in the proper use of this approach is a very serious constraint on the person's behaviour. Once the person takes an action based on decision theory calculations, he cannot intervene in the process initiated by the action. If he does intervene at any point, the mathematical quantification of the probability of success ceases to be valid. Once the die is cast, it must be permitted to roll uninterruptedly until it stops; once the croupier drops the roulette ball on to the spinning wheel nobody can interfere with the process until the ball falls into a cup. This constraint can be eliminated or relaxed when decision theory will be in a position to calculate the p_1's of the actions available to the person at any point in the process where he wants to intervene, as well as the probability that he will choose each of these actions, and include this in the initial p_1. At present this is impossible.

(c) *Game Theory, Statistical Decision Theory, etc., and Psychological Certainty*

It is a fact that in almost all experiments where human subjects are placed in a situation demanding the use of mathematically generated decision rules, they refuse to follow them rigorously. Such behaviour exasperates the experimenters who then call the subjects names. The experimenter should not be surprised. It is well known that upon examining man's economic behaviour we rarely find the ideal hedonistic man. It does no good to call man 'irrational'. Man's behaviour is reasonable in his crazy way.

A social psychologist once told me of trying to experiment with game theoretical predictions concerning a zero-sum game. He had a neat experimental set-up. He would get subjects, the standard college sophomore, and give them the rules of the game. Almost to a man the subjects would then rebel against participating in the experiment. Upon being asked why, their answer would again be almost unanimous: 'We don't want to behave like pigs.'

Human behaviour is not arbitrary, not random, not uncaused. If human behaviour is different from the behaviour predicted or recommended on the basis of mathematical models, it indicates that the causal nexus underlying human behaviour is different from the causal nexus underlying these models. In other simpler words, men, when deciding upon their actions take into account at least some different things from those taken into account by the mathematical theories.

This should not be construed to mean that men's decisions are better or worse than are mathematically determined decisions. It all depends. There are obviously conditions in which a mathematical solution is to be preferred to man's best attempts, and vice versa. What is important is that we should not feel that man is unreasonable, is perverse, in not doing what decision theory tells him to do. Once we understand how man goes about thinking, solving problems, and making his mind up, we will also know under what conditions man will disregard present dictates of decision theory, under what conditions he will apply them blindly, unimaginatively, and under what conditions he will apply them with insight, imaginatively. It seems obvious that a successful application of the insights of decision theory to human affairs cannot be achieved unless these conditions are known.

(d) *Minimum Level of Psychological Certainty – A Prerequisite for Action*

The title of this section and much of my preceding words make it obvious where I think the nub of the trouble is to be found: the men who formulated and are formulating mathematical decision theories are guided by the concept of logical certainty, whereas the men who make decisions primarily think and are primarily guided by considerations of psychological certainty. I will attempt to develop some of the consequences of this distinction.

Unless explicitly specified to the contrary, the word 'certainty' will refer to psychological certainty only. I will not cite specific experiments to support my convictions since these convictions are not based on any particular experiment, and I cannot imagine any particular experiment or small number of experiments that will, at present, undermine my confidence in them. I believe that enough of my assertions and/or their implications are amenable to empirical verification to take the whole matter out of the realm of armchair speculation, but I do not intend to develop this aspect.

In taking decisions whose outcome can affect *important* aspects of a person's life, uncertainty as such plays a minimal role. Such decisions are taken primarily on the basis of certainty considerations. To rephrase this in my technical terminology: decisions that lead to locomotion through and to *central* regions of the life-space are always based on certainty characteristics of these regions and not on uncertainty. This is a presumed law of behaviour that holds for every individual act. Acts which seem to contradict this law will yield, upon analysis, the fact that the person was coerced by forces external to himself that were more powerful than whatever forces he could mobilize to counter them. These coercions lead, in the longer run, to predictable behaviour which is generally undesirable.

In order to communicate a more tangible, palpable grasp of this law and what it entails, it will be necessary to explicate and develop some of the concepts presented above.

Certainty characteristics of a region refer to the meaning of a region, and the meaning of a region was earlier said to be the sum of things that the person believes can be done to him and what he can do while in the region. The meaning of a region refers to a range of possibilities only a few of which *will* occur when the person enters the region at any given time. This becomes obvious when we consider that the meaning of a region can include mutually exclusive contingencies; i.e. movies can be very thrilling or sickeningly boring but one movie cannot be both.

And with this we come to a basic distinction between psychological certainty and logical certainty; the latter is predicated upon what must occur when a person enters a new region – the former is predicated upon what *may** occur when a person enters a new region. The person seeks certainty by trying to determine what will not happen to him. In other words, the first thing a person will do before entering a new region will be to determine what the region may do to him. It is only after he is convinced that the set of possible consequences he may suffer upon entering a region excludes certain possibilities that he is not willing to face in any circumstance, that he will be ready to consider the idea of locomotion into the region. In simple figurative words: a person will not voluntarily take a step unless he is convinced that his foot will meet with solid ground and that he will not fall flat on his face. Unless this *minimum* level of certainty exists, no behaviour is possible. The consequence of lack of such certainty is clinical anxiety, the *sine qua non* for behaviour pathology.†

It is not enough for a person to know that a given decision has a high probability of success; he must, in addition, be certain that

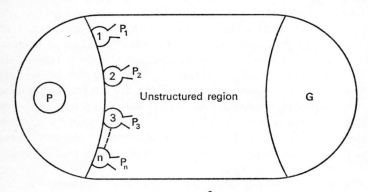

FIGURE 3

---

* 'May' is defined by: 'There is no reason for it not to'; the sentence: 'X may occur' is equivalent to the sentence: 'There is no reason for X not to occur'.

† The reader with a specialized technical background may recognize that the phenomenon here considered is what Goldstein [4] calls a 'catastrophic reaction'.

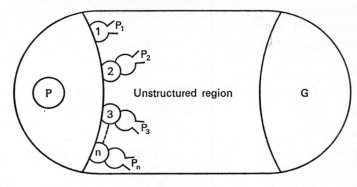

FIGURE 4

some outcomes will not occur. To the extent that he will not be certain about the latter the region will be insufficiently structured.* If all the person has to go by are decision rules giving a probability of success and nothing more, *Figure 2* becomes an improper representation of the psychological life-space. The first step into any means regions that may be a path to the goal is, because of the absence of a minimum level of certainty, open to some uncertainty, to some unstructure. *Figure 3* is therefore a better representation. Here the small numbered regions that represent possible actions, each associated with a p_1, are not fully structured, are opened to uncertainty.

Under these conditions the person will initially disregard the p_1's. Before considering them he will seek to establish a minimum level of certainty to guarantee his not falling flat on his face as a consequence of his decision. This can be represented conceptually by the closing of the numbered means regions. Supposing this can be done for certain of the means regions and not for others, a condition represented by *Figure 4* emerges.† We see here that a minimum level of certainty was reached for all possible actions but the one represented by means region 1. The law of behaviour enunciated above says that the person will not consider this action alternative regardless of the magnitude of p_1.

The guarantee of not falling flat on one's face is a necessary, but

---

* Of course, he may be certain that such undesired outcomes may occur and refuse to enter the region even though it is now sufficiently structured.

† It is necessary to add additional regions open to unstructure to those regions for which a minimum certainty has been achieved to retain their potential path properties; that is, they lead to another region which may lead to the goal.

insufficient, condition for the establishment of certainty. In addition, a person wants to be sure that if things go wrong, he will not be left holding the bag. In other words, he wants to be sure that if things go wrong, he will be able to retreat and try again. This is represented in *Figure 5* by single and double-headed arrows. *Figure 5* shows that if he undertakes the action designated by region 2, he cannot retreat and try other actions in case of failure. The actions designated by the regions 3 to n are not irrevocable, retreat is possible. It follows therefore from the law of minimum certainty that p will not consider the action represented by region 2 regardless of the magnitude of p_2.

A person is therefore not ready even to consider probabilities of success before he guarantees for himself a minimum level of certainty;

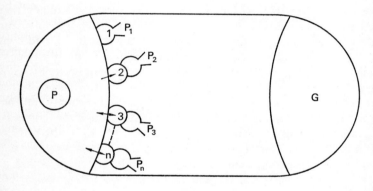

FIGURE 5

certainty that he will not suffer outrageous fortune and certainty that he will be able to retreat and try again if his attempt should come a cropper. Once these minima are satisfied he may pay attention to decision theory suggestions as to what he should do. Nevertheless, unless he is subjected to great pressures, he will still resist following suggestions. He will try to determine additional degrees of certainty before committing himself to a course of action. He will procrastinate as long as possible in order to achieve this additional certainty. And, to the degree that they are achieved, they too may override suggestions based on decision theory where appropriate. In fact, he will procrastinate as much as he can until reaching a state of absolute psychological certainty.

(e) *Absolute Psychological Certainty*

What is this absolute psychological certainty? Let us first denote it behaviourally, i.e. define it ostensively. It has been noted above that when an organism is figuratively glued to a spot when confronted with a choice point in behaviour, and refuses to budge, it is in a situation that is below the necessary minimum of psychological certainty. When an organism undertakes an action, but executes it in a faltering manner, hesitatingly, exhibiting anxiety or fear, it is in a situation of psychological uncertainty even though the minimum level of psychological certainty has been met. It follows, therefore, that when the organism is acting in a confident, assured manner, it is functioning under conditions of absolute psychological certainty.*

Under what conditions do men act in a confident manner? Men are confident in their actions when they are sure that nothing they will be confronted with in the course of this action will overwhelm them. In other words, they are sure that they will be able to cope with whatever will happen to confront them; and 'being able to cope with' does not mean 'necessarily succeeding'. It is important to note that an explicit spelling out of all the contingencies is not necessary to the feeling of absolute psychological certainty; all that is needed is the feeling that the environment in which the individual finds himself will not generate any situation with which he will not be able to cope. This is not surprising since this is the way our real environment functions. One thing we can all be certain of is that we can be confronted with unexpected, contingent situations of various degrees of urgency at almost any time. It is only after we lose our confidence to be able to cope with these contingencies as they arise, that we become 'nervous wrecks'.

Two factors seem to determine psychological confidence: the person's assessment of the environment in which he functions and his assessment of the resources he has at his command. Both of these, in turn, are determined by the person's frame of reference.

In 1 (c) above, the frame of reference was described as consisting of meaning dimensions determining the causal nexi of the real world. These causal nexi tell us what can happen to us in defined regions and what, given specified resources, we can accomplish in those regions, i.e. the meaning of the regions. Man assesses his environment by determining the possible situations he may be confronted

---

* The word 'organism' was used in this paragraph to indicate that these definitions hold for all life.

with, i.e. the possible regions that he may enter. He then assesses his resources, personal abilities, and material aids and implements. If he feels that he can cope with anything in the regions, he enters them confidently.*

Hence, in order to be able to function with certainty, man must have a mapping of the possible regions of the environment. He will then avoid those actions that lead to regions that may be catastrophic, i.e. he plays safe. To the extent that he has faith in his abilities, and/or arms himself with resources to cope with possible contingencies, the number of regions that may be catastrophic decreases and his range of possible movement increases.

Behaviour with psychological certainty does not mean that the person does not have to exert effort to achieve his goal. He does not get it free; he has to pay a price. What it means is that the prices he will have to pay, either for success or for failure, are acceptable to him. They are 'fair' prices. Psychological certainty exists when the person knows that in no circumstances will he have to pay certain prices, prices which he considers exorbitant.

Although it is implicit in all that has been said about psychological certainty, it is still worth while to say explicitly that a person can act with psychological certainty even though he does not know what the outcome of his action will be. All he has to know is that certain unwanted outcomes are excluded. When certainty exists the taking of risks and of chances becomes exciting, otherwise they are threatening.

(f) *The Nebulous 'In-Between' between the Minimum Level of Psychological Certainty Necessary for Behaviour and the Absolute Level of Psychological Certainty*

The behaviour that takes place in the in-between area is characterized by hesitancy, indecision, insecurity, etc. It changes 'monotonically' as the person moves from a situation just over the minimum level of certainty towards a situation that is absolutely certain, the hesitancy, indecision, insecurity, etc., becoming weaker and weaker. This is in marked distinction to the other two states discussed above. These states have an all or nothing characteristic. A situation is either below the minimum level of certainty or it is not, or it is

---

* This assessment need not be explicitly analytic or conscious. Experts generally operate on the basis of a feeling for what should be done without being able to explicate why they feel the way they do.

K

absolutely certain or not. These states admit to no quantitative differentiation.

The nature of the monotonic non-decreasing change in behaviour as the person approaches absolute certainty is not too clear. Two concepts which play an important role in clinical psychology seem, at first glance, to be of help in establishing a beginning for clarity. They are 'anxiety' and 'fear'. Unfortunately, what these terms mean and/or to what phenomena they refer is also not too clear. There is a general agreement that anxiety is more serious than is fear. A behavioural distinction between the two is explicitly mentioned in many theoretical analyses of these terms and is probably implicit in all of them. It is a distinction clearly formulated by Sartre [13]: anxiety hampers efficient behaviour in the face of a crisis; fear not only does not hamper behaviour but often facilitates it by mobilizing the organism's energy, sharpening its conceptual and perceptual abilities, etc. In addition, anxiety seems to generate ulcers and other similar afflictions, fear doesn't. Hence the in-between area can be said to consist of decision situations, some of which are under conditions of uncertainty which evoke anxiety and others evoke fear.

The various states of psychological uncertainty and certainty as just characterized are represented in *Figure 6* (this is not a formally rigorous representation). The ordinate consists of twelve discrete points. The lowest point indicates the state which is below the minimum level of psychological certainty. The next five points indicate five levels of anxiety. Five levels were chosen because attitude and opinion research shows that five levels of discrimination are what can be expected from the average human being.* Similarly the next five points were chosen to indicate five levels of fear. Finally the twelfth point indicates the state of psychological certainty. The abscissa consists of a set of points broken up into four subsets. Each point in the abscissa represents a possible event or state. All the points between a and b represent a subset of events in which the person, were they to confront him, would find himself in a situation of not meeting the minimum level of certainty. The points within this segment are not ordered. This means that the possibility of occurrence of any event or combination of events represented by points in this segment will have the same effect, will place the person in a situation below the minimum level of certainty. This is represented by the parallel line above this segment which is at the same level

* This is attested by the almost universal use of the Likert scale which has five positions: Very much +, Somewhat +, Neutral, Somewhat −, Very much −.

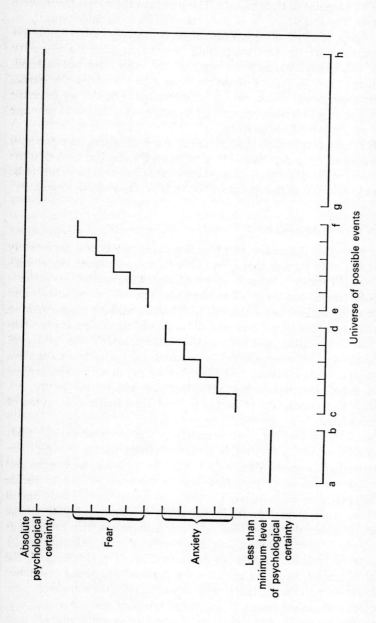

FIGURE 6

as the first point of the ordinate. The points in the subset from c to d represent events which, were the person to be confronted with them, generate a state of anxiety. This subset is partially ordered into five segments, each segment containing events that generate a specific level of anxiety. Within each segment the events are not ordered. Similarly, for the subset of points from e to f we have the partial order sequence of events which generate fear. Finally, we have the subset from g to h which represents those events that do not generate any psychological uncertainty.

The level of psychological certainty for each alternative facing a decision-maker is determined by a point on the abscissa such that the decision-maker is psychologically certain that none of the events to be found to the left of that point will occur if he chooses this alternative.

(g) *Decision-Making under Conditions of Certainty*

The preceding discussion on psychological certainty and uncertainty tautologically implies that men prefer to make decisions under conditions of certainty. When confronted with the necessity to make a decision under conditions of uncertainty they will procrastinate and take many actions in an attempt to achieve certainty before making the decision. These actions are of the nature of thinking and problem-solving, requesting additional information, asking the advice of experts, etc., i.e. they attempt to structure the situation to achieve certainty. Once certainty is achieved, they get down to the serious business of choosing the best path. Decision-making will be treated, first, under conditions of certainty, and then under conditions of uncertainty.

In decision-making under certainty the decision-maker finds himself in one region and is separated from the goal region by intermediary regions (*Figure 1*, p. 122). In addition, he can initiate various actions which may lead him to the goal. He has to decide which action he will initiate. The problem is trivial when only one of of these various actions leads through a distinguished path to the goal. If more than one distinguished path exists, the problem is somewhat more complex, but not much. If one path offers less resistance to locomotion than do others, i.e. if it is 'cheaper', the problem again becomes trivial – the path offering least resistance being chosen. If the alternate paths available offer the same resistance the decision-maker may take some stock before making a choice or may toss a coin. By and large, the latter action is not preferred; men do not like to depend upon chance; they prefer to make decisions which appear to them as being rational. The decision-maker will therefore delay the decision in attempting to find some additional reasons which will give him the grounds for preferring one of these actions to the other. Once he formulates such reasons, his decision emerges rapidly.

We will skip the condition where a distinguished path leading to the goal is perceived, but its resistance to locomotion is so great, i.e. its costs are so high, that the person does not, or cannot, take it. This can be viewed as a special example of the condition to be discussed in the next paragraph; the condition in which no distinguished path to the goal exists.

Up till now we have talked about paths to goals without going into details as to what constitutes a path. A path basically consists of two sets of elements. One set comprises the objective world with its causal properties; the other set comprises the resources available to the decision-maker. It was earlier stated that the meaning of a region consists of the things it can do to a person and the things a person can do in it. The meaning of a region therefore becomes a function of the objective causal properties of the world as perceived by a person and the resources he has available. Some of these resources enable him to modify what the region can do to him; if a person has a shelter he can keep himself dry when it is raining. Other of these resources determine what the person can do in the region; if a person has money, he can buy many goods, but he cannot buy true friendship – on a desert island, the money is useless. Resources are used up in overcoming resistance to locomotion; upon undertaking an action, resources are committed, i.e. are used up.

To return to our decision-maker. He finds himself in a region and wishes to locomote to another region. Several actions are possible; each may lead to the goal. Between the regions which indicate these actions and the goal region an unstructured region is to be found (see *Figure 2*). Unstructure represents ignorance; in trying to achieve a goal there are two basic types of ignorance. The first type is generally met with when the goal is an intellectual one, when a person has to solve a problem, has to figure out a rational connection between his present position and the goal. In the second type, all other things being equal, the rational solution is known. Ignorance, however, is due to the fact that the person does not know whether all other things are equal – the best-laid plans of mice and men gang aft agley. In what follows, we will concentrate on the second type.

We therefore restrict ourselves to the situation where the decision-maker has several alternative actions which, unless complications occur (i.e. all other things being equal), will lead him to the goal. However, this being a condition of behaviour under psychological certainty, not logical certainty, all kinds of contingencies are expected. These contingencies may hamper him from achieving the goal – they may be pitfalls; or they may facilitate the locomotion towards the goal – they may be windfalls. These contingencies stem from the person himself or from the action of others – whether nature or people. If the person is in error either in his perception of the regions or in the meaning of the regions he is bound to run into unexpected natural contingencies. In addition, the action of others can create unexpected conditions which the person could not have known at the start of his action, conditions which can be either benevolent or detrimental.

In order to maintain psychological certainty once a decision is being executed, the person must be vigilant – to be forewarned is to to be forearmed. Vigilance presumes adequate feedback as to how the locomotion is progressing. Vigilance enables the person to check the correctness of his plans as action proceeds, to spot and correct small deviations from the plan before they become serious, and to spot early those contingencies caused by others' actions which change the environment. Vigilance is necessary for control. Hence, once a course of action is decided upon, the person will be able to maintain psychological certainty in reference to this action only if the progress of the action is under constant supervision, that is, if it is observed vigilantly. Of course, the person himself need not do the supervision, although in most cases he would probably prefer to do so; in most cases he is forced to relegate the responsibility for the execution of the plan to a trusted staff. The staff does the supervising.

In a properly run hierarchical organization each planned action consists of a major goal broken up into a series of nesting subgoals. For each subgoal level there is a corresponding hierarchical staff level. Each hierarchical staff level is responsible for coping with those contingencies which affect its corresponding subgoal. To the extent that persons at one hierarchical level become aware of contingencies that may affect the subgoals at other levels, it is their duty to inform personnel at the other levels of this, but not to take action on it by themselves.

(h) *Decision-Making under Conditions of Uncertainty*

After making a decision under conditions of uncertainty, the person embarks upon action. This action is accompanied by fear or anxiety. We will treat fear first.

Following Sartre's definition we consider fear a situation where the organism's state of alertness is raised, his senses sharpened, and his reaction time speeded up. This enables the organism to cope better with the specific aspects in a situation which are dangerous. It has great survival value in coping with such specific aspects, but a price has to be paid for it. Under conditions of fear one focuses upon the specific and loses sight of the general; one finds it very difficult to focus upon the general. When travelling along a forbidding path, the frightened traveller will look for brigands behind each lurking bush and may meanwhile fail to see ominous clouds presaging a storm until it is too late to find adequate shelter.

Under conditions of certainty the person's focus shifts from the general to the specific, the specific often being dictated by what was previously observed in a general perspective and being pretty well anticipated. Figuratively speaking, one doesn't look under every bush but only under those bushes where, from earlier scouting, it is reasonable to anticipate that a brigand will be hiding. When a dangerous contingency is met with, fear may appear to mobilize the individual's energies to cope with this specific contingency. Once the danger is overcome, fear disappears and the ability to shift back to the general perspectives is regained. But this is basically different from starting out being fearful.

When a person acts or decides under conditions of fear, he operates in terms of a limited perspective. This affects both the quality of his decision and the efficiency of executing it once undertaken. Decisions made under fear are consequently nonoptimal. Man is not crazy when he procrastinates under these conditions and seeks psychological certainty.

Much more serious is the deterioration of the qualities of decisions and their execution under conditions of anxiety. Reality convolutes about the tortured ego and ceases to have a status of its own. Panic behaviour is a *sine qua non* of anxiety. Only one motive seems to dominate the actions of a person under conditions of anxiety: it is to escape. Extreme external pressures are needed to keep a person in such a region.

(i) *Fitting Decision Theory to meet the Behavioural Constraints of Man*

It may be true that the decisions based upon statistical decision theory are objectively the best that can be taken in a given situation. This is not too relevant as long as the responsibility for making and executing a decision rests with man. Man will not follow these dictates unless he has faith in them. There are many determinants of faith ranging from an almost pure emotional–instinctive determination through various intermixes with reason. Our nature being what it is, decision-makers will accept dictates of decision theory when it makes sense to them, when they do not entail a mystery.

Were every decision-maker a mathematical statistician, decision-making dictates would *ipso facto* make sense to him; he would know 'intuitively' how and where he can *cut corners*. Since most decision-makers are not mathematical statisticians, decision theory dictates must satisfy primary psychological needs of the decision-maker before they can begin to make sense. The two basic needs identified in this paper are the need to function under conditions of psychological certainty and the need to be vigilant.

I would like to suggest certain possible expansions of decision theory which would do much to increase its ability to satisfy these needs and thereby greatly increase its pragmatic utility. It should be added parenthetically that these needs are often met with intrinsically where decision theory has been applied successfully for the solution of problems in industry and large-scale organizations in peacetime. This because the administrator who decides to implement the proposed dictate is giving it a trial well knowing that the price of failure will not exceed certain bounds and never once relaxing his vigilance as long as faith in the dictate is lacking. In the military situation this condition does not exist. A mistake during war can have catastrophic consequences. Hence, the military decision-maker cannot simply depend upon decision theory. The suggested expansions would do much to help the military decision-maker to achieve psychological certainty where he does not have it, as well as to enable him to exercise greater vigilance. This in turn will increase his faith in the findings of decision theory and will enable him to use them more creatively and imaginatively. It can be expected that his overall performance will thereby improve.

Quite a lot of detailed analysis must be made before a statement can be formulated that a specific action in a specific situation yields a given probability for achieving a specific goal. This analysis, in itself, is most probably adequate for yielding some additional statements as to the probability distribution *of other possible outcomes* of this action. At worst, relatively little additional analysis will be necessary for this purpose. The decision-maker will then have not merely a list of probabilities of achieving some desired goal as a function of the actions he takes, but with a mapping of all possible outcomes of the possible actions he can take. This will be far more satisfying to him. He will have much more faith in it as a reliable guide.

To the extent that the action leading to the goal consists of discrete steps – that is, to the extent that the distinguished path leading to the goal consists of more than one region – decision theory can play another useful role. It should explicate the various alternatives and their associated probabilities open to the decision-maker at each discrete step – since a discrete step, a discriminable region, implies a choice point where the decision-maker can and should re-evaluate the decision, the progress of the action, introducing changes if he thinks it to be desirable. That is, it should explicate the many conditional probabilities which go into determining the initial distribution of probabilities confronting the decision-maker at the outset.

This complex manifold can be represented conceptually by means of point-graph theory, *Figure 1, b*. Every possible action and the associated probabilities of the outcomes of each action should be given simultaneously from the moment that the decision-maker has to choose a course of action, and updated as he locomotes to the goal until it is either reached in its purity, or a compromise goal is accepted instead, or it is judged to be unobtainable. Such a representation, if veridical, will almost guarantee that the decision-maker will function under conditions of psychological certainty. In addition, it will heighten his vigilance because it will alert him to the possible future choice points and the alternatives available at those points. He will therefore be in a better position to take advantage of the unpredictable windfalls, as well as to avoid and/or overcome the predictably possible and the unpredictable pitfalls with which he may be confronted.

If, in addition, we can add to this extended mapping of the decision and action space meaningful principles that explain why the probable consequences of the possible actions are what they are, and are not otherwise, we have what amounts to a conceptual representation of the frame of reference.

And with this decision theory changes its whole impact. Instead of being a pragmatic guide for action which is intrinsically blind, it now becomes a valuable tool and an aid to enrich man's general frame of reference as well as to help him in using it. As such it plays the role similar to other such conceptual aids for understanding which generally go under the name of scientific theories.

REFERENCES

[1] BARTLETT, F. C., *Remembering*. Cambridge University Press, Cambridge; Macmillan, New York, 1932.

[2] CARNAP, R., *Logical Foundation of Probability*. University of Chicago Press, Chicago, Illinois, 1950.

[3] CARNAP, R., *The Continuum of Inductive Methods*. University of Chicago Press, Chicago, Illinois, 1952.

[4] GOLDSTEIN, K., *The Organism*. American Book Company, New York, 1939.

[5] GOLDSTEIN, K., *Human Nature*. Harvard University Press, Cambridge, Mass., 1940.

[6] HEAD, H., *Studies in Neurology*. Oxford University Press, London, 1920.

[7] HEIDER, F., *Psychology of Interpersonal Relations*. Wiley, New York, 1958.

[8] LEWIN, K., *A Dynamic Theory of Personality*. McGraw-Hill, New York, 1935.

[9] LEWIN, K., *Principles of Topological Psychology*. McGraw-Hill, New York, 1936.

[10] LEWIN, K., *Resolving Social Conflicts*. Harper, New York, 1948.

[11] LEWIN, K., *Field Theory in Social Science*. Harper, New York; Tavistock Publications, London, 1951.

[12] LODGE, O., Johann Kepler. In J. R. Newman, ed., *The World of Mathematics*. Simon and Schuster, New York, 1956, pp. 220–38.

[13] SARTRE, J.-P., *The Emotions*. Philosophical Library, New York, 1948.

[14] WERTHEIMER, M., *Productive Thinking*. Harper, New York, 1945; Revised edition, Harper, 1959; Tavistock Publications, London, 1961.

9

Four types of learning
A phenomenological analysis

1. INTRODUCTION

The meaning of 'learning' in its everyday use has been practically lost sight of in various theoretical psychological contexts. On the one hand, it has been pre-empted by academic psychology to denote various mystical phenomena which are never met with in ongoing life and, very dubiously if at all, met with, as it is claimed, in a laboratory setting. On the other hand, the spirit in contemporary clinical thinking, predominantly influenced by Freudian thinking, attends to id psychology whereas 'learning' refers basically to the realm of the ego.

This gap between the prevalent scientific usage of the word and its common-sense meaning is disturbing – especially to the intelligent layman when he seeks help for his problems. Among professionals a similar sense of disturbance has also been expressed. In academic psychology, in particular, many professionals have expressed disagreement with the over-simplified, all-too-reductive definition of 'learning' entailed in almost every form of the so-called 'learning theories'. Years ago Tolman [7] protested against the treatment of learning as one simple process and pointed out that more than one type of learning can be discriminated. Others have followed his footsteps from time to time. By and large, the critics have had little impact upon academic thinking and 'learning' theories, though they have changed with time in form and content, have really not changed in spirit. Much of the blame for this lack of impact is perhaps due to the fact that the critics were inherently too committed to the spirit of the theories they were criticizing to be effective. Essentially they were criticizing the periphery, not the core.

And this brings us to what I understand by 'phenomenological analysis'. Many people find it difficult to define 'phenomenology'. The difficulty lies in their attempt to define 'phenomenology' substantively, in terms of the contents subsumed under the word. The contents vary much too much to yield an acceptable definition. Matters are simplified if we look upon 'phenomenology' as indicating a basic scientific attitude, a basic psychological predisposition. It seems to be correct to assert that, regardless of the specific context, whenever a scientist or philosopher uses 'phenomenology' he attempts to base whatever he has to say solidly and integrally on the hard stubborn facts of the world as simply seen by man. And what is simply seen by one man can generally be simply seen by every man. Phenomenological thinking in all its variations is irrevocably committed to the phenomenal world as a fundamental departure point; when all is said and done, the phenomenal world is the real world and science must explain reality. And, it may be added, common sense is the articulated expression of the phenomenal world.

The following discussion of learning is essentially a personal document. I have tried to make sense to myself, to simply see what learning is about. But since I am a man, what makes sense to me should make sense to any man. Hence, I take the liberty of writing down my inner discourse for public perusal.

This paper will treat 'learning' at a relatively low level of abstraction. It will focus on learning processes immediately abstracted from the phenomenal given, leaving open the more basic question of whether there is a unique process underlying all learning phenomena or not. It will distinguish a learning process found in the developing child, to be called 'maturational learning', which is not found in an adult. In addition, it will then consider three learning processes common to children and adults:

(a) Learning to do things,
(b) Acquiring knowledge,
(c) Learning to get along – with people or in groups.

The general concept of 'learning', or of 'the learning process' will be treated as an undefined primitive, an entity that is perceptually given. Those who claim that learning cannot be perceived will not be able fully to follow the discussion. They will be in a position analogous to a person blind from birth listening to a paper on colour mixing. It is assumed that a large enough set of events is perceived by a large enough number of people as being 'learning' to make the subsequent discussion potentially profitable. The fact that there probably also exists a large set of events that are perceptually unclear, i.e. one cannot be sure whether they constitute 'learning' or not, is immaterial for this discussion. One can hope that with increasing knowledge clarity will be achieved.

In discussing the different learning processes it will be necessary to specify what it is that characterizes the various instances of learning that are examples of a specific process and differentiates them from other instances of learning that are examples of other processes or that do not fit any of the discussed processes. This characterization will be made in terms of 'low level' concepts which will be co-ordinated as much as possible to a unique perceptual given or to a set of perceptual givens which sort of intuitively hang together in a meaningful fashion. The fact that concepts exist which differentiate between processes does not imply that concepts common to the disparate processes do not exist. The mere usage of the general word 'learning' denies such an implication. For the word 'learning' to be used meaningfully in a technical sense, a set of instances must exist characterized by a common property or set of properties ('property' is here synonymous with 'concept') on the basis of which they are differentiated from those instances that are not considered to be 'learning'. The learning processes discussed here constitute proper subsets of the more general 'learning' set, each characterizable by an additional property or set of properties.

Although the learning processes should be both perceptually and conceptually distinguishable, they need not be mutually exclusive for a given instance of 'learning'. In fact, except under contrived conditions, it is probably rare to find a learning instance which is a pure example of one or the other processes. An analogy: silver is a 'pure' substance, a chemical element, yet it is very rarely, if ever, found in a pure state in nature. Pure silver is contrived by man in a factory or laboratory. The lack of mutual exclusiveness is not crucial unless the processes interact in a noticeable manner. There is no reason to believe that they do. Therefore, as far as this discussion is concerned, they will be considered to be additive in their effects and will be discussed independently despite the probability that for many specific learning instances, some aspects will belong to one process being considered, whereas other aspects will belong to another process or processes.

For pragmatic reasons man has set up many contrived situations where these processes can be found in much greater purity, to a variable degree. Examples of such situations are educational institutions, training courses and/or programmes and psychological laboratories. Much of the knowledge we have about the 'learning processes' is obtained from our experience in these settings.

2. MATURATIONAL LEARNING

A child does not only grow, i.e. increase its physical mass, becoming bigger and bigger, it matures as well. Maturation can be viewed in terms of a dichotomy found useful in abnormal psychology: organic as against functional. Organic refers to the physiological locus of behaviour, i.e. an organic psychosis is a psychopathological state that can be related to a unique cerebral condition. Functional refers to behaviour without any knowledge or interest in its underlying physiological locus; i.e. a functional psychosis is a psychopathological state whose underlying physiological locus is unknown; hence, the investigator concentrates on its behavioural manifestations without considering problems of physiology. From an organic standpoint maturation refers to the development of organs and/or sundry physiological subsystems and the effect of this development upon the organism. Organs may be said to change from a passive to an active state with maturation. Physiological subsystems increase in differentiation and specialization with maturation. These changes affect organismic functioning at all levels in a non-additive manner. It does not seem proper to say that with a maturational change the organism has added some additional abilities to its previous repertoire; rather it seems more correct to say that with each maturational change the organism exhibits a reorganization of its abilities and that it functions in a new way in all important respects.

When trying to understand what learning as a phenomenon is, the organic standpoint is not very important. This would be true even if the connection between physiology and behaviour were known. This is even more true in the present state of our ignorance, where the little we think we know about this connection is quite speculative. From a functional standpoint, however, maturation exhibits patterns very similar to the physiological patterns thumbnail-sketched above. Suddenly what the child was unable to do or understand yesterday, it *can* do or understand today. And this ability is generally not a simple addition to the child's earlier repertoire, but also entails a reorganization of that repertoire.

Take walking as an example. Does the fact that the child takes a first step mean only that now the child's feet are strong enough to stand on one foot while moving the other forward? No! Walking entails a complete reorganization of body balance which in turn entails a different body image. In addition, a whole new world becomes literally available with this dramatic change in mode and efficiency of locomotion, and the organism must be ready to cope with this new world in all of its abilities; in addition, the old world is seen from quite a different perspective. It is true that walking involves other learning processes as well, especially the process called learning to do things, but the point made here is that even for the 'first' step to take place, a reorganization of the other abilities of the child must also occur. The subsequent learning processes then build upon this reorganization, rather than upon the new ability added to the old abilities.

Piaget [6] has studied the development of logical thinking in children and has demonstrated, to his satisfaction, a rather constant and interesting pattern. He argues that logical thinking emerges from non-logical thinking and then goes through a series of successive organizations characterized both by increased specialization and differentiation, on one hand, and by increased integration of the growing number of specialized and differentiated logical skills, on the other. Non-logical causality of the kindergarten child is characterized by mere contiguity of events imbued with animistic volition. With maturation the child begins to understand physical causality of simple events like pushing, weight, etc. Later these discrete causal events begin to be tied down into little groups based on common causal principles; or in Piaget's words, the child develops transformation rules which apply to a group of causal events. As the child grows older these transformations become more inclusive in a lawful manner and the number of groups decreases until, with the emergence of adult thinking, all causal principles are logically related by a set of transformations in one master group called a lattice. Piaget notes that the meaning of a causal principle or event changes with each change in transformation rules and change in group membership because the event now leads to a different set of conclusions and alternatives than it did earlier.

But it must be stressed that learning these principles and acquiring the use of transformation rules and logical lattices is not a simple function of maturation. While it is true that a child cannot learn a given set of transformations until it is *ready* to learn it, i.e. it is mature enough, mere readiness to learn does not necessarily result in learning.

When it is ready to learn, it has to be *taught*. Although all normal children pass the stage where their readiness to learn to read and write emerges, unless they go to school and are exposed to a didactic environment, they will most probably not acquire the skill.

Despite the fact that Piaget restricted his research to child solutions to logical problems and demonstrated that his formulations can account for the increasing efficiency and sophistication of growing children in solving such problems, his findings have wider implications. With each change in transformation rules leading to the inclusive lattice, the whole world of the child changes. Events are interrelated differently. The causal properties of the world become richer. Is it rash to believe that the appreciation of beauty, art, the adult sense of humour and of tragedy, so noticeably lacking in a child, is the result of a person living in a world that is causally connected and integrated into a rational, ergo meaningful, whole which is *unknowable* by a child. Hughlings Jackson demonstrated long ago and Henry Head [3] and Kurt Goldstein [2], among others, have shown since, that brain-injured patients who have an impaired ability to think abstractly or categorically also lose an appreciation for art, also lose their sense of humour and of tragedy.

Maturation is an unfolding of potentialities: virgin potentialities which have to be actualized in order not to atrophy. If a child is kept tied to a crib so that it cannot stand, it will suffer no harm as long as it cannot stand; but once it reaches a maturational state wherein it can stand, further restraint will definitely be harmful. After a given period of constraint its legs will atrophy and it will remain a cripple for life. To the extent that any potentiality of a maturing organism is atrophied, the organism is bound to function at a less efficient level than it could have and should have.

The organism seems to be aware of the danger of nonactualization of emerging potentialities. A child does not mind being tied down as long as it is not ready to stand, but once it is ready to stand, it is almost impossible to tie it down. Children of all ages demonstrate an 'exploratory drive' far more intense than almost all adults. Is this 'exploratory drive' anything more than their reaction to unfolding potentialities? Unactualized potentialities are virgin, unstructured; they cry for actualization; their actualization is a form of learning. They lap it up as dry land laps up water. Learning is very rapid and relatively permanent. There are many areas that are almost impossible for an adult to master, but are relatively easy for a child; examples are: learning an instrument, a new language, a host of motor skills and, probably most important, a culture and set of basic attitudes and meanings from which a person cannot free himself for the rest of his existence.

The adult has none of this. His potentialities have been unfolded. He has a fixed repertoire of adequately actualized potentialities, partially actualized potentialities, and atrophied potentialities. Most adults, with the exception of a small group of artists, gifted teachers, and some others who are characterized as being 'wonderful with children', have even lost the ability to empathize with this fantastic, ever blossoming, ever mushrooming world of the child. They cannot understand that often the 'perversity' of children is but an expression of this drive to actualize the potentialities as they unfold, that often the child's refusal to learn that which is offered him because of pragmatic considerations of a 'curriculum' is due to the fact that perhaps at the same time something which the child really needs to learn, really needs to know, is being denied him. A child will often not refuse to eat food it does not need as long as it also gets food it does need, but if its diet is inadequate, it will eat the food mother gives it with protest and crying, and then go to look for limestone which will give it the calcium it craves.

3. LEARNING TO DO THINGS

The classical example for this type of learning process is the acquisition of motor skills. It is this process that seems to serve as the model for most, if not all, associationist and connectionist theories of learning. Some phenomenal characteristics describe it in a clear-cut manner. First there is the classical learning paradigm with its relatively many repetitions and its small-increment increase in efficiency until a desired and/or maximum level of achievement is reached. In observing this process one can almost literally see the stamping in of correct responses and the stamping out of the incorrect ones. Concomitant with this increase in efficiency there is an increasing automatization of the performance accompanied by its recession from consciousness.

Take the learning of typewriting as an example. At the outset the pressing of each key stands in the centre of consciousness, generally involving a volitional decision on the part of the person. Slowly the letters recede from consciousness to be replaced by words. These, in turn, are replaced by sentences and/or lines. And finally, the whole process becomes automatic, the expert typist paying little attention, if at all, to the skill being executed. These two sets of phenomena, the incremental learning curve and automatization accompanied by recession from consciousness, seem to be significata for a skill-learning process.

But certain additional things characterize skill-learning. From the standpoint of the goal–means dichotomy, skills are related to means rather than to goals. Once they are mastered, automatized, and have receded from consciousness, they are called forth when needed to achieve a certain task, to help in reaching a desired goal. When the task is accomplished they retire, like good servants, not to be heard from again until needed. The products of this learning process emerge, after it has reached its optimum, as relatively finished abilities which, with appropriate practice, remain relatively unchanged and exist in relative isolation from the rest of the organism. At this point it is necessary to anticipate something to be discussed more fully in the next section. One should not confound the skill *per se* with the person's knowledge of his skills. The latter always plays an important role in behaviour, but it is distinctly different from the former.

Another interesting characteristic of learning to do things is its relationship with age and, consequently, with maturation. The younger a person is, the easier it is for him to learn new skills, that is, when he is mature enough and ready to master them. As just noted, there are many skills that are masterable with ease, if at all, only during the maturational period. Language is a good example. Children can master a new language with ease; with adulthood, however, many persons lose the ability to acquire a new language. Learning to play an instrument seems to be another good example. It is as if the newly matured potentiality is of unformed soft clay that will soon harden. While it is soft, it is easily moulded and structured by the use of fingers. As it hardens, moulding increases in difficulty until eventually a hammer and chisel are needed to produce any change at all. But the analogy of clay is perhaps insufficient. The hardness of the clay is not affected by its form, i.e. whether it is a shapeless lump or an articulated structure. This does not seem to hold true for a potentiality which has been actualized. The greater the efficiency of skill reached during the 'soft' period, the more it was learned and practised, the more difficult it is to change as time goes by. Therefore, to continue in terms of analogy, once a potentiality is actualized by developing a set of skills, once it becomes an articulated structure, it is more difficult to reutilize it for a different set of skills than if it had originally been neglected and had atrophied to a certain degree.

The discussion has, until now, restricted itself explicitly to motor skills, though some of the examples cited above are exceptions. Motor skills involve the use of muscles to effect some change in the physical environment. Does this mean that all skills are muscular? By no means. Motor skills were first focused upon because they are most open to immediate perception. Early in the discussion a criterion was suggested, that of incremental learning and auto-matization and recession from consciousness. By using this criterion 'mental' skills can also be identified. Let language be considered again. True, language does have a motor aspect: speaking. But reading and listening do not seem to have any significant motor components – they seem to have only 'mental' components. Learning a language, nevertheless, fits the above criterion. The mastery of a language is a slow process characterized by small increments; this holds for the child as well as the adult. Once a word is mastered it recedes from consciousness. It automatically appears in use when necessary without the reader or speaker explicitly having to call it up. The acquisition of language also conforms to the other characteristics of skill learning. Vocabulary is learned more rapidly by children than by adults. Once a word is mastered, it lies dormant, relatively isolated and unchanged until used. Words are means to achieve goals of expression and/or understanding, but they themselves play no part in setting goals up.

Rote learning, be it of nonsense syllables for the experimental psychologist, or poetry to be recited next day for the English teacher, also shares the characteristics of skill learning. Other 'mental' skills that will be discussed in some more detail below are skills in problem-solving, skills in interpersonal relations, and learning the multiplica-tion table. None of these acquisitions involve the motoric, as it is commonly understood, yet they all seem to share the properties which characterize the learning of skills.

Nevertheless, there seems to be a significant difference between the 'mental' skills and the motor skills. The latter are tied much more intimately to the maturation process. To consider language once more. Many do learn new languages despite being adults. But how many adults can learn to speak the new language without a foreign accent, i.e. the accent of a mother tongue learned in childhood? The motor skills involved in language are set relatively early in life. Danc-ing is another example. Many children dance 'naturally'. They take to it and master it like a duck takes to and masters water. How many adults can master dancing with ease, if at all, if they have had no experience with it as children?

Naïve psychology, another term for 'common sense', recognizes this uniqueness of skill learning. English reserves a special word to denote the learning of skills: the word is 'training'.

4. ACQUIRING KNOWLEDGE

Acquiring knowledge can be rephrased without any essential loss of meaning to learning things just as 'learning to do things' has already been functionally rephrased in the preceding section to 'acquiring skills'. The reason the two processes were described in dissimilar words rather than in similar words was to stress the differences between the processes.

It will be contended here that the two processes seem to be 'logically' complementary; that the opposite of what characterizes the one characterizes the other. But first it may be profitable to discuss briefly what is meant by 'acquiring knowledge' in general terms.

Naïve psychology also recognizes the uniqueness of this process by assigning a special word to denote it – education. The sentence: 'The pugilist is being educated', conveys a different meaning from the sentence: 'The pugilist is being trained'. The words education and knowledge refer to our awareness of the world, its nature and/or structure, its causal texture, its meaning.

It is this awareness which results as the end-product of the process of acquiring knowledge, so real yet so impalpable, so easy to see, yet so difficult to describe, that has served as the model for psychologists in formulating concepts as 'apperceptive mass', 'cognitive map', 'schema', and/or 'frame of reference'.

Knowledge and understanding imply each other, hence from a strictly logical standpoint they are equivalent. A body of knowledge is not an aggregate of isolated facts, idiot savants have shown remarkable ability in amassing such aggregates; it is some sort of integrated, interdependent, differentiated unity in which every element has a necessary place by virtue of the totality in which it is embedded. Piaget's concept of the adult logical matrix, although perhaps too simple, is nevertheless a good concrete model of what such an entity as knowledge might be.

The fact that knowledge is so difficult to conceptualize or to define in words does not mean that it is difficult to see. Take so simple a phenomenon as fear. No verbal conceptualization can really do it justice, yet the talented actor can present a picture on the stage to cause every individual in the audience to perceive fear as clearly as he can perceive a black square painted upon a white background. There are some who are dissatisfied with this state of affairs and devote much of their energy to a verbal and/or conceptual analysis of this tantalizing phenomenon. Attempts in this direction seem to end up in amputated, truncated pictures that are poor caricatures of the real thing. The genius who will successfully accomplish this task has yet to arrive. Nevertheless, fear is a real thing, and so is knowledge. Therefore, since the phenomenon is perceptually clear to all those who are not self-appointed solipsists of one form or another, one can talk meaningfully about how it is attained.

The acquisition of knowledge is not a process characterizable by the addition of small increments. On the contrary, it proceeds by means of noticeably discontinuous large steps. Naïve psychology discriminates: 'Either one knows or one does not know'. This discrimination does not refer to skills, it refers to knowledge. Take reading a book as an example. One does not read it over and over again until it is mastered. To be *known*, a book generally has to be read only once. Sometimes, a difficult book is read several times in order to be *understood*. But this is quite dissimilar to the process leading to a skill acquisition. Understanding is achieved by one or a series of noticeable discontinuities as the person proceeds from darkness into light. Although it need not be the only way to knowledge, the phenomenon of insight, the 'aha' experience, always indicates that a change in knowledge has taken place, and is, by definition, a discontinuous change. Plato's myth of the cave is a magnificent poetic description of such an experience; in it the light is not increased by increments.

Take a basic element of knowledge, the fact or datum, be it an object or relation between objects. It permits only of a discontinuity. Either it is perceived or it is not perceived. Knowledge grows from a body of discontinuous facts, through successive stages of discontinuous organizations and reorganizations, until it reaches a reasonable comprehensively integrated end-state.

The acquisition of skills has been characterized by increasing automatization and recession from consciousness. Exactly the opposite must hold for knowledge. The essence of knowledge is that that which is required emerges into *consciousness* where it is thought about to see how it fits the situation for which it is considered. If the constituents of knowledge were automatized they would appear machine-like every time a 'button were pressed'. How could they then be applied to the manifold situations in which knowledge plays a role. In planning how to achieve a goal, man uses his knowledge and intelligence to break up the task into a series of standardized procedures so that his automatized skills can then take over.

What is one of the stock phrases a person utters when he embarks upon a chain of thought in attempting to solve a problem? Isn't it: 'Now let me see!'

Skills were said to be related to means for goal attainment; knowledge is the basis for the *rational* component in goal setting, and is almost solely responsible in determining the means to be taken to achieve the goal. Skills were characterized as lying dormant in isolation, taking part in behaviour only when needed. The elements of knowledge, being parts of an integrated unity are certainly not isolated. They are not dormant. Any and every reorganization of the body of knowledge affects all of its elements by virtue of the fact that every element has to fit into the new organization.

However, since the whole body of knowledge does not emerge into consciousness at once, since only those elements of knowledge relevant to the existing situation seem to appear, it may be argued that in this respect knowledge is similar to skills. But what has already been said about perception and cognition holds for knowledge. The attended-to elements of knowledge constitute a conceptual figure, with the rest of the body of knowledge serving as a dynamic ground. We never can attend to all the details of our knowledge at one time just as we can never attend to all the details of the visual field at one time.

In some respects, although not in all, knowledge is also related to age and maturation otherwise than are skills. (Notice parenthetically that we do not speak of knowledges as we do of skills. This is a recognition by naïve psychology that knowledge is a unity.) In some respects it is true to say that the real job of acquiring knowledge begins once adulthood has been reached and the basic repertoire of skills are acquired. There are certainly many adults who will readily admit that they are too old to learn new skills, but will most vehemently deny that they are too old to learn. If we study human societies, both primitive and non-primitive, we would find upon excluding cases of senility, a very high correlation between socially recognized knowledgeable people and their age.

Nevertheless, skills and knowledge are closely related. The acquisition of skills affects the acquisition of knowledge; the acquisition of knowledge affects the acquisition of skills. Knowledge affects the application of skills, skills affect the application of knowledge.

Knowledge is conceived as a unified whole which determines the meaningful world in which the individual lives. It is a function both of the integrating ability of the individual, an ability presupposed by the concept of intelligence, and individual experience. Intelligence is not germane to the present discussion and need not be considered. The effects of experience upon the acquisition of knowledge is quite germane. The acquisition of skills, by increasing the repertoire of means at the individual's disposal, increases his mobility, increases the number and wealth of his experiences, and this in turn affects the body of knowledge at the individual's disposal. Hence, the acquisition of skills affects the acquisition of knowledge.

Knowledge, in turn, will affect the acquisition of skills in two ways. First it acts as a motivating agent. When one knows about a thing, one may become interested in that thing, and then try to do it. Certainly, it is impossible to get interested in a thing unless that thing is part of a person's knowledge. For instance, reading a book about sailing can get the reader interested in sailing, which will then motivate him to master the skills involved in sailing. But knowledge affects the learning of skills in a more subtle and important way. It seems to be true that a person will learn a skill more efficiently when the meaning of the skill is clear to him than when it is not. Knowledge is the repository of meaning.

Yet knowledge and skills are independent of each other, i.e. one can exist without the other. Or, to hedge somewhat, one can exist with very little of the other. Idiot savants have already been mentioned. They are examples of skills without knowledge. The other extreme is the traditional absent-minded professor of physics who cannot fix an electrical connection; his is a knowledge that is almost helpless because of the lack of skills. But these extremes, if they exist at all, are beyond the ken of most people. It may, therefore, be worth while to discuss in somewhat greater detail an example that is commonplace – the multiplication table.

One of the main forces that led to the modern revolution in education was the realization that a child may have perfect mastery of the multiplication table and yet not have the faintest idea of what multiplication is. This results in an inability to generalize or to multiply sets of numbers that are not found in the table. The slogan became that the child should not be taught blind skills, but should be taught to understand. In fact, teaching blind skills has become somewhat of an anathema. Some of the excesses of 'modern' education produced a pupil who understood multiplication perfectly but had no skill with the multiplication table. This pupil understood that 8×7 means adding seven to itself eight times or adding eight to itself seven times. Given a problem in the multiplication of digits he would do precisely that and come out with the correct answer. He also understood that the principle of successive addition also held for the multiplication of a three-digit number by a three-digit number. But lacking the algarithm based on the multiplication table on one hand, and lacking enough paper and patience on the other, he found that he could not solve the latter problem of multiplication.

Before leaving this discussion on knowledge, it is interesting to consider one more of its aspects. It has been mentioned several times that knowledge constitutes an organized body. But this understates the case. The person abhors discontinuities and disorganization within his body of knowledge. Each event and each experience that does not fit, becomes a personal challenge to the individual. He struggles with it until it fits somehow. If he is unsuccessful in this, the event becomes unpleasant *per se* and he avoids facing it. It is in these cases, when reason fails, that rationalization and/or repression step in. Two very interesting fruits of this requirement of total organization are religion and philosophy; both are characterized as yielding – in the case of philosophy 'seeking' would be a better word – ultimate answers. Theologians and philosophers are objects of extreme social respect in almost all societies because they represent the prime forces acting for the elimination of discontinuities of meaning, for the ultimate integration of all knowledge.

The conflict between science on one hand and theology and metaphysics on the other can be seen in a slightly different perspective in light of the above consideration. Scientific explanation does not oppose theological and metaphysical explanation, it obviates it.

5. LEARNING TO GET ALONG WITH PEOPLE OR IN GROUPS

This process concerns what is generally subsumed under the rubric Social Learning. However, it is not differentiated from 'thing learning' as 'social perception' is differentiated from 'thing perception'. In perception, the differences between the world of thing events and the world of social events is on the surface, stands out [4]. It is the commonalities that have to be sought out, that have to be elucidated. In learning, the opposite seems to hold. That which is common to thing learning and social learning stands out and we consequently neglect many differences. Skills and knowledge are involved in social learning just as they are involved in maturational learning, but, as with maturational learning, the context in which they are involved is different enough to merit separate discussion.

Since learning is intimately related to perception, it may be profitable to start this topic by reviewing some of the differences between social and thing perception. The first difference which seems to stand out is the fact that social perception is mediated by thing perception. This means that the perceiver can perceive the mediating processes in social perception. This condition does not exist in thing perception. One does not see the perturbations in the light rays which mediate vision nor the perturbations in the atmosphere which mediate audition; one sees the things and one hears the sound *per se*. Brunswik [1] points out, in discussing his lens model of perception and behaviour, that both in perception and in action, little, if any, clear relation exists between the processes mediating perception and action and the perceived objects and nature of action *per se*. Luckily for thing perception the mediating processes are invisible. They can be made visible by means of electronic equipment, but anyone who has seen sound or heard a television picture knows that these stimuli are meaningless as far as hearing and seeing the event represented is concerned. The matter is different for social perception. There the discrimination between the invariant stable social events that ought to be perceived and the thing events that mediate these perceptions is not always easy. This has been complicated by the fact that many philosophers have postulated that only thing events are 'real'. They in turn influenced many scientists who directed their research along this way. Hence the problem of variant mediation of invariant social processes was not easily recognized.

A second difference between thing and social perception is the difference in their causal textures, their causal nexi. Michotte [5] has demonstrated that when points of light move in a manner such that their future movement is a simple immediate extrapolation from their present and past movement, they are perceived as being thing events, i.e. mechanical, non-living. However, when this is not the case, when non-extrapolatable changes in velocity and/or direction take place, the movement is perceived as being animate. Mechanical, thing movement appears as determined once the initial position and velocity are perceived. When this phenomenal determinism disappears, living processes are seen. This is the perceptual basis for the concept of free will. The perception of a moving thing almost instantaneously tells you where it is going to, the perception of a moving man or animal does not.

Because of the visibility of the mediating processes, social perception is much less accurate than is thing perception. Confusion can and does arise, and in addition, it is much more difficult for an individual to correct for this confusion. Under such conditions learning becomes much more difficult too, in fact, under many conditions the difficulties become so great that the person defensively reverts to skills and knowledges of the thing world which are successful in their realm and applies them in desperation, blindly, to the social world. This leads to trouble.

The lack of accuracy in social perception is greatly complicated by the fact that the social environment affects the individual in several striking ways in a manner not found in the thing environment. The social environment is perceived as having powers to change a person, which, except under extreme conditions, the thing environment is not perceived to possess. This special power of the social environment stems, not surprisingly, from the fact that the perceiver has commerce with another person rather than with an inanimate thing. But not any living organism in any circumstances will do; it has to be a conscious, intelligent organism with the ability to perceive the person. When a person is looked at by such, he experiences a sort of self-consciousness that is lacking in all other environments.

Conscious awareness and ability to perceive on the part of an intelligent organism are necessary and sufficient conditions to evoke this self-consciousness. The fact that a person can use the knowledge he acquires by seeing another against that other, aggravates the feeling of self-consciousness. But this is not necessary. Two examples. People who have pets can attest to a fairly common experience. It occurs when looking into the eyes of the pet. In these circumstances one can suddenly get the feeling that the pet understands the person; concomitantly a feeling of self-consciousness emerges. Similarly, consider the circumstances where a person sits by himself in some public place or conveyance. A second person enters, a stranger who will soon leave, never to be met with again. The stranger sits down behind the person. Who can avoid a strong feeling of self-consciousness in such a situation?

This self-consciousness entails, among possible others, two strong irrational components; one wants the other to think well of him, and one has the feeling that one's thoughts and perceptions are open to the other. This may have effects on the person involved of which only one will be discussed explicitly. In social conditions it is much more difficult for an individual to appraise himself objectively. He finds it difficult to admit, if only to his innermost self, that he is in error. Rationalizations – that is, reasons attributing the inadequacies to any source but to himself – tend to overwhelm him. Any learning that depends upon recognition and elimination of personal error cannot but progress very slowly. In addition, the pressure to conform in areas where there is no question of error increases greatly. If a person or a group make their opinions known, and if one has the feeling, no matter how irrational he recognizes that feeling to be, that the person or group is aware of his private different opinions, the pressure for conformity becomes very great. Conformity can then occur without necessarily introducing a permanent change. When such a person leaves the group or other persons, he will generally revert to his previous way of thinking without great difficulty.

Here, as in many other instances, events involving life exhibit a complexity far greater than the events involving inanimate things.

The defensive attitudes and consequent rationalizations evoked by the presence of another person add to the difficulty of clear perception in social situations. One can 'escape' by attending to the mediating processes rather than on the relevant social process. Since mediating processes, by virtue of being mediators, can refer back to various different events, something can be perceived that has nothing to do with reality but is quite satisfying to the perceiver. The defensive attitudes also oppose a clear thinking-through of social issues so that the organized body of social knowledge of an individual can become, and actually is to a varying degree for all persons, autistic and not amenable to correction and change. For instance, the social world is populated with good and bad people, something unheard of in the physical world except when it is anthropomorphized.

One can still recognize and discriminate between skills and knowledge in social learning, but they are changed, both as far as their nature *per se* is concerned, and in their interrelationships. The previous paragraph indicated somewhat how knowledge changes where social learning is concerned, e.g. the difficulty in obtaining objective social knowledge. One of the most striking changes in skills is relatively incomplete automatization. The most skilful group leader cannot exercise his skills in a manner comparable to an expert machine operator. Once he permits them to recede from consciousness he cannot apply them. In addition, the relative independence of skills and knowledge is greatly weakened. There are no idiot savants in this area. In addition, when an erudite professor is met who is supposedly a repository of much of what is known concerning human behaviour, and the professor exhibits little skill in getting along with people, doubt will always arise as to what he really does know. In order to have skills in human relations, knowledge seems to be pre-supposed, and vice versa.

The acquisition of knowledge and skills in the social sphere is also somewhat different. Although formal courses in both are given in institutions of learning and at special seminars, the efficacy of these courses is yet to be proved. More than in any other field of learning, we learn to get along with others by trying to get along with others. And this latter, intuitive learning does not come with difficulty. Man does learn to get along with his fellow man reasonably well, all things considered. In fact, it is paradoxical that the persons with the most profound penetrating insight into the nature of man are not trained and educated psychologists, but psychologically self-educated playwrights and authors. Potential Einsteins and Newtons, however, cannot achieve eminence unless they receive a thorough formal education in their respective disciplines.

Men do learn to get along with each other and there are techniques that are effective in speeding up this learning and/or making it more effective. The *sine qua non* of learning to get along seems to be face-to-face interaction with others. In such an interaction the whole response of the individual to an action is perceived as well as the total action of a person towards another. All this evidence, this totality of cues, seems necessary to enable a person to integrate a body of knowledge about another in order efficiently to apply his repertoire of interpersonal skills in dealing with him. To the extent that the evidence is reduced, to that extent learning is hampered.

Of the different learning processes discussed here, social learning is by far the least clear perceptually, the most mysterious conceptually.

REFERENCES

[1] BRUNSWIK, E., *Perception and the Representative Design of Psychological Experiments*. University of California Press, Berkeley, 1956.
[2] GOLDSTEIN, K., *Human Nature in the Light of Psychopathology*. Harvard University Press, Cambridge, Mass., 1947.
[3] HEAD, H., *Aphasia and the Kindred Disorders of Speech*. Macmillan, New York, 1926.
[4] HEIDER, F., *The Psychology of Interpersonal Relations*. Wiley, New York, 1958.
[5] MICHOTTE, A. E., *La Perception de la causalité*. J. Vrin, Paris, 1946.
[6] PIAGET, J., *Logic and Psychology*. Basic Books, New York, 1957.
[7] TOLMAN, E. C., There is more than one Type of Learning. *Psychol. Rev.*, 1949, **56**, 144–55.

10

Training information-processing decision-making man–machine communication-systems

1. INTRODUCTION

As many another term in contemporary scientific discourse on man and his problems, the term 'man–machine system' has raised more confusion than clarification. As has been shown, 'system' is a problem by itself, but so is the hyphenated term 'man–machine'. At present, it is used to denote any collection of men and machines, beginning with the limited case of one man with one machine and extending to the huge 'information-processing decision-making communication-systems' which involve thousands of men and electro-mechanical monstrosities that serve as the subject for this essay. Consequently the term has become purely descriptive and has lost whatever unique and, as it turns out, important meaning it should have had.

Since 'man–machine system' can be and is applied nowadays to any collection of men and machines, and since the variety among such collections can be very great, hence, beyond the mere fact that the term denotes such a collection, it has very little additional meaning. With this we are confronted with a sort of paradox. Collections of men and machines have been with us for centuries, at least from the moment the first pulley or galley ship was invented, yet the term under discussion was coined after World War II and first appeared in print in the early 1950s. Why should the coining of a name have waited so long? It is reasonable to assume that something significant occurred, something new developed, which led to the coining of a new name.

Sure enough, if we carefully read the early papers where the hyphenation 'man–machine' is used we can see what happened. Two of the earliest, if not the two earliest, papers in which the term is used are by Bentley [1] and Birmingham and Taylor [2]. They use the terms 'man–machine' and 'man–machine system' respectively. Both make the same conceptual error or, more precisely, fall into the same conceptual trap. In both papers we find the assertion that the hyphenation 'man–machine' should be used whenever we have men and machines together but that the discussion will be restricted to limited systems as examples. Bentley discusses the problems of controlling supersonic aircraft whose flight characteristics exceed the speed of man's ability of discrimination and decision; Birmingham and Taylor discuss computerized control systems where man is considered as a link or module with a specific task of error detection and correction but where otherwise the system 'runs itself'.

The examples discussed in the two papers have a unique aspect. This aspect was lost sight of by the authors because of their phenotypical application of the term to all aggregations of men and machines; and it is this aspect that generated the need for this new term. In both examples discussed, the operator loses much of the functional control over the machine's operation – in the case of the aircraft by default and in the case of the control system by design – and therefore finds himself controlled to a large extent by the machine. The construction of machines whose performance characteristics are of such a nature that they, whether by default or by design, can take over control from the human operator is basically a post-World War II development.

The little we know about perceptual and cognitive organization is enough to explain why under conditions where the machine begins to exercise independent control a new name is called for. Machines, as well as tools of which they are an outgrowth, are means to help man accomplish tasks. As such they are extensions of man's motoric, and the process of learning to use them is identical with the process of acquiring motor skills. As soon as a person learns to use a machine or tool efficiently it 'recedes from consciousness' and ceases to be discriminated as a specific thing. The inattention to the machine continues as long as it obediently and efficiently functions as an extension of the motoric or, as in the case of instruments, as an extension of the sensorium. It becomes incorporated in the body image of the operator and one attends to it as much as, for instance, one attends to one's foot in normal circumstances. Because of the experience of complete control that man has over the average machine it therefore, psychologically, loses *independent* causal properties when used by a trained technician (this is what is meant by saying that it is incorporated into the body image).

Before the war all machines, as is true of most machines today, were experienced as being under the complete control of their operators and, within the task context, having no independent causal existence. Hence, as long as they functioned as designed, there was no need to attend to them as independent things.

To the extent that machines do not function properly, for whatever reason, and cannot be completely controlled, the operator experiences them as developing 'a mind of their own' and they emerge as an identifiable thing that demands attention and a name. It is not surprising therefore, that when man is given a task to do with a machine over which he has either lost some control, or is in constant danger of losing some control, the machine demands to be attended to and to be recognized as an entity in its own right. The key problem confronting the operator with many post-war machines was the loss of at least some control to the machine. This problem, though sensed, was obscured by the premature phenotypical generalization of the term 'man–machine' to all combinations of men and machines. But the problem did not disappear, men were still aware of it, or better still, sensed it, and were consequently confused by the fact that 'man–machine' *really* does apply to some such collections and *really* does not apply to others, while *formally* it applies to all of them.

2. INFORMATION-PROCESSING DECISION-MAKING MAN–MACHINE COMMUNICATION-SYSTEMS

With the increase of speed and the intensity of waging war as the result of the development of contemporary weapon systems, the military found it necessary to set up parallel electronic systems which could gather much information, at great distances, code, process, and interpret it, take local decisions on its basis and forward it above to higher headquarters for their information and for them to take decisions and action. This necessitated the construction of many information-gathering sites and a complex network of communication channels for transmitting the relevant information. These systems use hundreds and often thousands of machines, instruments, and men; each of the men being responsible for discrete jobs yet having to achieve a fairly complex co-ordination and harmony before the system could do even part of its mission successfully. Although, for the system to work, it was a necessary condition that each man in it know his equipment and know how to run it, it was certainly not a sufficient condition. Every individual in the system had to learn to function as a member of a team, and this entailed training as a team, or as it has euphemistically been called: 'system training'.

That the knowledge of skills is not a sufficient condition for effective system functioning is obvious now. But the Air Defence System, one of the earliest large-scale systems of this nature to be set up, did not have any 'system training' at the outset because nobody was explicitly aware of its need, and even were this need to emerge momentarily into consciousness, nobody would have known what to do about it. A successful system training programme for this system was developed and it will be described and discussed in the sections to follow.

The key element determining a man–machine system is the fact that the man in the system experiences himself as having lost control over the machine and being controlled by the machine, at least to some extent. While it is true that in the early communication systems no single machine managed to control its operator, as such – this changed later with the introduction of computers to store and process the information – nevertheless, the individual generally felt helpless in the face of the system, as such. No single individual in the system, including its commanding officer, felt he knew what was going on in the system; and it is impossible to control something if one does not know what goes on. As a result, the system did not perform effectively and all attempts to improve its performance had, at best, quite limited success. Many reasons can be adduced for the poor performance of the Air Defence System but only those relevant to the system training programme will be mentioned here.

Let us try to imagine an old Air Defence site before the introduction of computerized air defence. The standard day shift had a complement of from ten to fourteen men. It consisted of several 'teams'. The largest single team was a surveillance team of four to five men. These men monitored radarscopes and their responsibility was to identify aircraft tracks, determine their altitude, speed, and direction, and keep an eye on them as long as necessary. This information would be relayed via telephone to a plotting team of two to three men which would plot the tracks on a large plotting board for the

M

entire crew to see. Another team of two to three men identified the
tracks, i.e. they determined which tracks fitted advanced flight plans
received from the air traffic control authorities. Another team of two
to three men relayed relevant information of the air picture to
adjacent air defence sites and to higher headquarters. Finally, there
was a team called the weapons section which consisted of the commanding officer and several other men responsible for maintaining
contact with, and control over, the fighter aircraft which were to be
sent up to identify unknown aircraft. As can be seen, it was a complicated affair.

The mission of the site was to maintain surveillance over a defined
airspace by means of radar, to identify correctly all aircraft for
which flight plans were available, and to intercept all others that
were, by definition, unknown. In addition, the site had to co-ordinate
its activities with adjacent sites, keep higher headquarters informed
of significant happenings as well as execute the orders given it by
them. It was a complex mission and many men had to be involved in
many of its aspects before it could be accomplished.

It was the case that the men were reasonably well skilled as far as
their specific jobs were concerned. The difficulty lay in their lack of
knowledge as to how the system operated *as a system*, and how to
work effectively as a team (there was difficulty in social learning).
How did these difficulties come about?

First of all, no one person could observe the system in operation
so that no one person could know what actually was going on. It is
true that the commanding officer had overall responsibility and
generally did know how well it performed and, more important, why
and where it did not perform well as far as the mission was concerned.
But he did not know what went wrong in the system. He could and
did discuss the matter with the crew members, but they too did not
have a clear picture. Each individual crew member was tied down to
his piece of equipment, to his console, and not only did he not have
the time or objective ability to see what others were doing; he often
had no way of knowing what he was doing, i.e. he could make mistakes and had no way of checking upon himself or of correcting
himself. The mistake would enter the system, unknown and unnotice-
able, only to have its effect show up 'mysteriously' later in system
malperformance. And, to the extent that a person is technically
skilled, he does not experience himself as making mistakes; most of
the crew members are technically skilled. Hence, to the extent that
the commanding officer tried to reconstruct what went wrong he was

confronted with what appeared to be an endless buck-passing, even though this was often not the case. It is difficult to improve crew performance under such conditions and, when crew performance is 'mysteriously' poor, all involved have a feeling of helplessness and of lack of control.

A second area which caused great difficulty was that of team development. A team is more than an aggregate of specific individual technical skills, it is a harmonious fusion, a blending of skills, as well as a development of many things that are relatively independent of skills, such as load-sharing and spontaneous mutual aid among the team members, the timing of actions between team members, and group problem-solving. Research with military crews and teams, particularly bomber aircraft crews, soon reached conclusions that in addition to the skills in implementing *standard operating procedures* (sops) prescribed by military regulations, the crews could also be characterized by another set of skilled procedures, more nebulous and more difficult to define clearly, but nevertheless often of crucial significance for determining the quality of the crew. This second set of procedures eventually came to be called *crew operating procedures*. It was the quality of the crew operating procedures that determined the quality of the team, and, as a rule, it was the high quality team that made the high quality crew.

Crew operating procedures result from social learning, and social learning is something which, as yet, is very difficult to teach didactically. Rather it is learned 'intuitively', unawarely, as a result of 'normal' interaction of the team members in a 'normal' environment. By 'normal' interaction, face-to-face communication by means of a free, spontaneous use of the spoken language is meant; by 'normal' environment relatively clear perception of the nature of the team interdependence, the team mission, and how the actions of each individual of the team fit into and affect the successful accomplishment of the mission, is meant. Although those responsible for the training of aircrews may not have analysed the problem in terms of social learning, those responsible for the training of aircrews were obviously aware, in some manner or other, of its importance. If we look at the aircrew training environment we find that it is admirably suited to the development of crew operating procedures.

The interdependence of the crew both for the success of the mission *per se* and for just getting back to the ground safely was so obvious that it was known and felt without any necessary comment. What is most characteristic of the crew training environment is the many different ways and settings afforded the crew to interact with each other. Consider first the actual mission. A crew training mission lasts at least several hours of which only a small fraction, generally take-off, landing, and the target run, keeps the members so busy at their jobs that they cannot attend to other things that are going on. It is well known that during the rest of the time much talking goes on among the crew and that much of it is task-oriented (parenthetically one may add that this is probably more effective for crew development than if *all* the talk were task-oriented). In addition, the mission is both preceded and followed by formal crew discussions: a briefing before each mission where the mission is explained and discussed until every crew member feels he understands it to his satisfaction; and a debriefing after each mission with an immediate reconstruction and evaluation of the crew performance. Finally, it cannot be over-stressed that aircraft crews fraternize when off duty and between missions with, obviously, much informal talk going on, which also includes much shop talk.

Some may wonder why the stress on informal communication in the above paragraph, why not restrict oneself to the formal meetings, the briefings and debriefings, which were specifically set up for crew discussion and training. One may ask what use can informal, un-controlled, and personal discussions be? There is a very good reason for stressing informal communications; informal communication, at the very least, is the seeding bed for crew operational procedures and generally is the setting wherein they develop fully. Crew operating procedures often develop implicitly so that the crew does not realize its having solved a tricky problem in its informal discussions; this is the reason that most crew operating procedures can be identified only by rather subtle questioning or observation of crew members who are often unaware of the complex and efficient solutions they have found for crew operating problems.

In our society, formal meetings in hierarchical organizations are generally accompanied by an atmosphere of individual evaluation – and advancement in such an organization is predicated upon indivi-dual evaluation – hence, even with the best of intentions of all concerned, strong forces always exist to organize the content of the meeting so that the defence of the individual becomes the important constituent of the cognitive figure. Such forces do not facilitate effective and creative solutions to operational problems which are seen as stemming from individual weaknesses.

The importance of the formal meetings lies in their being the setting where what went wrong with the mission can be and is spelled out explicitly and convincingly. Then the informal meetings take over. In an informal meeting one tends to forget about oneself, the atmosphere of self-evaluation is either greatly weakened or disappears (alcohol facilitates this process noticeably). The problems raised in the formal meetings can now be faced, thought about, and discussed with others without the defence of the individual playing a noticeable part, i.e. they can be discussed much more objectively. It is not surprising that the kind of understanding of the problems that is a prerequisite for good solutions, is thereby facilitated.

The crew in the Air Defence site had none of this; it had neither a 'normal' environment nor was there a 'normal' interaction between team members. Reasons for the lack of a 'normal' environment have already been given when it was pointed out that nobody in the crew was in a position to know what was actually going on. In a 'normal' environment one generally can know what is going on, at least in the immediate vicinity of his responsibilities. 'Normal' interaction between team members was also greatly undercut by being tied down to consoles and telephones rather than talking to each other directly.

Finally, a significant difference between an Air Defence crew and almost all other operational military crews, and particularly air crews, must be noted. By and large, operational military crews have no job to do in peacetime except to train and prepare for war. Hence their peacetime activities are generally in a training context and generally follow a comprehensive plan, in which training the operational team to cope with wartime contingencies plays the dominant role. The Air Defence crews are among the few operational crews that have a full-time operational responsibility during peace – they have to maintain a constant surveillance of the air space around their site against intrusion by unknown aircraft. It is certain that the wartime demands upon the Air Defence crew will be quite different from the demands during peacetime operations, yet, by nature of the peacetime demands, it was very difficult to train the crew, as a team, in anticipated wartime activities. Those responsible for the Air Defence System had justifiable doubts whether, under these conditions, the various crews would be flexible enough to cope creatively with the many new problems bound to come with an outbreak of war.

3. THE SYSTEM TRAINING PROGRAMME – A THUMBNAIL HISTORY

The System Training Programme is a product of pure serendipity; it is also an excellent example of the strengths and pitfalls of serendipity. As such it makes for an interesting and important case study. Parts of the story have been told in RAND Corporation and System Development Corporation internally-published documents as well as in some papers that appeared in print. Perhaps, the best of the papers in print is a paper published in *Management Science* in 1959 by R. L. Chapman, J. L. Kennedy, A. Newell, and W. C. Biel [3]. Though, as far as I know, the story has never been told the way I will tell it here.

The RAND Corporation was founded upon the ideal that if one gets a group of competent scientists, exposes them to a complex problematic situation, and then *lets them alone* to follow their own interests and tastes, and lets them interact intensively with each other, enough of them will spontaneously come up with research that in both quality and scope will be of value towards the solution of many existing problems and the anticipation of many otherwise unanticipated problems highly relevant to that situation to make the whole effort well worth while. The RAND Corporation approached this ideal quite closely when it was still young and small.

A problem of both theoretical importance to psychology and of pragmatic importance to the military, concerned the nature of team or crew behaviour. A small group of psychologists at RAND, as well as a few professionals of other disciplines, became interested in this problem. Since RAND was an Air Force research organization, the RAND scientists 'naturally' focused upon military crews; after all, since there is no such thing as an abstract crew, one must, at least at the outset, consider some specific crew as a basic model, and a military crew is as good a one as any other.* As noted in the preceding section, it was common knowledge that the Air Defence crews were not functioning effectively, and the RAND researchers knew of this. In addition these crews had a rich complex job and were small enough to be studied. Is it surprising that in order to learn something about crew behaviour in general, a decision was taken to study an Air Defence site crew?

---

* Note to academics: this shows how, by being exposed to a complex enough living problem situation, a competent investigator can always find that his personal theoretical interests can be expressed through research that involves pragmatic problems.

It was impossible to study an Air Defence crew *in vivo* so the decision was taken to set up a special laboratory, called the Systems Research Laboratory – 'system' being a very popular and 'scientific' word – where a model of an Air Defence site could be set up; this was called, correctly, simulating an Air Defence site – 'simulation' being another very popular and 'scientific' word. As a crew for this simulated Air Defence site the standard subjects for psychological experiments were chosen – undergraduate students. The purpose of the experiment was to train the students as fast as possible to a skill level comparable to that found in the field in order to be able to observe and record their behaviour carefully and systematically. It was felt that an analysis of the recorded behaviour would yield valuable results. This was not an experiment in the accepted sense of the word where theories or hypotheses are tested and relevant variables are controlled, rather this was basically non-theoretical field research with the novelty that the environment to be field-studied was simulated in a laboratory.

The first step was to visit the site to be simulated in order to know what to simulate. The researchers came back from their visit with all the necessary information concerning the site environment, the nature of the air traffic picture that appeared on the radarscopes, as well as who did what with that input. Information which later was to become crucial was the size of the air load which the crews could 'hack' efficiently, under what conditions, on the average, the crews became overloaded and ceased to function efficiently, etc. Input scripts for the simulated sites contained loads which in real life would lead to crew overloading or system breakdown.

The second step, after setting up the simulated site and checking it through, was to train subjects. Since training the subjects was not the focus of research interest it was given little theoretical thought. The researchers intuitively set up a training programme which they felt would be efficient, the purpose being to bring the subject crew as fast as possible up to a skill level comparable to the skill level of the military crews. Considering the conceptual mess in which so-called learning theory finds itself and the fact that it has nothing to do with what normal men deem to be learning, including psychologists when they worry about what school to send their children to, this dependence upon intuition rather than theory in setting up the training programme was a 'stroke of genius' – had the RAND scientists become involved in theoretical considerations, they would probably not have been successful in setting up an efficient training programme, and their research would never have got off the ground.

The unexpected occurred with the second step. Not only did the student crews all too soon hack the loads normally hacked well in real life, but they also soon, with the greatest of ease, hacked loads that would overwhelm real crews. The original research purpose had to be abandoned because the prepared scripts which were intended to stress the crews proved to be too easy, there was not enough team behaviour worth recording. (But inadvertently a team training programme was born.) Military crews were brought in, subjected to the training procedures and given heavier and heavier loads, loads which could not conceivably be hacked in real life. Yet they managed to hack them effectively and efficiently. The military were alerted and, properly, requested that the training programme be implemented in the field. This was accomplished by setting up a special corporation to administer, and direct the implementation of, what by now came to be called, the 'System Training Programme'.

What occurred until then is not too rare in science; a group of scientists set out to study one area and find something which is very valuable in another area. But what followed is more or less unique to contemporary American academic social science in general, and to academic psychology in particular – no attempt was made to think through why the training programme was so effective. Four experimental crews were run through the Systems Research Laboratory. Almost everything the crews did and said during the runs was recorded accurately and systematically. A mass of originally invaluable data were accumulated. Yet nothing was done with all this.* They are probably still to be found, untouched, in filing cabinets.

Later, as the training was implemented in the field and involved hundreds of professional social scientists, primarily psychologists, very valuable lessons were learned concerning problems intrinsic to the training effort, and extrinsic to it, but relating to practical problems of implementing a training programme in an 'alien society'. Yet all these hundreds of man-years of experience have gone to waste. There are no publications sponsored by the scientists involved in this gigantic effort that attempt to reduce this rich experience to conceptual coherence. It is a mark of the failure of the profession as a whole which stems from its refusal to permit itself to think and from its reliance upon external criteria as to what science is and what 'respectability' is.

---

* Data tend to deteriorate with disuse, hence what was originally invaluable generally *becomes valueless* with disuse over time.

Since, however, the training programme was intuitively sound and made sense, both objectively and to the trainers, it was possible to describe it coherently – and there are many descriptions of the System Training Programme in print. The programme will be described in the section to follow and, in addition, it will be shown how the specifics of the programme met the training needs of the Air Defence sites and why the programme was successful.

4. THE SYSTEM TRAINING PROGRAMME – DESCRIPTION AND ANALYSIS

In order better to grasp the description of the System Training Programme, it is useful to know something more about the Air Defence System.

The mission of the Air Defence System is to keep the air space over the United States free from hostile aircraft. In order to achieve this mission, three things have to be done: (*a*) an accurate, up-dated radar picture of the air traffic over the country must be maintained; (*b*) the aircraft in the picture must be identified on the basis of prior information (flight plans forwarded to the system by air traffic control authorities); and (*c*) those aircraft in the picture that are unidentifiable on the basis of prior information must be physically intercepted and identified visually. The 'old' air defence system consisted of many individual radar sites maintaining an around-the-clock surveillance of a specified section of the air space controlled by several echelons of higher headquarters culminating with the headquarters for the entire continent. As such, it was organized both 'vertically' and 'horizontally'; i.e. the sites and lower headquarters had to co-ordinate their activities with the adjacent parallel sites and headquarters as well as maintain constant co-ordination with the higher headquarters. Since time was of the essence, it involved precise co-ordination with little opportunity for error checking between the many teams having responsibilities for limited aspects of the mission.

The hierarchical structure consisted of individual sites, divisions, forces, and finally the entire command. According to original system training plans, the basic unit of the system to be trained was the division of several sites and division headquarters. However, almost from the outset, individual sites also used the programme for self-training without involving the other adjacent sites of the division. Later, with experience, force exercises were introduced involving several divisions. Eventually successful command-wide exercises were run as well. It was also found that the training programme could be run successfully for teams within a crew, i.e. not even involving the entire crew at a site – this latter finding was resisted since it conflicted with uncritically accepted theoretical principles that underlay the thinking of the professionals involved; this will be discussed in greater detail in the next section.

Each system to be trained was a specifiable geographical unit of men and equipment embedded in an environment. When a site was being trained, the geographical unit was a room called the direction centre, which contained the crew and its equipment; when a division was trained, it contained the direction centres of the division sites and a similar room at the division called the control centre plus the communication linkages between the rooms, etc. The environment consisted of all aspects that had an effect upon the system but which were not part of the geographical unit. In the field the system to be trained was not simulated, i.e. the men to be trained sat in their regular position with their regular equipment, but the embedding environment was; in the Systems Research Laboratory the physical aspects of the system were also simulated – the only thing not being simulated was man.

The embedding environment can be conceptually broken up into three sections which, for the lack of better terms, I will call: (a) the task environment, (b) the operational environment, and (c) the support environment. The task environment includes that part of the environment that directly concerned the mission of the system; in the case of the Air Defence System it includes the air space for which the system is responsible, the air traffic within that space, and the interceptors stationed at assigned air bases available to the system for interception of unknown aircraft.

The operational environment includes all those military and/or civilian organizations and/or systems with which the system being trained interacts in normal operations and which are also responsible for air defence. For the Air Defence System being trained this included adjacent sites, divisions, and/or forces (depending upon the scope of the training effort) as well as other relevant organizations in the Army and Navy.

The support environment includes those organizations that are necessary for the proper functioning of the system being trained, though they are not directly responsible for the mission; in the present case they are not directly responsible for air defence as such.

Originally this aspect of the environment was restricted to the federal organizations responsible for forwarding flight plans to the system so that they could identify the aircraft in the air. Later, as the training became more sophisticated and battle damage was introduced, this environment became more important since the destruction of support normally taken for granted could be simulated and the system had to devise means of functioning without this support.

The system being trained interacts with its embedding environment by means of inputs into it from the environment and outputs from it into the environment. As already mentioned, the embedding environment was simulated. This meant that a script had to be written as to what would be input at the proper time in the proper manner. In addition, it meant that simulators should also receive the system output, and input back into the system the consequences which followed the system actions and which, in turn, affected the system. This enabled the men in the system being trained to function, as they normally do, within reasonably realistic circumstances.

The most important input into the system was the air picture or, as was generally the case, the attack. It was possible to project upon the radarscopes a realistic air picture and the job of the men in the system was to detect the attack and take the appropriate actions, many of which were output to the simulators. The important outputs of the system were the speed and effectiveness of identifying the planned unknown flights (that is flights for which the script did not provide flight plans), the actions taken by the system upon such identification, and the observed errors committed – whatever they might be.

It follows therefore that simulation equipment, a corps of simulators, and a corps of people who could construct the necessary scripts, are a fundamental prerequisite for the success of the training programme; without them, or without the simulation being done well, there could be no training programme. This whole area of endeavour was subsumed by the term 'simulation' and, as will be seen in the next section, it also played a very important negative role in the training programme.

Given an ability to simulate the embedding environment, it is possible to conduct exercises in which the system being trained acts as in real life.

The second aspect of the training programme is an accurate recording of the system performance. Since the script is known, the nature of the crucial events and the time of their occurrence is known as well. It becomes possible to alert trained observers to record how the system reacts to the crucial events as they occur. For instance, since the time that a simulated enemy aircraft is scheduled to penetrate the embedding environment is known, the observer can record how long it took for the system to spot and correctly identify the aircraft – it is obvious that the speed and accuracy of spotting and identifying hostile aircraft is of primary importance for an air defence system. Furthermore, since the scheduled path of the aircraft in the simulated embedding environment is known, it is relatively easy to evaluate how accurately the system tracked the aircraft once it was identified as a simulated hostile aircraft. Finally, since the scheduled target of the aircraft is known, it is possible to evaluate objectively the efficacy of the tactical actions taken by the system in regard to the aircraft, etc. It is therefore possible to get accurate records of system performance or the performance of selected parts of the system as it related to events crucial to the system or to selected aspects of these events.

Having completed the exercise, the crews gathered in selected meeting rooms for a debriefing. The trained observers presented the record of the crews' performance objectively, i.e. they presented the record of the times of action, the nature of the action, the outcome of the action, etc., in a factual, impersonal, non-evaluative manner. This was presented in conjunction with the simulated input to the system so that the crew could see how their actions related to the simulated 'real world'. Upon finishing the presentation (the feedback) and answering factual questions by the crew, the observers left the meeting and the crews took over to discuss what had occurred.

It is proper to assert that most of the learning that occurs as a result of the System Training Programme occurs in this meeting that follows the feedback of system performance. This is not to say that what preceded the meeting was either less necessary or less important; experience has amply demonstrated that learning in the crew meeting is vitiated to the extent that what precedes it is done ineffectively. However, most of the effort that precedes such meetings would go to waste if the meetings, or something functionally equivalent to them, were not held. The crew meetings following the feedback of their performance are, figuratively speaking, the moment of harvest of the System Training Programme.

These meetings were conducted in a special manner, different from the standard military briefing and debriefing. The meeting leaders, generally the commanding officers, were sent to special workshops to learn how to conduct themselves. The spirit of the meetings followed the spirit of the feedback in being objectively task-oriented. The focus was upon what went on rather than upon who did what. The meetings can be characterized as being objectively evaluative and personally non-evaluative. The events were analysed as to their successes and failures and, in the latter instances, attempts to identify causes for the failures as well as possible corrective actions were followed up until a consensus was reached (hopefully). The consensus was then written out explicitly in a special log for all to be able to read.

Reflection shows that this training programme meets the various difficulties confronting the Air Defence System presented in section 2 above. Let us summarize them and see how the programme fits.

It was argued that the crew members, including the commanding officer, felt that they had lost control over the system because of various lacks of knowledge of what was going on. They did not know how their actions in the team related specifically to the objective relevant events in the air space, since they had no knowledge of what went on objectively in the air. In the System Training Programme this was available through knowledge of the script, the knowledge of crucial events, and alertness to record the crews' behaviour in light of these crucial events. In real-life operations it was generally difficult to identify where the initial error was made in the system and how it snowballed into ineffective system performance. This was corrected by the observation of system performance as well as by the crew meeting.

The difficulties of exposing the Air Defence System, with a peacetime mission, to expected wartime situations were, of course, easily solved. The scripts could input any desired or imaginable air picture into the system. It was in fact possible to expose the system to extreme situations which were impossible to imagine occurring in real life but which would explicate a principle or a problem worth explicating.

As has already been indicated, the greatest difficulty confronting the crews was in the area of social learning. The vehicle in the training programme which facilitated social learning was the meeting of the crew, after the feedback session. It pays to discuss this meeting in some detail.

The meeting would begin after the results of the exercise were reported to the crew and the reporters had left. The first and most important principle underlying the meeting was that it be task rather than person oriented. This meant that, based upon the feedback, the group would try to identify what went wrong, why it went wrong, and what the *crew* can do about similar circumstances in the future in order to improve its performance, without attributing *individual* blame as such. Because of this de-emphasis upon individual blame, the meeting was mis-described as being non-evaluative – and, as will be seen in the next section, this mis-description led to many unnecessary difficulties.

Although, on one hand, the substance under discussion would be the same whether task oriented or person oriented, on the other hand, the nature of the discussion would differ radically under these two conditions. Man finds his malperformance, within large limits, a challenge to be overcome if the recognition of the malperformances will not result in his being penalized for them.* The fear of penalization makes it difficult for an individual objectively to face malperformance; rather than face the issue openly, he will, willy-nilly, so restructure the situation as to minimize his blame and project it elsewhere. Men are aware that they do this to some extent, but it is almost certain that they are not aware of the total extent of their doing this. Improvement becomes difficult to the extent of their partial awareness; it becomes impossible to the extent of their unawareness. To the extent that man can face the issues, both publicly and privately (the two are highly correlated), his malperformance does become a challenge and a spur for an efficient and creative overcoming. A group discussion led by a skilled discussion leader where individuals are supported in their attempts to achieve an objective picture of things rather than being blamed for their personal weaknesses becomes a royal road to self and group improvement.

A second important principle underlying the meeting was the achievement of group commitment through participation. To the extent that individuals participate creatively in an activity, they become committed to it and to its outcomes. To the extent that they are committed to an activity and its outcomes, both their participation and support of the outcomes becomes more efficient and responsible. A discussion leader can create a group atmosphere fostering commitment by seeing to it that the discussion is not monopolized by an individual or small subset of individuals in the meeting, while

---

* Penalization for malperformance can stem from internal as well as external sources. Not only do individuals fear the exposure of their weaknesses to their peers and superiors; they often fear to face them themselves.

facilitating and *encouraging* every person in the group to participate in the discussion and express his opinion. It may sound trite to warn discussion leaders that encouragement does not mean coercion, were it not the case that confusion between the two is so widespread. Coercing a person to participate in a discussion may have effects as undesirable as not enabling him to participate in the discussion when he wishes to. Individuals will feel committed to a discussion and its outcomes when they have the feeling that, *had they wanted to*, they could have expressed their opinions and would have been listened to seriously.

The third principle of the discussion was 'the debriefing log'. Those acquainted with the System Training Programme may raise eyebrows at this point. The ostensive purpose of the debriefing log was to record for future reference the conclusions reached at the meeting so that were a situation to arise similar to the one discussed, the crew would have a reference telling it what to do. In practice this did not work, and the entries into the log were rarely read after having been entered. It is fair to say that the ostensive purpose of this log blinded most to its dynamic effect on the discussion. The necessity for summarizing the consensus of the discussion in a terse and objective fashion fitted for the log acted as a disciplining framework to prevent the discussion from wandering off into irrelevancies or becoming individual oriented. In addition, the public formulation of the entry by the log recorder before its being entered into the log brought a closure to the discussion, facilitated understanding of the consensus on the part of all concerned, and strengthened commitment to the consensus. It is true that this can be achieved by other techniques as well, but the debriefing log served the purpose admirably in these circumstances. Hence, it was somewhat irrelevant that once entered into the log, the entry was rarely, if at all, re-read.

Finally, it should be noted that the meeting, ideally, was not restricted to the information fed back to it. Rather the feedback and the meeting often served as a springboard for the crew members to bring up whatever problems they felt worth discussing. As such, the feedback played another significant role. It served as a goad for 'stimulated recall'. It is known that if a person is confronted with a concrete aspect of a complex situation in which he participated, the recall of other aspects of the situation is facilitated. The presentation to the crew of an objective record of significant aspects of its performance, followed by a task-oriented discussion which stresses crew actions, could not but stimulate crew members to recall problems which, under other conditions, they would have 'normally' forgotten.

The effect of such meetings seems obvious. To the extent that they succeeded, crew members came to know the consequences of their actions upon overall crew performance (this was called 'enhancing system awareness') and social learning was greatly facilitated as individuals got to know each other's responsibilities, abilities, and disabilities; as such, the group of relatively isolated individuals confronted with a console, in relative ignorance of much of what was going on about them, changed into an integrated team well aware of their environment and of the means available to them to cope with the actual and potential demands of the environment. As such, they became a better crew.

5. SLOGANS, RED HERRINGS, AND AVOIDABLE PITFALLS WHICH WERE NOT AVOIDED

Man cannot engage in an activity which makes no sense to him, hence he makes sense out of whatever he does; however, the sense he makes need not be valid even though it 'works' under the special situations for which it was formulated. When the sense man makes of what he does is valid, man truly understands his actions, how they fit the environment in which they take place, and how they accomplish that which he wishes to accomplish. With true understanding, no conceptual difficulty confronts man when either his wishes change or the environment changes, and he clearly sees how he ought to change his actions, and the reasons for making the change.

To the extent that these reasons are general or abstract they are relevant to more than a specific situation. As such, they become maxims that guide behaviour in many situations and can be called principles for action. To the extent that principles are based upon understanding, they become valid guidelines for behaviour when they apply and to the extent to which they apply. Principles for action cannot be applied blindly, mechanically; the actor must analyse the situation in which he finds himself in order to determine which principles apply to it, and the extent of their application; this he can do effectively when he understands the situation.

But the sense that a person makes of his activities need not be valid. Consider an imaginary primitive who follows a ten-step procedure in planting his food crops. The ten steps consist of various dances and offerings aimed at persuading and assuaging various deities who, he believes, have some control over the growth of the crops. Part of one dance contains, from the primitive's standpoint, the 'trivial' act of putting the seed into the ground, and as part of another dance we find a similarly 'trivial' act of watering the seed.

The ten-step procedure works and the crops grow. Were we to ask this primitive why the procedure works, he would explain with ease and show how the dances and the offerings propitiate the various deities involved, who then see to it that everything proceeds in order; trivial details such as putting the seed into the ground and watering it would not be mentioned. And the more intelligent primitive may even come up with two principles underlying the success of the procedure: (*a*) the intensity of the dancing, and (*b*) the size of the offering. As has just been acknowledged, the procedure works, hence the principles have been vindicated. Let us continue to imagine that because of the 'triviality' of the task, the depth of seed planting is disregarded and in order to conserve energy for greater 'intensity', it soon becomes too shallow for efficient germination; the crops begin to fail. Following his principles the primitive increases the intensity and violence of his dancing and increases the size of his offerings – the pragmatic effect of this very rational behaviour is predictable.

Some may argue that the above example should be restricted to the most primitive, if it has any validity whatsoever, and that any reasonably intelligent man would not perseverate in following invalid principles, but would soon question them. It is true that intellectual progress is predicated upon the questioning of principles, but it is also true that such questioning is surprisingly rare; in our society we tend to call those who question principles and get away with it: 'geniuses'.

In the imaginary example just given, the enunciated principles were wrong, were invalid, but the procedure itself was valid since it 'caused' crops to grow. But the degree of validity of procedures is irrelevant if and when they are used blindly, without understanding. He who accepts them uncritically cannot tell what is right about them and will not know how to apply them correctly to changing situations and to unexpected contingencies that crop up. When used without understanding, the most correct principles must be accepted uncritically and, as such, they soon turn into Baconian idols. Rather than guidelines for effective action which generate creative thinking towards the solution of problems, they become slogans which blind

N

the mind and steer it towards rationalization and scapegoat seeking. On one hand, it is surprising to note how much of this occurred when the to-be-expected difficulties were met with in the implementation of the System Training Programme; on the other hand, knowing the propensities of academic psychologists not to think issues through, it is not surprising at all.

'Simulation' soon turned from a valid principle into a slogan and a red herring. This was facilitated by several aspects of the situation: (*a*) the role of the professionals in implementing the training programme; (*b*) the split between the field professionals and those in the home office; (*c*) the pernicious influence of academic learning theory; and (*d*) the role of the military.

Although the professionals implementing the training programme had the real responsibility for seeing that the programme worked, they did not have the official responsibility for administering the programme. The responsibility for administering the programme rested with the military themselves, the professionals served officially merely as advisers to the military. Being an adviser meant that they had little formal control over what was going on. On the other hand, the corporation, and because of this the professionals who represented it, did have the responsibility for setting up the scripts and the problems, i.e. they did have control over the 'simulation'. When things go wrong, man's attention is 'spontaneously' centred upon those aspects over which he can exercise control (one of the psychological bases of scapegoatism – one always has control over the scapegoat). Hence, when the inevitable troubles emerged, it was all too often the case that the professional responsible for advising the military first focused his attention upon the quality of the simulation.

Once this was done, other factors reinforced this direction of attention and made it relatively difficult to change. The professionals within the corporation were themselves split into two groups: those at the home office preparing the materials for the programme and those out at the field working with the military. The professionals out in the field were first confronted with difficulties in the programme. By attributing the cause of many of the difficulties to faulty simulation, they shifted the responsibility from their shoulders to those at the home office, in addition it enabled them to take 'positive' action. Very much of the correspondence between the field and the home office consisted of detailed accounts of how and where simulation is faulty.

Since the professional staff, both in the field and at the home office, was, by and large, a representative cross-section of academic psychology, the majority of its members were both emotionally and intellectually committed to academic learning theory which is predicated upon blind rote learning, meaning and understanding being relegated to the realm of epiphenomena. It is a strict derivation from learning theory that the more accurate the simulation, the better the learning must be, since learning takes place solely through action. This harmony between theoretical implications and the 'natural' inclinations of the field personnel to attribute as many faults to simulation as possible, enabled this to be done by all concerned rather uncritically – they felt that this was dictated by *Science*. The professionals at the home office were relatively helpless in the face of this criticism; they too were committed to learning theory and the whole thing made *a priori* sense to them. In addition, if they were able to demonstrate that improved simulation does lead to improved learning, they would be able to contribute papers to the professional journals – the treatment being scientifically respectable.* Finally, the military also bought the argument that most of what was wrong with the programme stemmed from faulty simulation. For that shifted the onus of responsibility from their shoulders to that of the professionals and the corporation, an onus, which as just indicated, the professionals did accept.

As a result, for much of the time 'improvement of the training programme' became synonymous with improving simulation. The art of simulating the embedding environment reached a degree of truly impressive sophistication while many serious problems bedevilling the System Training Programme were either intelligently patched up *ad hoc* by those on the spot, botched up, or neglected. The most obvious effect of this 'idolization' of simulation occurred while planning for training the to-be-introduced computerized (SAGE) air defence system. With this new system an almost perfect simulation was achievable, and planning started out with enthusiasm, with the feeling that all basic problems were resolved and that it was only a matter of fitting the details to the new system. Very bitter experience subsequently showed that nothing could have been further from the truth.

What is the role of simulation in training? Obviously, simulation must be accurate to a certain degree to have any effect; if one gives a

---

* It should be noted, parenthetically, that the great frustration of many dedicated professionals associated with the programme was their inability to do research as defined by the standards of academia.

broom to a basic trainee and tells him that it is a simulated rifle, it is an ineffective simulation for learning rifle drill, whereas a weighted wooden rifle is excellently suited for that purpose. On the other hand, it is just as obvious that to 'simulate as accurately as possible' is unimplementable. One hundred per cent accuracy in simulation is approached asymptotically and, no matter how accurate one simulates, with additional effort it is always possible to increase the accuracy. Hence there must be a cut-off point to accuracy. It is possible to formulate a rational principle to serve as a guideline for determining the degree of necessary accuracy: simulation should be accurate enough to achieve the degree of learning desired by the teacher. This principle does not tell you what to do in a specific case, rather it indicates that you spell out to yourself what you wish to achieve in your training effort, and what degree of accuracy is reasonably necessary for this achievement, recognizing full well that experience may show that you either oversimulated or undersimulated in your initial planning. For rifle drill a piece of wood shaped like a rifle and weighing close to a rifle is a very effective simulator; for bayonet practice a sack full of damp straw hanging from a pole is an effective simulation of a man's stomach, etc. No such analysis was ever seriously attempted for the System Training Programme, rather the principle of simulation soon came to resemble the increased intensity of dancing.

The second principle that rapidly turned into a slogan was 'training the system as a whole'. The 'great' discovery of the System Training Programme was that individual skills are not enough for efficient crew operation, and what was needed was to train a team.* And a team has to be trained as a unit, as a whole. Unfortunately, it was difficult to identify the team to be trained in the Air Defence System. No criteria were worked out to define the whole system to be trained; hence, the principle became inapplicable and, rather than serve as a guide, it became a blinder hampering rather than helping the solution of operational problems. An Air Defence site is part of a larger system – a division; the division is part of a larger system – the force; and the force is part of a larger system – the North American Air Defence Command, etc. As in Ezekiel's picture of heaven, we find wholes within wholes within wholes. Pragmatically, the division was chosen as the basic unit to be trained, but this choice was dic-

---

* The mere fact that this homely truth of the necessity to train a team was 'camouflaged' under the pompous then popular phrase 'training a system' also indicates the basic lack of understanding of what was going on.

tated by material, not theoretical, circumstances, i.e. it was too difficult to train the force or the entire command except on rather rare occasions. As a result, training the division as a whole was felt to compromise the principle of training the system as a whole, and many things that went wrong and that probably could have been corrected were shrugged away with the rationalization that 'if we could only train the system as a whole, we would take care of it'.

Actually, it is possible to conceptualize the 'whole' that needs to be trained as a unit. This conceptualization is based upon the central role that social learning plays in team training.

A man–machine system is set up to do a job, i.e. to turn out a product. Hence, something is always put into the system, processed within the system, and then put out of the system. It can be seen that people within the system can interact with each other either *only* via the product or, also directly, over and above the product. In interacting only via the product, the two people have no direct contact with each other, i.e. one person processes the product in the pre-scribed manner and then puts it in a prescribed place from which the second person takes it (if the product is directly handed to the second person, we do not have interaction only via the product since there is direct contact between the two persons). In all other cases where people talk directly to each other, hand things directly to each other, etc., in order to get the job done, we have interaction over and above the product. Persons who interact only via the product do not constitute a team. All that is necessary is that the first person be able to turn out the product according to specifications – he need not ever even see the second person. What he needs is 'skill learning'. To the extent, however, that persons have to interact over and above the product, we find the makings of a team. To the extent that the inter-action is intense and/or important for the systems job, the need for team training increases and 'social learning' is called for.

For example: those persons engaging in surveillance and plotting in the manual Air Defence site constituted a team. The product of this team was a display of the air tracks in the air space over the site. Other teams in the crew functioned on the basis of this display and had no need to contact individuals of the surveillance-plotting team directly, they referred to the plotting board.

Unfortunately, in military hierarchical man–machine systems there are teams within teams even according to the rather stringent definition given above. The senior individual in the surveillance-plotting team does interact directly with senior individuals in other teams. The commanding officer directly interacts with persons from all the teams in the crew as well as with persons at the adjacent sites and at higher headquarters. Rather than despairing at this, we will argue that in such cases individuals are members of more than one team. It then becomes possible to reduce a man–machine system to a set of teams, each turning out a relatively well-defined product, with some individuals being members of more than one team. The unit to be trained then becomes a team and the environment embedding this team can be simulated for effective team training. Of course, to the extent that a member of a team being trained is simultaneously a member of another team in the system which is not being trained, his individual training suffers, but this does not have too great an effect on the team being trained, as such. The pressure towards training as much of the Air Defence System as possible can now be understood, since the senior officers of the system are members of teams which reach down deep into the system. For the best training of the officers, all the teams of which they are members must be trained simultaneously. This is the objective pressure which led to the misinterpretation of the principle of 'training the system as a whole' to 'always training as much of the system as possible'. It is only when the training is aimed at the senior officers that training large segments or the entire system is necessary. For the training of teams at the lower hierarchies, individual site exercises and individual team exercises are eminently sufficient, and were actually practised. But if one believes that by doing so, one violates 'basic training principles', one is very unhappy when one is forced to do so, and, consequently, doesn't do too good a job at it.

Two principles relating to the post-exercise meetings also turned into slogans: they concern objective feedback of system performance and non-evaluative debriefing. But before they are discussed *per se* it pays to discuss some of the difficulties accompanying the post-exercise meetings in general. These meetings became a bone of contention among the professionals themselves. As already mentioned, the majority of the professionals adhered to academic learning theory and in terms of this approach only the action under conditions of veridical simulation makes sense, the post-exercise meetings being relegated to the limbo of epiphenomena. The minority of professionals were under influence by academic clinical and social psychology. They latched on to these meetings as a vindication for their approach and the conflict that rages within university departments emerged. The conflict was aggravated by the fact that the 'soft-headed' clinical and social psychologists were more correct than their 'hard-headed', 'rigorous' experimental brethren, but the latter were more powerful in the corporation.

Since the meetings, as such, did not make theoretical sense to the 'hard-headed' experimentalists, they could not speak about them with much assurance. They felt more at ease with 'feedback' however. For feedback they could apply the principles of accuracy and rigour so important in the psychological laboratory. The quest for accurate feedback of 'system' performance became the main vehicle for their activities. Unfortunately for them, the system performance was recorded by human beings, who are notoriously inaccurate and unreliable and, what is even worse, do not record 'objectively' everything that happens as it happens, but organize and synthesize whenever the opportunity permits. This inability to depend upon getting complete, 'objective' feedback became an excuse for many things that were going wrong with the post-exercise meetings.

Not long after the training programme went into effect, planning for the automated Air Defence System began. This system was to have a computer which could keep a temporal record of every action taken by the crew during an exercise. Here then was the solution to all the feedback and, by implication, the post-exercise meeting problems. A complex computer program was prepared to print out the 'system' performance after each exercise. The program worked reasonably well and did print out in detail everything that happened, but it was self-defeating. The reams of detail were next to useless for the meeting; there was much too much information to be used for immediate feedback and the meetings were designed to be held immediately after the exercise.

The soft-headed clinical and social psychologists focused their attention upon the meetings *per se*, since that was their element. The 'mythoses' of group therapy and group dynamics became their guidelines. Togetherness, *Gemütlichkeit*, calling each other by the first name, etc., became that which primarily has to be achieved in the 'properly' run meeting, and with it all serious problems would be solved. That such aims are at variance with the entire military culture was considered to be unfortunate, but then the military culture is not a 'democratic' culture and therefore it is a 'bad' culture which the training programme would do something to improve. This of course generated both conflict among the professionals administering the programme and resistance among the military as well. As a result of all this, the post-exercise meetings, the setting wherein most of the 'system learning' actually did occur, became the weakest link in the entire training programme.

The difficulties just enumerated, and others, all sprang from the fact that the programme emerged as a by-product from research that had another purpose, and then was not thought through carefully. Hence, the professionals did not really know what they were doing and the basically correct principles underlying the programme turned into blind slogans. As such, the professionals also did not know what they were training for, they lacked a tangible purpose. But since man cannot act unless he has a purpose, a new slogan emerged. The purpose of the System Training Programme became training for 'system flexibility' and 'system awareness'. The trouble with this slogan is that it says too much and it says too little. Flexibility and awareness are general purposes of each and every training programme – one does not train people to be inflexible at their job or to be unaware of what their job entails. Hence, the slogan says too much. It says too little because it gives no indication how one achieves this kind of training. In order to know this, it is necessary to think the issue through, and this, of course was not done.

6. POSTSCRIPT

Some may ask: with all this going wrong, how is it that the training programme worked at all? Let us recall the imaginary example of the primitive who followed a ten-step ritual while planting seeds, only two of the steps being necessary and sufficient for planting seeds. That primitive did grow enough food to feed himself and those dependent upon him. But let us also remember that primitives do not make efficient farmers and their crops are poor. Poor crops are not adequate substitutes for rich crops.

Others may wonder why my criticism levelled against the profession is imbued with bitterness. It is annoying to see professionals behave like primitives – one has the right to expect more.

REFERENCES

1] BENTLEY, M., Forecasting, Timing, and other Primary Factors in Government of Certain Bio-Mechanical Systems. *Amer. J. Psychol.*, 1952, **65**, 329–45.

[2] BIRMINGHAM, H. P., and TAYLOR, F. V., A Design Philosophy for Man–Machine Control Systems. *Proc. Inst. Radio Engrs.*, New York, 1954, **42**, 1748–58.

[3] CHAPMAN, R. L., KENNEDY, J. L., NEWELL, A., and BIEL, W. C., The Systems Research Laboratory's Air Defense Experiments. *Mgmt. Sci.*, 1959, **5**, 250–69.

11

The social science practitioner and his client

*Experience with the military**

Before getting down to the brass tacks of this paper, a case description of concrete experience in implementing what may be called social engineering in a military setting, I would like to make two general introductory comments.

First, the title of this programme is: the social science practitioner and his clients. It consists of four papers describing experiences with various clients. This poses the danger of conceptually separating the practitioner from the client and considering the client and the problems he poses in isolation. The danger is aggravated by the fact that no clear-cut role distinction between the practitioner and the scientists exists in the contemporary social sciences; we all like to see ourselves as a bit of both. As scientists, however, we conscientiously and properly try to study the phenomena objectively and not interact with them. Would that this were possible in applied social science. But it is not. All understanding into the problems of applied social science will be vitiated if we slide back into separating the practitioner from the client and focus exclusively upon the latter. In social science application, the social whole to be observed, the dynamic unit to be studied, is the practitioner *and* his client. The case I am about to discuss serves as a good example of this point.

Secondly, I would like to think out loud as to why the presentation of cases is important in the present social science milieu. When all is said and done, the social sciences have no theory that can be applied

* Presented at the American Sociological Association meetings held at St Louis, Missouri, 28 August–2 September 1961.

directly for the solution of specific concrete social problems – the area of immediate interest to the practitioner. At best, if the practitioner is theory-conscious, he comes up with a working solution to his problem and then, if it is successful, he shows how his pet theory can explain its success. As far as practice is concerned, we find ourselves in a position very similar to that of the medical profession, where even today so much of its success is based upon a careful recording and studying of individual cases. But even more. We stand in awe, admiration, and jealousy at the success of our professional younger brother, the physical sciences.* In our hope and desire to achieve even some measure of his success we have emulated his techniques, methodology, and philosophy as formulated by the great epistemologists who have evaluated him after he achieved his first of a spectacular series of accomplishments. What we have forgotten, or overlooked, is that when this younger brother of ours started out on his scientific adventures, he too concentrated almost exclusively upon individual cases. Those who doubt this would do well to look up the agenda of the British Royal Society, or its functional European counterparts, during the seventeenth century. There may be more than mere pragmatic utility in studying cases. Perhaps the lesson to be learned from the success of the physical sciences is that careful experimentation and control, and all that that implies, is the magnificent tool it is only after a discipline reaches a minimum level of theoretical sophistication, but that before that level is reached, the best thing to do is to study cases carefully.

Well, let's get down to brass tacks.

THE SETTING

The case here presented is on the introduction of a novel training technique for training selected military personnel. As such, it was part of a much larger ongoing training effort. In order better to have a feeling for the uniquely social problems that were met with in introducing this new technique, the larger training effort must be understood. This effort involved the training of military operational crews as units at military bases. The training *per se* involved the running of simulated exercises for the crews, feeding back to them an objective account of their performance during these exercises, and

---

* As a functioning entity, the social sciences are older than the physical sciences. Plato and Aristotle's psychology and sociology should still be read by students of human behaviour; their physics are naïve.

then generating a crew discussion based upon group dynamic principles in order to evoke self-criticism with an aim of self-improvement.

The programme, as such, was the administrative responsibility of the military, but the functional responsibility for the success of the programme lay in a corporation especially set up for the purpose. The corporation prepared the material for the exercises – no mean job in itself – maintained a research and development staff whose responsibility it was to evaluate and improve the programme, and maintained a staff of field representatives who acted as a liaison between the corporation and the military as well as guiding and helping the military in administering the programme. The personnel of the research and development group and the field representatives were almost exclusively social scientists.

Although, on one hand, obviously, the introduction of this special training technique involved the interaction of individual social science practitioners and individual clients, on the other hand, it is also fair to say that the social science practitioner was a differentiated social entity – the corporation, and the client a differentiated social entity – the military command. For the purposes of the present discussion, it is sufficient to distinguish the research and development group and the field representatives within the corporation, and the division headquarters and the bases within the military.

THE TRAINING PROBLEM

As just mentioned, the heart of the training effort consisted of crew discussions aimed at self-analysis and critique. On the whole, the crews numbered between ten and fifteen men. One member of the crew had a unique and individual job – and it was a very important job. Since he was one among so many, in conjunction with several other factors, his job was left out of the discussion. It was common knowledge among all concerned with the training effort that these key crew members got little if any benefit from the overall crew training programme. There was of course an on-the-job individual training programme available for these crew members, but it was the almost unanimous consensus of all involved with that programme that it was quite poor. There were rumblings.

But first things first. It was necessary, and of paramount importance, to get the crew training programme to work reasonably well. Before this was achieved, no attention could be paid to problems of individuals. As this was being achieved, the rumblings grew louder and reached the windows of the higher echelons. Finally, the top command echelons in the military indicated to top management of the corporation that they would be very happy if some way could be found for using the highly developed and available techniques for crew training to help the poor neglected key crew members. Management thought it was a good idea and handed the job to the research and development group. And with this our actual case begins.

A POSSIBLE SIMPLE SOLUTION TO THE TRAINING PROBLEM

The people in the research and development group had enough experience with the programme to be able to figure out an adequate way of using the crew training programme to train these individuals without ever leaving their offices. It was mentioned earlier that the training involved simulated exercises for the crew. It was relatively easy to extend the simulation and simulate all the other members of the crew with the exception of the individual to be trained. Hence, all that was needed was to describe clearly how to accomplish this. Then both top management and the military command would send this description to the individuals involved with an order to implement it as a new programme. But as every practitioner knows, nothing would have better guaranteed failure than such a direct approach. Even had the research and analysis people been able to take this step, which they weren't for reasons to be immediately given, both the field representatives and military personnel involved would look upon the order as an increase to their already heavy load of duties, as an imposition from the outside, and would implement it most perfunctorily, if at all.

But the situation was such that the research and development people could not even consider this step. Such a step was interpreted by them as using 'expertise', as relying on experience leavened by common sense. And their whole academic training was predicated upon the proposition that common sense is untrustworthy, that the only thing worthy of the name 'knowledge' is that which was rigorously checked out in a laboratory or experimental setting. In the present case, the experimental study had to be conducted in the field and previous very sad experience with such attempts showed that this is fraught with many difficulties.

A very important lesson had been learned the hard way. It is almost impossible successfully to conduct an experiment in the field unless the individuals involved are intrinsically interested in the success of the experiment; and that, with the exception of the professional investigators, nobody can be expected to become interested in the research on the basis of elegance of experimental design, beauty of rigorous controls, or the profundity of the hypotheses being tested. Interest on the part of those involved can only be obtained when they feel that their effort and activity in the experimental setting *may* lead to solutions to problems that are real for them.

INTRODUCING THE NEW TRAINING PROGRAMME

Although the research and development team responsible for introducing this new training programme was armed with authorizations to do their job, authorizations signed by vice-presidents and by generals, they decided not to use these directly if at all possible. Nevertheless, they did use them implicitly, and the authorizations were a necessary prerequisite for the success of the effort. The press upon individuals in our modern mammoth organizations is so great that they will not permit themselves to become involved in anything unless they are assured that their superiors look upon this favourably. We have here the paradox that it is very difficult to get individual involvement of the organization man with orders and very difficult to get involvement without orders. Throughout the effort, the practitioners trod a cautious path between telling people what to do and facilitating on the part of those involved the spontaneous desire to do what had to be done.

The basic principle guiding the efforts of the practitioners was that all those whose effort was needed for the success of the project should see in that effort a means to achieve at least some of their personal goals. This demanded spadework that actually took more time than the testing of the new programme, but it was this spadework that assured the success of the programme.

The general strategy followed in the initial contacts with the individuals whose involvement was sought was the same for all. First a short, objective account of the history of the problem was given (it was in this context that the interest of higher levels of management, or of the higher echelons of command was indirectly and non-threateningly communicated). Then the individual was asked whether he himself was confronted with the problem and, if so, how. This enabled the person to unburden his troubles and enabled the practitioner honestly to play the role of an able specialist who earnestly wishes to help him. Then the practitioner would outline what he intended to do and how it might help the person. At the same time, he would solicit advice as to what else could be done that would make the project even more useful. Finally, a plan for future action based upon this discussion was summarized and approved by all. A cover letter containing this summary for final approval was then sent to the person interviewed.

This technique was applied first to the field representatives, and the representative indicating greatest enthusiasm for the project was chosen. Then it was applied to the military personnel in that representative's division, starting with the highest echelon and going downwards. It was relatively easy to achieve reasonably real approval on the part of every person contacted. As an additional result of these discussions, the practitioners obtained a very good picture of the various problems confronting these individuals as well as the nature of the social environment in which the experimental programme was to be tried out. It was only after all discussions were concluded that the final details of the programme were set and the actual implementation begun.

Space limitations preclude the presentation of the fascinating history of this implementation. Suffice it to be said that many of the difficulties to be expected in field experimentation emerged; difficulties which would have destroyed the project, had the psychological burden of responsibility for the success of the project rested mainly upon the shoulders of the small group of practitioners from the research and development group. But because all involved were also psychologically involved, they immediately took steps effectively to cope with the difficulties without waiting for the harassed practitioner to run over and fix things. But even more. Despite the lengthy preparation, the practitioners' definition of the military situation and their unique problems was faulty. The suggestions by the field representatives and the military involved, both during the initial spadework and the actual testing of the programme, did much to refine the programme and make it more adequate.

THE IMMEDIATE OUTCOME

From a hard-boiled experimental standpoint the outcome was a dud. Subject attrition in the military environment being what it is, the final number of subjects and controls at the end of the trial was too small to be able to get any statistically significant results. All that could be demonstrated quantitatively were possible trends. From a qualitative standpoint the picture was entirely different. To a man, the military personnel who were directly involved in the programme both as trainers and as students, liked it very much and wrote testimonials to that effect. Formal letters were sent to division headquarters strongly recommending that the technique be adopted for use throughout the division.

The work of the research and development group was done. They issued two reports: a quantitative report that said very little tangible, and a description of the technique used with a summary of the testimonials. They then left the scene.

EPILOGUE 1

The recommendations from the base were disregarded by the division training officer, and the training technique was not implemented. The practitioners had made a serious error in their strategy. They had contacted the division training officer at the outset of the programme and achieved his involvement. But they failed to maintain and systematically to reinforce it. The recommendations reached his desk more than six months after the initial contact and by that time all involvement was gone. The division officer perceived these recommendations as entailing additional work and worry to an already crowded workload emanating from someone else and not himself. They died by a pocket veto.

EPILOGUE 2

Military transfer policies being what they are, the division officer was transferred to another post within a year. Division headquarters looked around for a replacement and chose the officer who was directly involved in testing the new training technique. Within several months after his appointment a new overall training programme was introduced into the division. As part of that programme, without being identified as such, the training techniques developed experimentally the year earlier were incorporated without any significant change.

Question: Was the training officer who ran the experimental training programme appointed to the position of division training officer by chance?

12

The allocation of functions between man and machines in automated systems*

In a document published recently entitled: 'Factors Affecting Degree of Automation in Test and Checkout Equipment', which, among other things, reviews the problems of allocation of functions, Swain and Wohl assert: '. . . A rather stark conclusion emerges: *There is no adequate systematic methodology in existence for allocating functions* (in this case, test and checkout functions) *between man and machine.* This lack, in fact, is probably the central problem in human factors engineering today. . . . It is interesting to note that ten years of research and applications experience have failed to bring us closer to our goal than did the landmark article by Fitts in 1951' [5, p. 9]. Two competent and experienced observers summarize ten years of hard and intensive labour as having basically failed. This is a serious problem. Why this failure?

We can attempt to seek a possible answer to the question by seeking a similar case in other fields of scientific endeavour and seeing what can be learned from it. And another case is easy to find; it is in fact a classical case. In their book *The Evolution of Physics* [3], Einstein and Infeld spend some time discussing the problems that beset pre-relativity physics, focusing upon the concept of 'ether'. They point out that ether played a central role in physical thinking for over a century after having first been introduced as a necessary medium for propagating electro-magnetic waves. But during all this time all attempts to build and expand upon this concept led to difficulties and contradictions. A century of research on ether turned out to be sterile in that no significant advance was made during that time. They conclude: 'After such bad experiences, this is the moment to forget ether completely and try never to mention its name' [3, p. 184].

* First published in the June 1963 issue of the *Journal of Applied Psychology*.

And they do not mention the concept any more in the book. The facts underlying the concept were not rejected, however, and it was by focusing upon the *facts* while rejecting the *concept* that Einstein could solve the problems that bedevilled the physics of his day.

The lesson to be learned from this momentous episode is that when a scientific discipline finds itself at a dead end, despite hard and diligent work, the dead end should probably not be attributed to a lack of knowledge of facts, but to the use of faulty concepts which do not enable the discipline to order the facts properly. The failure of human factor engineering to advance in the area of allocation of functions seems to be such a situation. Hence, in order to find an answer to the question: 'Why this failure?', it may be fruitful to examine the conceptual underpinnings of our contemporary attempts at allocating functions between men and machines. And this brings us back to the landmark article by Fitts mentioned earlier [4].

This article gave rise to what is now informally called the 'Fitts list'. This is a two-column list, one column headed by the word 'man' and the other, by the word 'machine'. It *compares* the functions for which man is superior to machines with the functions for which the machine is superior to man. Theoretically this leads to an elegant solution to the allocation of functions. Given a complex man–machine system, identify the functions of the system and then, based on such a list which was expected to be refined with time and experience, choose machines for the functions for which they are best suited and men for the functions for which they are best suited. This is a clean engineering approach and it is not surprising that great hopes were placed upon it, in *1951*. The only gimmick is that it did not, and does not, work.

The facts to be found in all the existing versions of the 'Fitts list' are all correct, just as the facts underlying the concept ether were all correct. Hence the inutility of these lists must be attributed to what we are told to do with these facts, to the instruction to *compare* man with the machine and choose the one that fits a function best. I question the *comparability* of men and machines. If men and machines are not comparable, then it is not surprising that we get nowhere when we try to compare them. Just as the concept of ether led to inutility, perhaps the concept of man–machine comparability does the same. Let us explore somewhat the background to the concept *comparability*.

The literature on the place of a man in man–machine systems converges to two posthumous articles by K. J. W. Craik published in

1947 [2]. These articles are recognized by almost all as being the basis upon which much that followed is built. Craik argues that in order best to be able to plan, design, and operate a complex system, man functions and machine functions should be described in the same concepts, and, by the very nature of the case, these concepts have to be in engineering terms. In other words, Craik recommends that we describe human functions in mathematical terms *comparable* to the terms used in describing mechanical functions.

In fairness to Craik's memory it must be stressed that these two papers published after his death were notes for a discussion and probably not meant for publication. Hence, he should not be blamed for failing to recognize the simple fact that any time we can reduce a human function to a mathematical formula we can generally build a machine that can do it more efficiently than a man. In other words, to the extent that man becomes comparable to a machine we do not really need him any more since he can be replaced by a machine. This necessary consequence was actually reached, but not recognized, in a later paper, also a fundamental and significant paper in human factor engineering literature. In 1954 Birmingham and Taylor in their paper: 'A Design Philosophy for Man–Machine Control Systems', write: '. . . speaking mathematically, he (man) is best when doing least' [1, p. 1752]. The conclusion is inescapable – design the man out of the system. If he does best when he does least, the least he can do is zero. But then the conclusion is also ridiculous. Birmingham and Taylor found themselves in the same paradoxical situation in which Hume found himself some two hundred years earlier where his logic showed him that he could not know anything while at the same time he knew he knew a lot.

This contradiction, so concisely formulated by Birmingham and Taylor yet not recognized by them or, it seems, by their readers, should have served as a warning that something was wrong with the conceptualization underlying the thinking in this area. But it didn't.

Now we can see why the 'Fitts lists' have been impotent. To the extent that we compare, numerically, human functions with machine functions we must reach the conclusion that wherever possible the machine should do the job. This may help to explain a curious aspect in designers' behaviour which has annoyed some: an annoyance expressed trenchantly by a human factors engineer over a glass of beer, thus: 'Those designers, they act as if they get a brownie point every time they eliminate a man.'

Let us return to the 'Fitts lists'. They vary all over the place in length and in detail. But if we try to abstract the underlying commonalities in all of them, we find that they really make one point and only one point. Men are flexible but cannot be depended upon to perform in a consistent manner, whereas machines can be depended upon to perform consistently but they have no flexibility whatsoever. This can be summarized simply, and seemingly tritely, by saying that men are good at doing that which machines are not good at doing and machines are good at doing that which men are not good at doing. Men and machines are not comparable, they are *complementary*. I suggest that *'complementary'* is probably the correct concept to use in discussing the allocation of tasks to men and to machines. Rather than compare men and machines as to which is better for getting a task done, let us think about how we complement men by machines, and vice versa, to get a task done.

As soon as we start to think this way, we find that we have to start thinking differently. The term 'allocation of tasks to men and machines' becomes meaningless. Rather we are forced to think about a task that can be done by men *and* machines. The concept 'task' ceases to be the smallest unit of analysis for designing man–machine systems, though still remaining the basic unit in terms of which the analysis makes sense. The task now consists of actions, or better still activities, which have to be shared by men and machines. There is nothing strange about this. In industrial chemistry the molecule is the fundamental unit for many purposes and it doesn't disturb anybody that some of these molecules consist of hundreds, if not thousands, of atoms. The analysis of man–machine systems should therefore consist of specifications of tasks and activities necessary to accomplish the tasks. Man and machine should complement each other in getting these activities done in order to accomplish the task.

It is possible that with a shift to emphasizing man–machine comparability, new formats for system analysis and design will have to be developed, and these formats may pose a problem. I am convinced, however, that as soon as we begin thinking in proper units, this problem will be solved with relative ease. Regardless of whether this is so, one can now already specify several general principles that may serve as basic guidelines for complementing men and machines.

Machines serve man in two ways: as tools and as production machines. A tool extends man's ability, both sensory and motor; production machines replace man in doing a job. The principle underlying the complementarity of tools is as follows: Man functions best under conditions of optimum difficulty. If the job is too easy he gets bored, if it is too hard he gets fatigued. While it is generally silly to use machines to make a job more difficult, although this may be exactly what is called for in some control situations, tools have, since their inception as eoliths, served to make a difficult job easier and an impossible job possible. Hence, tools should be used to bring the perceptual and motor requirements of a task to the optimum levels for human performance. We have had a lot of experience with tools and they present few, if any, problems.

The problem is more complex with machines that do a job in place of man. Here we can return with benefit to the commonalities under-lying the 'Fitts lists'. To the extent that the task environment is predictable and *a priori* controllable, and to the extent that activities necessary for the task are iterative and demand consistent perform-ance, a production machine is preferable to man. To the extent, however, that the environment is not predictable, or if predictable not controllable *a priori*, then man, aided by the proper tools, is required. It is in coping with contingencies that man is irreplaceable by machines. This is the essential meaning of human flexibility.

Production machines pose a problem rarely posed by tools since they replace man in doing a job. They are not perfect and tend to break down. When they break down, they do not do the job. One must always then take into account the criticality of the job for the system. If the job is critical, the system should so be designed that man can serve as a manual back-up to the machine. Although he will then not do it as well as the machine, he still can do it well enough to pass muster. This is another aspect of human flexibility – the ability for graceful degradation. Machines can either do the job as specified or they botch up; man degrades gracefully. This is another example of complementarity.

Planning for feasible manual back-up is a difficult job in the con-temporary complex systems that we are constructing. It has generally been neglected. In most simple systems explicit planning is not neces-sary since man's flexibility is generally adequate to improvise when the relatively simple machines break down. But this changes with growing system complexity.

It is here that 'automation' should be mentioned. Some of you may have been bothered by the fact that 'automation' is in the title of this chapter but has, as yet, still to be introduced. The reason is rather simple. Although automation represents a significant techno-logical breakthrough, which has generated many specific problems, the allocation of tasks to men and machines being one of them, conceptually, an automated machine is just another machine, albeit radically different in its efficiency and performance characteristics. The problems that were generally latent or not too critical in the older, simpler man–machine systems became both manifest and critical, however, with its introduction. One of the most critical areas is manual back-up.

We customarily design automated systems by allocating those functions that were either difficult or too expensive to mechanize to man, and the rest to machines. As many articles in the literature indicate, we have looked upon man as a *link* in the system and have consequently given him only the information and means to do the job assigned to him as a link. When the system breaks down, a man in a link position is as helpless as any other machine component in the system. We have tended to design out his ability to take over as a manual back-up to the system. At the same time the jobs performed by the machine have become more and more important and the necessity for a manual back-up consequently greater. How to design a complex automated system to facilitate its being backed up manually is a neglected area. One thing seems certain. It will most probably call for 'degradation' in design, that is, systematically introducing features that would not have been necessary were no manual back-up needed. This is an important area for future human factors engineering research.

Another area of complementarity which is gaining in significance as the systems are getting more and more complex is that of responsibility. Assuming we lick the problems of reliability, we can depend upon the machines to do those activities assigned to them consistently well, but we never can assign them any responsibility for getting the task done; responsibility can be assigned to men only. For every task, or for every activity entailed by the task, there must be a man who has the assigned responsibility to see that the job be done as efficiently as warranted. This necessitates two things: the specification of clear-cut responsibilities for *every* man in the system and supplying the men with means which will enable them to exercise effective control over those system tasks and activities for which they are responsible. You may think that this is obvious – yes it is. But it is surprising how rare, and then how ineffective, our planning and design in this area are. Experience to date with automated systems shows that the responsibilities of the individuals involved are generally nebulous, so that when something unexpected occurs, people often do not know who is to do what. Even to the extent that these responsibilities are clarified with time and experience, the system hardware often makes it difficult for men to assume these responsibilities, the means for man to exercise control over the areas of his responsibility being either inadequate or lacking.

The complementarity of men and machines is probably much more profound and subtle than these aspects which I have just highlighted. Many other aspects will undoubtedly be identified, elaborated, and ordered to the extent that we start thinking about how one complements the other. In other words, to the extent that we start *humanizing* human factors engineering. It is not surprising that the ten years of lack of progress pointed to by Swain and Wohl were accompanied by the conceptual definition of treating man as a machine component. Man is not a machine, at least not a machine like the machines men make. And this brings me to the last point I would like to make in this chapter.

When we plan to use a machine, we always take the physical environment of the machine into account; that is: its power supply, its maintenance requirements, the physical setting in which it has to operate, etc. We have also taken the physical environment of man into account, to a greater or lesser extent; that is: illumination and ventilation of the working-area, noise level, physical difficulties, hours of labour, coffee breaks, etc. But a fundamental difference between men and machines is that men also have a psychological environment for which an adequate physical environment is a necessary condition but is ultimately secondary in importance. This is the truth embedded in the adage: 'Man does not live by bread alone.' The psychological environment is subsumed under one word: 'motivation'. And the problems of human motivation are at present eschewed by human factors engineering.

You can lead a horse to water but cannot make him drink. In this respect a man is very similar to a horse. Unless the human operator is motivated, he will not function as a complement to machines, and the motivation to function as a complement must be embedded *within the task itself*. Unless a task represents a challenge to the human operator he will *not* use his flexibility or his judgement, he will *not* learn nor will he assume responsibility, nor will he serve efficiently as a manual back-up. By designing man–machine systems for man to do *least* we also eliminate all challenge from the job. We must clarify to ourselves what it is makes a job a challenge to man, and build in those challenges in every task, and activity, and responsibility which we assign to the human operator. Otherwise man will not complement the machines but will begin to function like a machine.

And here too men differ significantly from machines. When a man is forced to function like a machine, he realizes that he is being used inefficiently and he experiences it as his being used stupidly. And men cannot tolerate such stupidity. Overtly or covertly men resist and rebel against it. Nothing could be more inefficient and self-defeating in the long run than the construction of man–machine systems which cause the human components in the system to rebel against the system.

Herein lies the main future challenge to human factors engineering.

REFERENCES

[1] BIRMINGHAM, H. P., and TAYLOR, F. V., A Design Philosophy for Man–Machine Control Systems. *Proc. Inst. Radio Engrs.*, New York, 1954, **42**, 1748–58.

[2] CRAIK, K. J. W., Theory of the Human Operator in Control Systems: I. The Operator as an Engineering System. *Brit. J. Psychol.*, 1947, **38**, 56–61. II. Man as an Element in a Control System, *Brit. J. Psychol.*, 1947, **38**, 142–8.

[3] EINSTEIN, A., and INFELD, L., *The Evolution of Physics.* Simon and Schuster, New York, 1942.

[4] FITTS, P. M. (Ed.), *Human Engineering for an Effective Air Navigation and Traffic Control System.* National Research Council, Washington, D.C., 1951.

[5] SWAIN, A. D., and WOHL, J. G., *Factors Affecting Degree of Automation in Test and Checkout Equipment.* Dunlap and Associates, Inc., Stamford, Conn., 1961.

13

Motivational problems in human–computer operations*

It seems fair to say that, as a profession, human factors engineering has neglected the area of the operators' motivation. The index to McCormick's textbook, *Human Engineering* [1], a book that is rightfully respected and quite widely used, does not contain the term. Within the book proper, motivation is mentioned only once, and that within the context of the Hawthorne experiment, i.e. the author warns that subjects in an experiment may be motivated differently from operators in real life situations so that generalization from experimental results to real life situations should be made with caution.

As a profession, human factors engineering has concentrated on making the task allocated to an operator less fatiguing, as such; making the physical environment within which the operator has to work more fitting to his physiological requirements; making the displays the operator has to monitor more readable and the controls he has to manipulate more graspable and distinguishable in order to reduce errors, etc. The responsibility for solving motivational problems has generally been relegated to management and its consultants, to personnel psychologists, and to human relations experts.

The profession's neglect of motivation seems to be attributable to two interdependent causes: the treatment of motivation by academic experimental psychology, and the standards the profession has set up for itself.

Academic experimental psychology views goal-directed behaviour almost exclusively from an instrumental standpoint. It views behaviour as a means for achieving goals, for the obtaining of rewards, or the avoidance of punishments. It has generally neglected

* First published in the June 1962 issue of *Human Factors*.

the fact that all behaviour has satisfying properties *per se*, that it can also be viewed from a consummatory standpoint, even though it has recognized this by accepting the concepts of 'functional autonomy' and 'secondary reinforcement.' But recognition is not enough; active interest and research are also needed. And both of these have been lacking. As a result, motivation as an area of interest became almost the exclusive property of the 'soft-headed' and therefore looked-down-upon specializations of clinical and social psychology. Since human factors engineering has its roots in experimental psychology, this neglect of motivation was carried over as a matter of habit.

Early in its development, human factors engineering accepted the standard of treating the human operator as just another component within a complex man–machine system. As such his behaviour had to be represented in a quantitative language compatible with, and comparable to, the functioning capabilities of the machine components within the system. While it is relatively easy to measure speed of performance and accuracy of performance, it is notoriously difficult to meaningfully measure motivation. It is not surprising, therefore, that the profession concentrated upon the former and neglected the latter.

In the good old old days, when machines were crude and could not 'think' for themselves, this neglect was not too critical. Because of the limitations of the machines, one could not design a man–machine system that would make it very difficult, if not impossible, for the human operator to function effectively in it. With the rapid development of automation, however – and with automation I include complex mechanical control based upon elaborate feedback loops as well as information processing and decision-making by computers – we are becoming able to do so. In fact we have already designed man–machine systems which make it very difficult for man to function effectively. As I write these words, I have in mind the SAGE system, many variants of automated checkout equipment, and the Advanced Reflex Logistic System which was introduced in the Air Materiel Command.

When we look upon goal-directed behaviour from a consummatory standpoint rather than from an instrumental standpoint, we are confronted with the following problem: what is it in a job, what is it in action *per se*, above and beyond the terminal state to which the action leads, that satisfies the operator. The problem can be answered in one word: challenge. To the extent that a job challenges the operator, it is intrinsically satisfying. But, although this answer is useful in that it clarifies the issue and shows along which dimension, or dimensions, we should direct our thinking, by itself it is quite inadequate, since it is too general. We now have to clarify to ourselves what it is in a job that is challenging and what it is in automation that eliminates or vitiates the challenge.

First, however, a common set in regard to challenge should be discarded. We tend to associate challenge with the spectacular: running the four-minute mile, conquering space, solving a problem which has baffled the best minds, etc. Yes, these are challenges, striking challenges, and as such they stand out and tend to monopolize our attention to such an extent that we forget that there is a challenge in the unspectacular also. Nothing will be done well unless it is a challenge to the doer. The good janitor is as much challenged by his job as the good scientist by his. And conversely, the poor janitor is as much bored by his job as the poor scientist by his. If we look at the meanest of so-called unskilled labour, be it ditch-digging, stevedoring, or rickshaw-pulling, we cannot help but discriminate the good worker from the poor worker. The good worker is seen as doing whatever he is doing skilfully, quite skilfully, whereas the poor worker is seen to be clumsy. And with this we have taken the first step in clarifying an important aspect of what goes into making a job challenging. It must involve the use of skills.

What is it in a job that necessitates skills? There are several things. First the tasks to be done must be, by definition, difficult. If something is easy, then no skills are required. At the same time it cannot be too difficult. Hence, for a task to demand skilled performance it must be of optimum difficulty, not too easy and not too hard. Second – and this is rather hard to grasp – the task must permit degraded performance. It must be do-able in many ways, some of which are much better than others, and the better ways can be achieved to the extent that the human operator becomes more skilful. If we set up a task which the person can perform in one way, and in one way only, he can never develop skills. Hence, there must be more than one degree of freedom as to how the job can be done. On the other hand, we have to set bounds to the degree of permissible degradation; inefficiency beyond certain levels just cannot be tolerated. Again the concept of an optimum is reached, each task must have a built-in optimum range of permissible degraded performance on the part of the human operator. Third, and finally, the operator must have relatively immediate feedback as to how efficiently he actually is operating so that, to the extent that he is inefficient, he can improve his skills, and, to the extent that he is efficient, he can maintain them. Feedback that is either too late to be of any use or irrelevant in helping the operator in his skills is not only not helpful but, as such, even damaging.

The demand for skills is a necessary, but insufficient, condition for a job to be challenging. The skills have to be used in a meaningful context – the job for which the skills are utilized must make sense. This means that whatever an operator does should fit meaningfully into a larger context. How large need the context be? Again we meet with the word 'optimum'. It has to be large enough for the operator to achieve a meaningful closure yet not so large as to overwhelm him with irrelevancies and things he is not interested in. When a task is not seen in a meaningful context it is experienced as being arbitrary and, consequently, as being stupid. Men cannot be satisfied by doing stupid jobs. Meaning is therefore another necessary condition for challenge.

The final condition that seems to be necessary for an operator to experience his job as challenging is his being delegated real responsibility over that which he has to do. It is pretty well recognized that efficient management practice calls for giving a man a job which is within his ability, explaining to him clearly what has to be done and giving him the means that enable him to do it, and then leaving him alone until he completes the job. There is nothing as demoralizing as 'snoopervision' on the part of the supervisor.

To summarize what has been said so far: In designing a complex man–machine system one should consider the human performance necessary for the system, not only from an instrumental standpoint, but also from a consummatory standpoint, that is, how satisfying the job is *per se*. For jobs to be satisfying three conditions seem to be necessary and sufficient: they must demand of the operator the utilization of skills; they must be meaningful; and the operator must have real responsibility. It was also asserted that although human factors engineering neglected the consummatory standpoint, as long as machines were relatively crude, this neglect was not critical. With the mushrooming development of automation, however, we cannot afford this luxury any more. In designing and thinking about our new complex automated man–machine systems we *must* take the consummatory standpoint into account, we *must* learn to design for men jobs that are intrinsically interesting and satisfying. The latter part of this paper will be an attempt to defend this thesis.

The argument that we attend to the consummatory aspects of

behaviour in complex man–machine systems is a modern version of a rather old school of thought, the school of thought that insisted upon humanizing production. It first appeared when the guild craftsman was replaced by the factory, with a division of labour where no one worker produced the article manufactured from start to finish. It was revived with added vigour with the introduction of the production line with arguments that this turns the worker into a machine. The dire predictions as to the effects upon the human as a result of these changes did not materialize and the arguments were therefore discredited. But this does not make the arguments invalid. The arguments raised with the introduction of factories and then later with the introduction of the production line are psychologically sound and, therefore, valid. The error made by the early proponents of these arguments lay in their overestimating the capabilities of machines and in underestimating the ingenuity of man, if but given half a chance, in turning the most seemingly routine task into a challenge. And even the most elaborate machine of the era before World War II managed to give man half a chance. Let us take that *bête noire*, the production line, as an example.

The production line has been looked upon as one of the most dehumanizing of production techniques. Chaplin, in his celebrated movie *Modern Times*, presents the argument against it in a striking manner. And, it is true, the production line in that movie is deadening and revolting. But what happens in real life? The workers do not seem to mind the line too much, in fact most of them get to like their work, that is, they find a challenge in it. From whence this challenge? A clue to the source of the challenge may be found when we consider an unexpected problem with which industry was confronted when it began to automate production lines. Bright reports, in his important study on the impact of automation upon management [2], that with the automating of production lines management discovered that the tolerances of the components being supplied to the line had to be tightened. The automated system could not cope with the variability in components with which the manual system had no trouble. Is it unreasonable to speculate that this variability gave the human operator the half a chance he needed? In compensating for this variability he could develop the skills necessary for making the job interesting. Enough of the components required special care and treatment to serve as a challenge to the operator. The meaningless, completely skill-less task presented by Chaplin rarely, if ever, did exist in real-life production lines.

Production lines also had 'built in' responsibilities and meaning. To the extent that the worker had to compensate for, and fit the varying components together, he experienced real responsibility within his sector of control, and to the extent that he improved his skills, he obtained the means to assume this responsibility. And finally, since he worked in a factory which produced an end item, his job also became meaningful by being perceived as a necessary step for the production of that item. Hence, although it wasn't planned that way, a production line did contain the necessary and sufficient conditions for meeting the needs of the human operator for job satisfaction *per se*.

With the development of our contemporary giant computers and their incorporation into our complex man–machine systems we can, and do, design jobs for human operators that eliminate all skills, that take away most, if not all, real responsibility, and often make the job of the individual operator meaningless. I mentioned earlier that in writing these words I had the SAGE system, automatic checkout systems, and the Advanced Reflex Logistic System in mind. Examples of at least one of these lacks can be found in each of the three types of systems.

One notices a striking difference when comparing the behaviour of the crews in the old manual Air Defence Command sites to the crews in the SAGE direction centres. In the manual site almost every crew member took pride in his job. I had occasion to visit many of them, and in every site the crew members to whom I talked would eagerly go to great trouble to explain to me the intricacies of their job and what it demanded of them for good performance. A comparable pride and eagerness was almost completely lacking in the SAGE direction centres I visited. Perhaps the reason for this lack can be found in the answer given to the following question: What is the characteristic most common to the various positions in the direction centre? The answer was: Ennui. This answer was given by a senior social scientist who had much experience in setting up and running the SAGE System Training Programme. Men just cannot be proud of something which bores them.

If we look closely at the job demands in a SAGE direction centre, we find several striking differences between it and the manual sites it replaced. First, for most jobs, skill requirements have been reduced to a bare minimum. Second, most of the jobs have become so isolated and fractionated that they have become meaningless in terms of the overall crew mission responsibility. One clear-cut example of this isolation and fractionation will here be given; there are many others.

Most of the jobs in an air defence system involve relaying information, i.e. information is processed or acted upon and then relayed to another position for further processing and action. Each job by itself, although clearly defined, generally has little meaning when the total picture of crew's actions are lacking. In the manual sites there was a central plotting board which showed such a picture for all the crew members to see. No such summarizing display is available for a member of a SAGE crew.

Third and last, because of the fantastic performance ability of the computer, because of the inflexibility of even the most so-called flexible program, and because of the mystery, to the crew members, of what goes on inside the computer, and reinforced by the effect of the preceding two conditions, the roles of the human operator in SAGE and the computer have functionally been reversed. Rather than the machine being an aid to the man, the man becomes an aid to the machine. In addition to boredom generated by the reduction of skill, there is a feeling of futility generated by the feeling of having lost control over what is going on. Maybe this is all we desire of the men in our emerging complex automated man–machine systems, that they merely be aids to the machine, but it is legitimate to raise the question whether this desire is itself desirable.

Whereas the designers of SAGE did not intentionally set out to reduce skills, reduce responsibility, and reduce control as such, the designers of automated checkout equipment generally did set out to do so. The vocabulary surrounding this equipment contains terms like: 'the trained ape operator', 'idiot jobs', and 'goon meters'. Luckily, or unluckily – depending upon one's point of view – this equipment generally did not perform satisfactorily, so the operators in the field had either to use it in an improvised manner or to circumvent it entirely to get the job done. But what would have happened had it worked? We would have had a corps of human operators in the field whose only motivation for doing the job would be the alternative of being court martialled. What good would such a corps be in time of an emergency when things are bound to go wrong and the machines necessarily begin to function inadequately?

When we turn to the newly automated logistic systems, we find a most fascinating development. Here a large computer was set up to relieve man of routine bookkeeping and routine processing of supplies – a boon to the harassed clerk and administrator. But what actually happened? The responsibilities of the men in the system remained the same but, because of the machine taking over and implementing so much of the system's mission in its inexorable, mechanical, and coldly logical manner, the men lost functional control over the areas of their responsibilities. What could be more frustrating than this – it is an ulcerogenic situation *par excellence!*

In designing complex systems, regardless of our good intentions, we can often create a situation that becomes intolerable for the human being, and as a result he either leaves the system or, if he cannot, he subordinates himself to the system and ceases to play the role which is the ultimate role of men in man–machine systems, *to see to it that the system works.*

I conclude and repeat: human factors engineering cannot any more afford the luxury of neglecting the role of motivation in designing complex man–machine systems. We have focused upon making jobs easy; let us now enlarge our focus and also try to make the jobs interesting for every human operator at *every skill level.* In doing this we will not only improve the lot of the human operator as a man, which is not a bad thing as such and not to be sneezed at, but, and necessarily, we will improve overall system performance as well.

REFERENCES

[1] MCCORMICK, E. J., *Human Engineering.* McGraw-Hill, New York, 1957.
[2] BRIGHT, J. R., *Automation and Management.* Harvard University Press, Cambridge, Mass., 1958.

P

14

The application of human relations research to administration*

Those who have tried to apply the results of academic research on human relations to real life problems in organizations are well aware of the pitfalls that bestrew this path. These pitfalls have at times had so undesirable an effect that the opinion is voiced, occasionally in print but more often after a cocktail or two, that academic research is inapplicable, is irrelevant. But this may be the throwing of the baby out with the bath water. There are very good reasons why the results of academic research cannot be simply applied to line organizations. Many of the pitfalls met with in their application stem directly from not taking these reasons into account.

The purpose of this paper is threefold; an attempt will be made:

I. to spell out at least some of the reasons which make the application of academic research difficult;

II. to show that this research, even as it is, can be of help to administrators;

III. to suggest a way of facilitating communication between administrators and academic investigators to their mutual benefit.

I. THE GAP BETWEEN ACADEMIC RESEARCH AND ITS PRACTICAL APPLICATIONS

At least three reasons seem to stand out as important contributors to the difficulties met when men of goodwill attempt to apply the results of research in academic human relations laboratories to live situations. They stem from:

* First published in the December 1961 issue of *Management Technology*.

1. The goals of the academic investigator.
2. The analytical techniques used in academic investigations.
3. The research settings and research problems available in the universities.

1. *The Goals of the Academic Investigator*

The liberal arts college, where most of the research in human relations takes place, is by and large dedicated to 'pure research'. Pure research is abstract-theory-oriented and attempts to answer ultimate questions as to the nature of the world. It is, as a result, rarely oriented to solve specific everyday problems. Just as the laboratories studying physical phenomena attempt to set up 'ideal' situations, never met with in the world at large, in order to identify the laws of physics, so do the social psychologists who try to study human relations. They too try to set up ideal situations, uncontaminated by many of the contingent factors to be found in real life, to enable them to identify and quantify the laws of human relations.

Society has to pay a price for this kind of research in 'sterile, antiseptic' laboratories. The results of this research, be it in the physical or psychological domains, cannot simply or directly be applied to specific problems in the everyday world. The formula showing that an atom bomb was possible was enunciated by Einstein in the first decade of our century. It took more than three decades and the threat of a war to translate this formula into an actual atom bomb. Many of the disappointments and frustrations encountered in applying academic research to real-life situations can be traced to an over-enthusiasm of both the academic investigators and the practitioners. It takes much work and often a long time before that which is found to hold in an academic laboratory can be efficiently applied to a real-life situation.

The goal of academic investigators determines to a very great extent the analytical techniques used in academic research. And this leads us directly to the second reason.

2. *The Analytical Techniques used in Academic Investigations*

The classical model of laboratory research is the essence of simplicity. In order to identify the laws underlying observed phenomena one must first identify the factors which affect the phenomena studied.

Then one must set up a laboratory situation containing these factors in such a manner that the experimenter can control them. Once this is achieved the experimenter varies the factors systematically and records the effects of this *controlled* variation. To the extent that these effects can be reduced to some logical order, laws of nature are identified. This has worked excellently for the physical sciences. In attempting to apply this model to the social sciences, investigators ran into a serious difficulty. Although it is often possible to set up a laboratory situation containing many of the factors affecting social phenomena, it is generally impossible to exercise the kind of control achievable in a physical laboratory. It is generally possible to vary one or two factors systematically, but it is almost never possible to keep the others constant. In order to mitigate the uncontrolled variation of these other factors, the social scientist has had to have recourse to statistics.

Again a price has to be paid. Statistics enables the investigator to formulate general laws of a special sort. These laws take the following form: if for a given situation a person will take an action A, he can expect *on the average* that it will lead to the result B. The academic investigator is generally satisfied with such results and he goes on to explore other problems which interest him. But statistical laws, by their very nature, cannot predict the outcome in individual cases, and the manager of a real-life organization is always confronted with an individual case. The statistical law cannot tell him, for his particular problem, how far he actually will deviate from the average outcome and how costly that will be. It is often the case that because of contingent circumstances to be found in a particular situation the law found in academic laboratories should not be applied for that situation.

3. *The Research Settings and Research Problems available in the Universities*

Social science laboratories are at a distinct disadvantage when compared to the laboratories of the physical sciences in this area. Despite the fact that the physical laboratories set up 'ideal' situations not to be found outside the laboratory, the physical microcosm of the laboratory is essentially identical with the physical macrocosm of the world at large. This does not hold for psychological laboratories. The psychological microcosm of the laboratory is generally quite different from the psychological macrocosm of the world at large.

This for two simple reasons. The overwhelming number of subjects in psychological experimentation on human relations are undergraduate adolescent students; they are available to the investigators and relatively easily coercible to become subjects. In addition, most of the group tasks that can be set up within the confines of a university laboratory have the psychological nature of a game; that is, regardless of how subjects perform in the laboratory, this performance will have no effect on their real-life situation.

It is dangerous to generalize from how a person plays 'monopoly' to how he behaves as a manager of a real-estate investment firm. A professional gambler exhibits an entirely different style of playing when he plays with his peers for 'fun', than when he plays with a 'pigeon' for business. Many factors that play a very important role in real life which involve an individual's economic future, his social status, his self-respect, etc., just cannot be introduced into most psychological experimentation. If these are not taken adequately into account in applying the results of academic research, the consequences may be quite undesirable.

Nevertheless academic research should not be belittled. It enables us to clarify concepts by carefully observing the effect they have in the controlled laboratory situations. Most of these concepts are not revolutionary. They generally underlie the actions of the successful administrator. But he tends to follow them in an implicit intuitive manner, having neither the time nor the facilities to make these concepts explicit. To the extent that these concepts can be made explicit *per se*, as well as showing how they do effect organizational life, it will enable the administrator to function more effectively. He will find himself in a better position to evaluate objectively the consequences of his actions. It is in making these concepts explicit that academic research is already of use to the administrator. Some significant concepts, and their implications for effective administration, that have been identified by academic research will be presented and briefly discussed in the next section of this paper.

II. CONCEPTUAL CONTRIBUTIONS OF ACADEMIC RESEARCH ON HUMAN RELATIONS

1. *Group Atmosphere*

In a series of what can now be called classic experiments, White and Lippitt [5] investigated the effect of different styles of leadership on the behaviour of small groups of children. These groups were given the task of constructing masks for an exhibition. The group leaders, assigned by the experimenters, were trained to act in three roles: as 'democratic' leaders, as 'authoritarian' leaders, and as 'laissez-faire' leaders.

When playing the 'democratic' role, the leaders encouraged the group and facilitated the reaching of decisions on the masks to be made and on how to organize the work. As 'autocrats' the leaders just told the children what to do without any consultation on their part and without any explanation for their decisions. And finally, as 'laissez-faire' leaders they just sat back without intervening with the group activities but just answered questions if and when asked.

Every leader played each of the three roles for at least one group, and every group was subjected to each type of leadership. The type of leadership generated an atmosphere that was quite striking. Almost all the observable aspects of group functioning were affected in a striking manner by this atmosphere. Individual differences, both among the leaders and within the groups, played a small role in the differences of behaviour that were observed.

Some of the major observed differences can be summarized, all too inadequately, as follows: Groups subjected to 'authoritarian' leadership made many masks. They showed very little initiative, however, and almost always stopped their work when the leader left the room. In addition, the masks they did produce were quite unimaginative; were quite dull. Under 'democratic' leadership, the groups made a slightly smaller number of masks, but the quality of masks was quite superior. The groups set their own pace and worked industriously whether the leader was present or not, i.e. they were self-motivated and the leader could depend upon them to do the job spontaneously to the best of their ability. With 'laissez-faire' leadership the group found the task dull and boring. They produced a small number of relatively unimaginative masks. The significance of leadership upon group behaviour and performance, and the many different subtle ways by which the leadership has its impact, has rarely been demonstrated in so clear and brilliant a manner as in these experiments. By studying them carefully we truly get a tangible feeling for what 'group atmosphere' actually is.

In these laboratory studies the leadership roles were prescribed by the experimenters; in organizations the behaviour of the leaders, of the bosses and foremen, will, willy-nilly, induce an atmosphere. All too often this atmosphere is unknown to them and contrary to their intentions. It is easy to find leaders who try to be 'democratic' but induce an 'authoritarian' atmosphere; or who try to be 'authoritarian' while inducing a 'laissez-faire' atmosphere. Things cannot go smoothly under such conditions. The consequent frustrations and tensions of both the leader and his group cannot but generate organizational conflicts which cause an overall decrement in organizational efficiency.

Group atmosphere is so general a concept that most, if not all, of the concepts to be discussed below can be considered to be special aspects of it.

2. *Commitment*

A person will administer a policy or do a job better if he is committed to it. How does one achieve a greater degree of commitment on the part of members of an organization?

One of the most effective ways of inducing commitment is by involving the persons concerned either in formulating the policy or, more commonly, in formulating those aspects in the policy implementation for which they will be responsible. People will feel themselves committed to policies to the extent that they feel that they were given an opportunity to participate in their formulation. It is not necessary for them to take advantage of this opportunity; all that is needed is for them to feel that had they wanted to, they could have.

It follows, therefore, that when it is desirable to introduce procedural changes in a hierarchical organization, the specific changes should be formulated, to the extent that it is feasible, by the members of the lowest hierarchy to be affected and then forwarded upward for approval. When an administrator at any hierarchical level approves a policy formulated from below, he has the feeling that, had he wished, he could have modified it, i.e. he has 'freely' accepted it and it was not imposed upon him. This feeling would be lacking were the identical policy to be handed to him for implementation from above. The commitment of the entire staff is consequently greater to policies which they know were formulated at the lower levels of the organization and which were reviewed and 'freely' accepted by all concerned. This overall commitment would be maintained despite many modifications of the procedures that higher-echelon management might introduce. (The next section will touch upon the conditions under which lower-echelon people are tolerant and acceptant of decisions coming from above.)

In doing a specific job, an individual's commitment to the job is directly related to the degree of actual responsibility delegated to him. If no actual responsibility is delegated to a man, he cannot experience any commitment to the job. And this responsibility must be really delegated. It happens all too often that despite the delegation of formal responsibility to an individual, his superiors do not trust him and express this by overbearing supervision. Under these conditions formal responsibility is meaningless; in fact, it may create conflicts within the individual so that his performance will be poorer than were he given no responsibility whatsoever.

In a fascinating account of how a textile factory using semi-automatic production machines was introduced in India A. K. Rice [3] of the Tavistock Institute in London tells of the great impact upon efficiency in production that followed the real delegation of production responsibility to teams of five – each team responsible for a group of machines. The teams, in turn, allocated responsibility to each individual within them.

It is easier to induce individual commitment to the extent that the morale or *esprit de corps* of the organization is high. And this leads us to the next concept to be discussed.

3. *Morale or Esprit de Corps*

Research on morale, both in military and industrial organizations, seems to lead to the not surprising conclusion that the level of morale is most closely related to how the individuals involved perceive the administrators who have power over their destiny within the organization. To the extent that such administrators are perceived as being fair and able, morale is high.

An administrator is perceived to be fair if it is believed that before making a decision he takes into account, to the *best* of his ability, the interests of all those who will be affected by the decision. If an administrator is so perceived, then individuals will tend willingly to accept decisions even though they may harm them slightly. People are quite reasonable when they have faith in the fairness and ability of the administrator; they will accept the fact that the demands of the objective situation forced the administrator to make a decision which has adverse effects upon them. Since they believe that the administrator did weigh the interests of all involved to the best of his ability, then it follows that had he been able to make another decision, he would have done so.

Finally, if an administrator is perceived as being fair, he is permitted to make a larger than average number of reasonable mistakes before being perceived as incompetent.

4. *Non-evaluative Feedback on an Individual's Performance*

This is a poor formulation of a principle that has caused much trouble to those attempting to apply it. These words mean that in discussing the performance of another person in relation to a specific organization or team goal the objective efficacy of the performance for reaching the goal should be evaluated, not the person *per se*. It is relatively easy for two intelligent people to reach a consensus about a concrete practical problem which, so to speak, stares them in the face if personal considerations as to whether they are good or bad do not enter into the discussion. When personalities enter a discussion, this is generally accompanied by an emergence of defensive behaviour which masks the real intentions of the actor and is consequently ruinous to effective problem-solving. It is not by chance that the word 'personality' has evolved from the Latin word *persona* which means 'mask'.

The need for this type of objective feedback on one's performance grows greater as our organizations become more complex and the dependency among individuals grows. The specific jobs assigned to individuals tend to contribute less and less to the goals of our growing organizations as they become more and more complex. It becomes difficult, if not impossible, for an individual objectively to evaluate his strengths and weaknesses in his contribution to the organization effort. Something he does well may be vitiated by actions of the man who takes over after him; a mistake he makes may be discovered so much later that it is difficult to identify its specific cause. In order to be able to do their job efficiently and in order to be able to improve themselves in their job, men need to know where they stand.

Lack of objective knowledge of one's performance leads to refusal to assume responsibility, passing the buck, window-dressing, etc., leads to a host of undesirable phenomena. For efficient organizational function it becomes quite important to develop channels to feed back objective, non-evaluative information on an individual's performance.

The problem of feedback is more inclusive than merely the individual's performance. And this leads us to the next concept.

5. General Feedback and the Meaning of a Situation

People do not like to do meaningless jobs and/or be subjected to meaningless constraints. No person will deliberately ask another person to do something the other does not understand. In training a person to do a job, a good training programme always includes an explanation of the meaning of the job. What is often neglected, however, is the fact that the meaning of a job or task *per se* is dependent to a very large extent upon its role or meaning for the entire system or organization in which it is embedded. No matter how well an individual knows his specific job, this knowledge is often useless unless he also knows how his job fits into the larger picture. The neglect of this aspect is generally due to the fact that to the supervisor or experienced person who teaches the novice, this knowledge appears to be self-evident. But this is often not so – what is self-evident to an expert may be quite a mystery to a novice.

Unless the novices are given reliable information on the subject, they will formulate their own explanation which will most probably be wrong. And this latter development can lead to trouble in human relations, especially in times of change or crisis. When a person has a wrong model of things, then the actions of others relating to these things appear to be either meaningless or stupid. This causes misunderstanding and conflict. In addition, as mentioned earlier, a person will tend to accept constraints if he sees them as being meaningful and fair; he will resent them if they are not understood. There are many ways in which resentment can be expressed by a group or team member, and almost always they are detrimental to the group or to the team.

Since an organization is a dynamic entity, i.e. it exists in a changing environment and is subject to its own internal changes, it is preferable that permanent channels of feedback exist that inform the members of the organization of relevant changes that take place. Of course, if such channels are perceived as being management propaganda outlets, they will have an undesirable rather than a desirable effect.

6. Creativity in Organizations

Almost more than any other aspect of behaviour, imaginative and creative behaviour are subject to the dictates of group atmosphere. This has been eloquently argued by creative thinkers throughout time, since it was part and parcel of their personal experience. In the eighteen-nineties the philosopher–psychologist Josiah Royce [4] instructed groups of students to draw abstract line drawings. To some of the groups he added the suggestion to be imaginative. These latter groups produced far more drawings numerically and of a more complex nature qualitatively than did the group who were not reminded to be imaginative.

Let us not jump to conclusions, however. If creative behaviour is sought, it is insufficient that it be just enunciated as a desirable policy. The total organization must be such as to encourage and facilitate creative behaviour. And this is easier said than done.

A necessary, and perhaps sufficient, condition for generating creativity is the creation of a setting that facilitates a type of critical discussion rarely found nowadays. We seem to have lost the knack of criticizing another person's ideas objectively. Criticism of another is generally perceived as a statement that the other is stupid. Since it is impolite to call another person stupid, unless we wish to harm him, we tend to tone criticism down until it becomes ineffective, or to interpret it as a personal attack. It is only by subjecting ideas to a harsh honest critique that the 'fool's gold' among them will be differentiated from the real precious metal. But even more than that, living in the challenging and exciting environment generated by honest criticism sharpens individuals to formulate the most precise ideas that they are capable of.

We recognize the lack of this atmosphere in establishing the 'brain-storming' session. What is the definition of such a session? Aren't the participants in such sessions told, either implicitly or explicitly, that the ideas they are expected to toss out will not be perceived as their considered judgements so that they ought not take umbrage at criticism? Such sessions succeed only to the extent that the participants manage to overcome the inhibitions imposed by the cultural atmosphere and do get involved in a heated argument, no holds barred.

7. *The Role of Personality in Organizational Functions*

It may be questioned why the concept of personality should be introduced in the present context. After all, this is one concept that organizations have accepted from the academic world and have applied in various ways in attempts to solve administrative problems. There is an opinion gaining ground, however, that were we able to add the accounts on both sides of the ledger, we would find that the net effect of paying attention to 'personality' has been detrimental rather than beneficial. 'Personality' has been overused and misused. And this for several reasons.

First, it must be remembered that both the tests measuring personality and the relationships between the measurements and various kinds of performance are based upon statistical analyses. Their predictive power, their reliability as guidelines for action in individual cases or when an administrator has to choose between a few people, is consequently quite tenuous. Now add to this the creeping suspicion that the personality tests are basically not valid, i.e. they certainly measure something, but how that something is related to personality is nebulous; Whyte's critique in *The Organization Man* [6] of the use of personality tests by industry is very well taken. It is therefore reasonable to suspect and doubt the extent to which administrators should depend upon personality tests in making administrative decisions concerning people.

Secondly, even were the tests valid, and an ideal person for a given slot could, in theory, be found, for most organizations this would be functionally impossible. They just do not have a pool of people large enough from which to select the ideal personality. They have to learn to make do with what they have. Although it assuages his ego if the administrator, when things go wrong, can sit back and sigh to himself: 'Damn these personalities; if I only had the right guy for the job', it certainly is of no use in solving the problems that exist. To achieve an efficient organization, the administrator has so to structure the jobs to be done that the people he is stuck with can hack it well. This is not too difficult; this is actually done every time an administrator solves a knotty conflict in his organization, even though later, when he sits back to contemplate and evaluate his actions, he may again sigh yearningly for the ideal personality and order the purchase of the newest edition of a well publicized personality test. And this leads us directly to the third, final, and probably most important point.

Careful, controlled observation of experimental groups attempting to achieve a common goal has forced investigators to the conclusion that personality conflicts are generally symptoms rather than causes. They are the symptoms of difficulties that the groups have with objective problems they cannot solve and that hamper the achievement of their goal. In a paper presented at the 1961 American Psychological Association annual meetings Jensen, Jordan, and

Terebinsky [1] argued that personality reared its ugly head only to the extent that the team could not solve its objective difficulties. When a team member would propose a working solution, people would forget their personality difficulties and try the solution out.

Of course, once personality conflicts do develop, they can have a serious effect upon the organization, primarily because they can act as a red herring and can distract those involved from identifying the real, effective cause of the difficulties. An excellent example of how personality conflicts can becloud issues is given in a paper by Kurt Lewin entitled: 'The Solution of a Chronic Conflict in Industry' [2]. What appeared to all as being a severe personality conflict between a forelady and the chief mechanic in a clothing manufacturing plant turned out to be the consequence of a poorly defined allocation of responsibilities which led to difficulties in repairing machine break-downs. Given half a chance, most people, despite large personality and ability differences, will learn to work together efficiently and then will learn to enjoy each other.

III. BRIDGING THE GAP BETWEEN ACADEMIC RESEARCH AND ITS PRACTICAL APPLICATIONS

It was mentioned earlier that the gap between laboratory results and their application in real life is not restricted to the social sciences, but is also true for the physical sciences. Yet there is no great problem in applying the results of academic research in the physical sciences to the needs of industry and the government. This is the result of the development of a large and highly competent, experienced, mediating profession – the engineers. Chemical engineers, mechanical engineers, electronic engineers, etc., are, as a profession, at home both with the basic research done in the universities and the actual needs and realities of the line organizations.

The social sciences lack a similar profession. True, social scientists are playing a greater and greater role in industry and government and a social engineering profession is slowly emerging. But it is growing up like Topsy; it is developing in an unplanned manner. This is a rather inefficient way of doing things A reasoned plan, even though it may be mistaken in many ways, is generally more efficient in getting things done than letting 'nature' take its course unaided. Steps should be taken to set up a viable social engineering profession as soon as possible. Industry, government, and the interested professional disciplines should organize a social engineering curriculum in the

American colleges and universities, modelled after the physical engineering curricula. It should lead to a terminal Bachelor or Master degree – not a Doctorate – and turn out people who are at home in the world of both the academic investigator and the practical administrator. The prime responsibility of these engineers will be to eliminate the pitfalls and difficulties to be found in the present attempts of applying academic research. In addition, such a profession can have another important impact: it can revitalize many aspects of contemporary academic thinking and research in the social sciences.

The gap between practical problems and basic research has affected the nature of the basic research. Unfortunately, many of the problems that intrigue the university investigators *are* inapplicable and irrelevant as far as the administrator is concerned. He is not altogether wrong in his criticism. Many of the problems confronting the administrator are as challenging, are as exciting as are the so-called most profound problems in basic theory. If only they could be communicated to the academic investigator in a language which would excite his interest. This the administrator cannot do effectively. But this a social engineer would probably do most effectively since one of his main areas of specialization would be the speaking and understanding of two languages, the language of the academic and the language of the administrator.

With this we see something that is rather common when proposing solutions to social problems – what appears to be a good solution for one problem, can, upon closer consideration, be seen to serve as a solution for other, seemingly independent problems as well. A social unit is generally a complex, interdependent whole. A problem in such a unit is a result of some underlying dislocation and hence is generally a symptom among other symptoms. A good solution, by going beyond the symptom, is therefore found to have a greater overall effectiveness than originally expected.

REFERENCES

[1] JENSEN, B. T., JORDAN, N., and TEREBINSKY, S. J., The Development of Cooperation Among Three-man Crews in a Simulated Man–machine Information Processing System. *J. Social Psychol.*, 1963, **59**, 175–84.

[2] LEWIN, K., The Solution of a Chronic Conflict in Industry. Chapter 8 in *Resolving Social Conflicts*. Harper, New York, 1948.

[3] RICE, A. K., *Productivity and Social Organization: The Ahmedabad Experiment*. Tavistock Publications, London, 1958.

[4] ROYCE, J., The Psychology of Invention. *Psychol. Rev.*, 1898, **5**, 113–34.

[5] WHITE, R. K., and LIPPITT, R., *Autocracy and Democracy: An Experimental Inquiry*. Harper, New York, 1960.

[6] WHYTE, WILLIAM H., *The Organization Man*. Simon & Schuster, New York, 1956; Cape, London, 1957.

15

Whither scientific psychology?

There can be no doubt about it, contemporary American scientific psychology is the sterilest of the sterile. Years of arduous labour and the assiduous enterprise of hundreds of professors and thousands of students has yielded precisely nothing. Most American academic psychologists would probably agree, to the extent that they are aware of their own history, that the birthdate of American scientific psychology is 1913, the year in which Watson published his first paper on Behaviourism. Almost all the work prior to that date has long since been relegated to the status of literal nonsense: nonsense as meant by circa 1925 Vienna Circle positivism – that which cannot be rigorously defined operationally. A challenge can be thrown down. In the fifty-three years that have passed since that 'momentous' occasion can *one* positive contribution towards any increased knowledge of man be pointed to? None such can be found; no substantive contribution can be named. The canard that 'psychology is a new science' has long outlived its explanatory-away usefulness; the unpleasant and discouraging facts must be faced honestly.

Behaviourism, however, is but a phase of a much more comprehensive process of sterility. Words and concepts that had their origin in the primitive 'arithmetic' association theory of Hume, or the more sophisticated 'chemical' association theory of John Stuart Mill are still being used, despite the fact that the centuries of their use have not contributed one whit to our real knowledge of man. In 1890, in summarizing and reviewing the academic psychology of his day, William James left no doubt as to what he thought about it in many a barbed and eloquent expression: 'It would be difficult to believe that intelligent men could be guilty of so patent a fallacy, were not the history of psychology there to give proof' [1]. In reviewing what was basically German scientific psychology, whose 'official' date of birth is 1872 – the year in which Wundt set up 'the first psychological laboratory', Karl Mannheim found it necessary to characterize it as late as 1929 as: 'a trained incapacity to deal with problems of the mind' which 'accounts for the fact that it offers no foothold to living human beings in their daily life' [2, p. 21].

Yet Behaviourism deserves to be treated separately. Despite its consistent record of failure and sterility it has managed to capture position after position in the academic world. It is not only the dominant, but practically the exclusive force in contemporary academic psychology. In addition it has already made serious inroads and threatens to overwhelm the academic disciplines of economics, sociology, political science, and anthropology. It is a real and present danger for which our society has already paid too great a price if only in the wasting of limited and needed mental resources. But there is probably a more profound reason for focusing upon Behaviourism. The overall sterility, the overall ineffectiveness of man's attempt to understand himself throughout the ages is a vast problem. The fact that we have advanced so little, if at all, from the state of knowledge of Socrates who literally meant what he said when he asserted that he was the wisest man in Athens because he knew he knew nothing – and it should be recalled that Socrates' sole interest was the problem of man – is instructive. Perhaps we are in no position directly to assail the over-all problem of our inability to understand ourselves. Many frontal assaults have been launched against this problem since Socrates' time, but the results clearly indicate that they have all, all but failed. Perhaps, to use terminology currently popular, the more effective strategy is to focus upon a more limited problem. To the extent that the lesser problem is clarified, the enrichment of our conceptual armamentarium and the increased sensitivity of our feeling in such matters will place us in a more advantageous position with respect to the larger more comprehensive problem.

Not too long ago logic (which for the present purpose includes mathematics as well) was considered to embody the laws of thought. This was obviously wrong; human thinking is far too complex a phenomenon to be reducible to the simple laws of logic, no matter how elegant and coercive the latter may be. So the pendulum swung to the other side. Nowadays both logicians and psychologists tend to assert that logic is independent of human thinking, even though it is a product of human thinking. But this extreme position is also, most probably, wrong; careful consideration of how logic operates can probably teach us much of importance concerning human thinking. Logic can teach us something of importance with respect to the problem under discussion.

Contemporary logic and 'foundations of mathematics' are currently enjoying an unprecedented spate of activity. Logicians can, and do, construct, for their research purposes, all kinds of logics based upon differing syntactic and semantic rules. However, despite the variety of logical systems available at present, they all, if I am not mistaken, share at least one common prerequisite: there is no logical system that permits a statement which implies its contradiction.* Such statements are, to use Carnap's terminology, logically false, and all logical deduction breaks down in a logical system that contains a logically false statement. In other words, no logical deduction is possible in a system that contains self-contradictory statements. It will be asserted that conceptually self-contradictory statements accepted by a man are as debilitating to action within the realm relevant to the self-contradiction as they are to logical systems; the inability of logic to cope with self-contradictions merely reflects a more basic human inability.

Whenever men of reasonable ability and goodwill labour conscientiously for a long period with little to show in the way of accomplishment, it is almost always a sign that they labour under conceptual confusion, and most likely conceptual contradiction. Conceptual contradiction does not permit its captive even to face the problem directly, let alone make progress towards its solution. The conceptual contradiction inherent in every step taken by behaviourists is not hard to find. It has been expressed very concisely and neatly in a recent paper by a prominent spokesman for contemporary scientific psychology. In discussing some actions which he, as an individual, had engaged in, Osgood writes that one source for the concern he had which led to the actions discussed 'was an intense devotion to rationality' [3, p. 111]; when discussing the 'psychologists' conception of the nature of man' he lists first among several other ideas 'the notion that man's behaviour is deterministic in terms of both innate and acquired factors . . .' [3, p. 116]. Now the phenomena denoted by 'rationality' and 'deterministic' are mutually contradictory; both cannot co-exist in the same person. If 'rationality' is

---

* I may be mistaken in this and some enterprising logician may have gone to the trouble of formulating a logical system where this is permitted. Such a system, however, would be a degenerate system of no intrinsic interest or value to logicians.

to make any sense, it denotes an event where a person being confronted with an objective state of affairs considers it carefully, weighs and judges the issues involved to the best of his ability, and *as a result* decides upon a course of action which best fits the objective realities in the situation. 'Deterministic', as used in scientific psychology, means something contrary; it denotes an event where a person being confronted with a state of affairs necessarily reacts to it in a predetermined manner which is a function (in the mathematical sense) of his innate physiological structure and his prior personal experience. There is no conceptual room here for choice or judgement and, consequently, for rationality. We are faced with a special instance of the more general modern dilemma that contemporary science cannot cope with the phenomena of free will and personal responsibility, phenomena which serve as the rock-bottom foundation for both personal and social order. It is interesting to note, parenthetically, that Osgood uses 'rationality' in discussing his own, living actions, whereas he uses 'deterministic' in discussing abstract psychology from a scientific standpoint.

So here we are. Are we to back the old, and historically demonstrated sterile, nomothetic, ideographic dispute which 'raged' in the German universities towards the end of the nineteenth century, i.e. that disciplines devoted to the study of man in all his manifestations cannot hope to formulate scientific, nomothetic, laws but are restricted to careful studies of the individual case in the quest for intuitive ideographic understanding of the case studied? Yes and no. Yes, because the problem here posed is the same problem that generated the controversy; no, because I propose to try to avoid the impasse in which the old dispute ended up.

The ideographic approach had two weaknesses which contributed much to its having lost the battle with respect to the application of science to the problems of man in the United States. First, it posited an unbridgeable gap between the nomothetic, physical sciences and the ideographic disciplines – in many cases it went so far as to refuse to use the word 'science' when discussing the study of man in all its aspects. Secondly, it replaced the concept of laws, be they nomothetic or any other, with the concepts of intuition, understanding, or wisdom, which at best are nebulous, without ever trying to clarify what is clearly meant by them. It is difficult, if not almost impossible, to maintain the position that unbridgeable gaps exist in knowledge, particularly when men whose nature led them to be scientists are involved. Gaps are there to be bridged; the greater the gap in knowledge, the greater the challenge it poses. It is not by chance that mankind generally considers the greatest intellects to belong to those men who have attempted to formulate the solutions to ultimate problems rather than to those who have successfully solved explicitly limited problems. And when the gap is functionally unbridgeable, for whatever reason, it is a common reaction to 'bridge' it by refusing to recognize its existence and to act as if it 'wasn't there', as if it was an epiphenomenon. Added to this that the nebulous 'intuition', 'understanding', and 'wisdom' cannot compete, at least in the scientist's mind, with the coercive clarity of the logical and mathematical analysis which serves as a *sine qua non* for the nomothetic sciences, the victory of the nomothetic, positivistic, behavioural approach became almost an inevitability.

But, as already seen, it was a hollow victory based upon a false-hood and, consequently, yielding nothing. Despite its defeat, the ideographic contention is truer to the facts as we know them today.

Let us accept the gap as it stands, let us assume that it is unbridge-able; after all, as scientists we should be able to discipline ourselves and not be seduced by a simulated bridging of the gap despite its painful challenge. We can model ourselves, nay, we must model ourselves after a man who is recognized throughout the world as one of the most significant intellects known to have lived and who met his death proclaiming that he was the wisest man in Athens since he knew how little he knew. Does it follow that we also have to give up the conceptual clarity of the physical and the logico/mathematical disciplines and regress to some mystic intuitionism? It does not.

An area where psychology, as a discipline, can point to accomplishment is that of sensory psychology. We have accomplished much in ascertaining the limits of perception, the sensitivity of discrimination, and, most important from a pragmatic standpoint, the external conditions that facilitate accurate perception. Human engineering, in its broadest sense, has continued along this line and has developed principles, which have stood up with time and much implementation, that reduced the errors of the human machine operator as well as speeding up the tempo of his operations.

The admitted achievements of these two areas of specialization within psychology do not belie the earlier assertion that academic psychology cannot point to any *positive* contribution towards an increased knowledge of man. Careful consideration will show that the accomplishments here discussed are 'negative' in nature; the conditions hampering clear vision or causing an operator to make errors are identified and eliminated. In order to make a positive contribution a theory, or something, must be propounded that leads to understanding why men see the way they do and why men make errors under certain conditions. There are many theories propounded, but as long as there are many theories there will be no theory and the sought-for contribution will not be attained. We can talk here about ameliorative psychology but not about a positive science of psychology.

The above is not meant in a pejorative sense; rather the opposite. Anything serving to ameliorate the human condition is to be blessed. Medicine, after all, throughout most of its history and still to a great extent today, is basically an ameliorative discipline consisting primarily of the art of diagnosis and the knowledge of therapeutic actions to be taken, it being quite irrelevant and generally unknown why the indicated therapy is effective. A tried compendium of diagnosable disease entities and their cures is as invaluable as a good dictionary; but neither the compendium nor the dictionary is a positive contribution to our knowledge of disease or of language.

Much of psychology, and probably all of psychology that has made any contribution whatsoever towards man's welfare, can be characterized as being an ameliorative and not a positive science. Abnormal and clinical psychology, to the extent that it is successful, identifies the factors that 'cause' mental disturbance and the therapeutic techniques which alleviate and, hopefully, cure it. It is interesting that both the psychiatric and clinical psychological literature have no positive definition for mental health similar to the medical profession's definition of physiological health. The available definitions of mental health all tend to be 'negative', characterized by a lack of 'abnormal' symptoms – be they in behaviour or in answers to tests. Psychological disease seems to be an easy thing to see, to point to, and to conceptualize, whereas psychological health, normality, is quite elusive and slips through our fingers every time we try to grasp at it. One is tempted to characterize abnormal behaviour as being determined, 'mechanical', predictable, whereas normal behaviour is anything but that because of its harmonious fusion with the 'here and now', which is always in many respects unique.

Research and activity in social psychology, especially in the area of group dynamics, to the extent that it made contributions, shows a similar pattern. We have identified the 'factors' which hamper the reaching of a group consensus, which hamper a group from resolving

236 · *Themes in speculative psychology*

its conflicts; in other words, *that which vitiates* group action, which hampers its progress and renders it relatively ineffective, has lent itself with some success, to study. The current popular leadership training programme effort, in its many and various guises and forms, is based upon these successes and attempts to train group leaders to be sensitive in this area so they can keep these 'factors' from appearing and playing their undesirable role. The effect of these factors is predictable in the way they hamper the group from acting effectively; but the actual resolution of the conflict, the consensus, the 'good' group decision is not. It seems that the latter can be recognized only after their occurrence.

And what do we find in the research areas of education and training for creative problem solving? Almost the same thing. The factors hampering effective teaching or creative problem-solving seem to be easily identifiable and all proposed reforms in these areas consist primarily of attempts to eliminate them. The nature of effective education or of effective teaching to be creative are basically defined negatively by what not to do; here, too, positive knowledge is sadly lacking. The effects of the 'bad' factors are known and predictable, but we are not in a position to know and predict the effects of the recommended practices by which they are replaced. May this not be the reason why so much of our educational reforms and changes are basically puerile?

A model seems to emerge. To the extent that psychology has been 'successful', applicable to real-life problems, it has been in identifying factors that hamper man from acting and behaving effectively. Only these seem to be conceptually identifiable and predictable in their effects. Effective behaviour seems to be nebulous and residual, defined 'negatively' by what it is not. Effective behaviour, that is, optimum adaptation to ones' environment and creative solution to the problems posed by that environment, seems, by its very nature, to be difficult to discriminate conceptually and to be unpredictable. We seem to be able to predict only those aspects of psychological causality that dehumanize man which, as an ameliorative discipline, we seek to overcome. It follows that in order to humanize man to the fullest extent possible, we must use science to make him as unpredictable as possible.*

* This seems to be the significant message in Henry A. Murray's important paper: 'The Personality and Career of Satan' [4]. Murray points out that throughout time and in all great religions Satan seems to have been conceptualized as the dehumanizing agent, *par excellence*, with 'an incapacity to love and an incapacity to create any variety

With this, the self-contradiction inherent in behaviourism disappears. Psychology is redefined from making man predictable to making man unpredictable. The task of amelioration is vast and demanding and it is socially inexcusable to paralyse and waste our intellectual resources by getting involved in conceptual contradictions. Medicine is an excellent example of the benefits to follow from such a course. Where would medicine have been today had most of its practitioners bogged down in premature, sophistic theory-spinning and theory-proving?

But the gap is still there, and it is disturbing. In fact it is even more disturbing than before.

We may accept the analogy with medicine as a palliative since it does point to a way of action that makes sense on the face of it. And the extent to which this way can lead to an actual improvement of man's lot upon this earth will be rewarding. But it is also a blind way of proceeding, which, despite the amount of pragmatically useful knowledge it may yield, can never lead to understanding.* A compendium of diagnosable undesirable states and effective cures for them, no matter how important, is in and of itself indistinguishable from successful magic; its only justification is that it works.

It is true that we assumed the gap between science and knowledge about man at the outset; but it was not assumed in good faith. We had a slight reservation, a sneaking hope that the assumption would lead to a *reductio ad absurdum* and would have to be discarded. Now we seem to be stuck with the gap more than ever. A scientist can discipline himself and admit to his ignorance much more easily if he has hope that the ignorance will eventually be overcome, that it is temporary. Ignorance in principle dispirits science and leads to mysticism.

Again the analogy of medicine may be of help. Whereas it is true that during the heyday of medicine in the nineteenth century the discipline was most strictly empirically pragmatic – the discovery of Salvarsan 606 being a representative model of medical research, as was the discovery of the antipolio sera in our generation – nevertheless medicine did not remain a strictly empirical discipline. As it

---

of new forms that are valuable to humanity' (p. 52). He concludes the paper with the accusation: 'I shall leave you with the question of whether, by any chance, the current Ph.D. system is one of the Devil's cunningest contrivances' (p. 54).

* I disregard the problem: what is understanding? It happens to be a fact that man feels ill at ease when confronted with phenomena he does not understand and is restless and disturbed until he achieves understanding – whatever that may be.

238 · *Themes in speculative psychology*

progressed and more and more diseases were 'conquered', viable scientific theories of health and disease did develop. Today, despite its still being 'blindly' pragmatic in many areas, medicine, nevertheless, can also boast of a healthy theoretical development as well. Increasing knowledge of cures leads to theory development; may not such also be expected for psychology?

Well, this is some sort of a solution; but it too is not really satisfying. First of all it is not based on reasoning but on a 'blind' analogy and a hope; and although we cannot dispense with hopes for the future, expectations based upon reasons are far more desirable. Secondly, the analogy with medicine is not really well taken. Upon examination of the physiological theories extant we find that they reduce themselves to the physical sciences, as currently known, and are all predicated on the concept of physical causality and simple determinism. But this leads back to the conceptual contradiction with which we started, and if this is the best that medical theorizing can do, our problem is not solved. Somewhere in *Process and Reality* [5], Whitehead, in discussing contemporary physiological theories, wryly quips that life resides in the interstices of the cells. By this I understand him to say that no matter what light has been shed by physiology on physiological processes, it has yet to shed any light on what life as such is. This is our problem in a nutshell.

The medical analogy is not well taken in another way as well. It can easily be imagined that for early medicine there was no inherent connection between disease and cure. What it was in the nature of the treatments that led to a cure was phenomenally un-understandable; treatments were generally discovered by hard and laborious effort, often pure trial and error, and crystallized and proved themselves only with the accumulation of experience of decades and centuries.* But normal behaviour is not a sequence of inherently unconnectable events or actions which just happen to be there. We may not be able to predict what a normal person will do, but once he does it, it fits. And if it doesn't fit, questions force themselves into consciousness that demand solutions: Why the devil did he do that? In other words, whereas there is no experienced fitting order between a disease and its cure, behaviour is perceived to constitute, and is expected to constitute, a continuous fitting order. And where there is order, an analysis of the order is also required. For psychologists to start out as did physicians is regressive; because they start out with phenomena

* Whether this is factually true is not too relevant for the present argument.

that are far more ordered and which make far more intrinsic sense than do the phenomena of disease and cure – in fact, because of this immediately given order – it becomes well-nigh impossible for a psychologist to emulate the early physician, even though he conscientiously attempts to do so. The observed order will force him into theorizing despite the best of his intentions. The immediately experienced order of human behaviour, and – it can be added parenthetically – of all social phenomena, can only be disregarded at the investigator's peril of becoming untrue to the facts.

But does this get us out of the box? It doesn't seem so. So there is an order? The dragging in of this experienced order is irrelevant to the opening arguments of this paper. Even if there is this order, the opening arguments contend, 'prove' that this order cannot be reduced to a scientific explanation; the example from physiology can be recalled. There it was argued that to the extent that physiological phenomena have been reduced to a scientifically theoretical schema, life disappeared.

Offhand, two ways seem open to react to the above. First, we may ask what is so holy about science. Admittedly it would be nice and highly desirable to study man in a scientific way. But if the application of the scientific method to the study of man entails a contradiction of terms, then it cannot be done. The observed order remains, however, and is still a challenge. So let us try to study it to the best of our ability, let us try to explicate the inherent sense underlying the order and not pay any attention to whether the study is scientific or not. And many students of man have reached this conclusion which is essentially the ideographic approach. But many are not happy with this way out; they feel that science is too important to be dismissed so cursorily.

A second way opens up. We have tacitly assumed the currently prevailing definition of science and have not questioned it. Let us submit it to an examination and see whether the contradiction that troubles us stems from too limited a definition. And this turns out to be the case. The difficulties confronting us seem to reside not in the study of man, but in the current conceptualization of science prevalent among those self-pronounced and socially accepted guardians of scientific purity, the academic psychologists.

What characterizes this conceptualization? Two concepts: determinism and prediction. Of these, prediction assumes far greater importance than does determinism since, it is argued, determinism cannot be differentiated from *post hoc* rationalization (which *ex*

cathedra is not science) unless it can predict. Functionally scientific
effort has concentrated on finding techniques for the prediction of
future events either in an experimental setting or in real life.

The slightest reflection seems to lead to the conclusion that the
contemporary preoccupation of scientific psychologists with prediction is an arrogant aberration. It, by fiat, excludes a host of well
established disciplines which have long been considered sciences by
both the intellectual world at large as well as by their many practitioners. What is there predictive about such disciplines as: zoology,
geology, anthropology, philology, history, oceanography, or even
physiology? And many others can be named. In fact, one of the most
significant and impressive scientific accomplishments of the human
mind must also be excluded: what is there predictive in the theory
of evolution? Even more surprising is the fact that mathematics in
its broadest interpretation, the discipline which serves as the prime
vehicle for scientific prediction is, in and of itself, not predictive.
The consequence of a deductive chain of mathematical reasoning
cannot be predicted, in principle, prior to the act of deduction – at
the end of which it is discovered. True, scientific studies in several
specialized fields of basic physical phenomena and in astronomy
have led to successful predictions which have enabled man to trans-
form his environment; so what?

Upon consideration we find that this focusing upon prediction does
not make any conceptual sense either. Men recognize an essential
difference between magic and science, though magic is also
considered to be a technique used to control and/or predict future
events. Let us assume a successful practitioner of magic; are his
predictions and control of the environment indistinguishable from
scientific prediction and control. Let no one argue that this cannot be,
that there can be no successful magic. It is too easy to turn the
proposition around: is a scientific theory which is wrong, which fails
to predict, indistinguishable from magic? Schrödinger seems to say
the same thing differently and somewhat more elegantly:

> There is, of course, among physicists a widely popular tenet, informed
> by the philosophy of Ernst Mach, to the effect that the only task of
> experimental science is to give definite *prescriptions* for successfully
> foretelling the results of any future observations from the known results
> of previous observations. If this contention is taken at its face value,
> then *not only* is it irrelevant whether the prescription makes use of a
> visualized model or only consists in definitely prescribed mathematical
> operations, to be performed with the previously observed values in order

to obtain predicted values; *but also* the said operations would apparently not even have to be mathematically correct, as long as they are precise and enable us to prophesy correctly. Indeed the lack of rigour in a theoretical deduction is nowadays sometimes followed by the remark that what vindicates the procedure is its success, its leading to results that agree with observation. The neo-Machian principle covers this argument not only pending the proof that the theoretical deduction is correct, *but even if it should prove to be wrong.*

Nobody will agree? But why? If our task is only to predict precisely and correctly by any means whatsoever, why not by false mathematics? [6, p. 154, italics in original].

In this connection it is of interest to see how a 'hard-nosed' physicist defines his science. Heisenberg implicitly defines science in characterizing the power of contemporary physics:

... When modern science states that the proton is a certain solution of a fundamental equation of matter it means that we can from this solution deduce mathematically all possible properties of the proton and can *check* the correctness of the solution by experiments in every detail. This possibility of *checking* the correctness of a statement experimentally with very high precision and in any number of details gives enormous weight to the statement that could not be attached to the statements of early Greek philosophy [7, pp. 74–5, my italics].

Nothing in this statement deals with or even implies prediction. What is talked about is the checking of conclusions. Granted that the checking of conclusions by means of an experiment is a very powerful check and that it may look, from a certain standpoint, like a prediction and may be described in terms of being a prediction, but this shifts conceptual schemata in midstream and causes us to lose sight of something very important. Experimentation, admittedly a most powerful tool for checking the correctness of scientific statements, is assuredly not the only tool for such checking. The scientific disciplines which do not entail prediction merit being called science because they have all developed techniques for checking the correctness of their statements even though these techniques, by the very nature of the disciplines, are not experimental nor can they take recourse in prediction.

Prediction has been dispensed with, as such, but problems still remain. The mere checking of statements as to their correctness does not characterize science adequately. Not all statements that can be checked are scientific statements, nor are all possible ways of checking scientific statements accepted as scientific. Obviously this issue cannot be dealt with adequately here, if it can be dealt with adequately at all at present. We will take much for granted and plunge in immediately into what we consider to be the essence of scientific activity and the essence of scientific checking. The discussion will be too short, obviously oversimplified, but essentially correct (the latter is an intuitive judgement, an opinion, rather than a demonstrable assertion).

Man has been characterized in many epigrammatic ways: a featherless biped; a political animal; a rational animal; an animal who laughs; etc. Each of these characteristics is true, relatively prominent, and widely known. Man can be characterized in another way, queerly enough, not prominent: Man is an animal who is restless and disturbed unless he has reasons or explanations for the phenomena surrounding him. What is one of the first expressions that toddlers learn by which they often drive their parents to distraction? *Why!* It would be interesting to determine what percentage of chit-chat, when people speak freely of what spontaneously interests them, is devoted to explaining things to one another: Why x did that. Why y happened, etc. I daresay that we would discover the percentage to be extraordinarily high. Given time and leisure, man tends to become preoccupied with finding explanations and reasons, or, what amounts to the same thing, causes. And to a great extent this quest for reasons is neither pragmatic nor extrinsically goal-directed; Aristotle's belief that the highest form of knowledge is disinterested knowledge is based on substantial psychological truth.

Man's earliest reasons for explaining the happenstances of the world surrounding him generally took the form of anthropomorphic theology. Powerful unseen beings or spirits were postulated who moved the world just as man moves his limbs. The causes of events in the external world were then attributed to the wishes of these beings in a manner identical to our experiencing our wishes to cause the movement of our limbs or the actions of our bodies. And so things remained for a long time.

It was the Greek genius that discovered science. Actually it is probably more correct to say that it was the Greek genius to discover logic (it is true, of course, that men used logic before its discovery, but they knew not what they did); with the discovery of logic, the development of science became just a matter of course. The essence of logic is the realization that conceptual properties entail consequences. These are experienced as being absolutely necessary, as that which could not be otherwise than it is. And this necessity is independent of the unseen beings or spirits, is not subject to their will. Two plus two must make four; it is impossible to conceive of any God willing it otherwise. This absolute necessity, independent of the wishes of men or Gods, is what makes logic objective. To the extent that explanations could be phrased in logic they were experienced as being eternally and objectively true, and this is what made them the most powerful and desirable ultimate explanation, the most satisfying explanation.

Man perceives/conceives of objects and, consequently, events in terms of properties; another way of putting this is that that which cannot be conceptualized by man cannot be either perceived or conceived. Many of these properties can be phrased logically; and once so phrased the consequences entailed by them can be deduced. If event *a* is phrased/represented logically, its consequences deduced, and event *b* which follows event *a* is perceived to embody those consequences, man experiences having obtained an ultimate, objective explanation of event *b*, event *a* being transformed into its cause. This is the essence of a scientific explanation. It should be noted that 'logic' as used in this paragraph intends its most general meaning; it is a fascinating fact that to the extent that the sciences 'use logic' they use it at the extremes, either the most highly specialized form of numerical logic – mathematics – or a nebulous logic embedded in the common discursive language. Is there a science which uses general abstract formal logic as its vehicle for checking scientific statements? Does this lack of use have any implications for formal logic?

With this we reach a position where we may begin to understand what constitutes a scientific statement and scientific checking. A scientific statement is a statement about a state of affairs in our world which is couched, either explicitly or implicitly, logically. Scientific checking consists of making the logic explicit, where need be, and verifying that the logic has been used correctly, that is, following logical rules and prescriptions. The existence of non-predictive sciences now ceases to be a problem. To the extent that such a science, e.g. geology, can classify the phenomena which interest it into sets defined by general properties (concepts), a logical operation *par excellence*, it is being scientific. This is the Linnaean stage of science and many disciplines may not go, or have not as yet gone, beyond this. Other disciplines can achieve something more complex. They, e.g. history, can demonstrate that if events *a* and *b* are conceptualized in a certain way, a logical connection between them can be demonstrated and with this event *b* is explained objectively. Some disciplines, e.g. either cultural or physical anthropology, show that the phenomena under their purview can be characterized as being parts of an articulate, logical structure which discloses the objective unity and meaning underlying what is otherwise seen as a plethora of discrete, disjunctive events.

A radical, exciting, and not to be underestimated significant shift occurs when sciences consider events that can *logically correctly* be characterized by numbers. *The significance of this change is primarily pragmatic and not necessarily theoretical.* When phenomena can be thus represented mathematically, it becomes easy to deduce consequences of their logical characterization which as yet have not been observed. These deductions will also tell us in what circumstances these consequences ought to become observable. If we then go out and either seek out these special circumstances in nature or set them up in a laboratory, and then the expected consequences are found, we experience this as the most powerful checking of scientific statements available. Pragmatically this experience has been well justified in that these sciences have enabled man to master much of the world in which he finds himself to an extent that puts all the other sciences 'to shame'.

Let us return now to the problems of psychology. Once we realize that science is not restricted to the formulation of laws that yield 'mechanical' predictions, that the latter are but a special aspect, no matter how striking, of a larger, more comprehensive, more significant endeavour, new ways seem to open up for psychology and the 'unbridgeable' gap between the nomothetic approach and the ideographic approach seems to fade in significance. There is no *a priori* reason why the study of psychological events cannot be so conceptualized that the logical connection within events (structure) and/or the logical connection between events (dynamics) becomes manifest. The experience of order inherent in all manifestations of human enterprise and being seems to guarantee the existence of a logical connection; it is very difficult to conceive of an order that has no underlying logic. Rather than commit ourselves to prediction and slavishly model the prestigeful physical sciences which have been able to use mathematics, thereby getting ourselves involved in all kinds of contradictions, let us be humble in the face of our ignorance and resist the deceptive, elusive, siren charms of high-speed computers and complex calculations. Let us return and directly face the phenomena which we presume to study and see to what extent we can reduce them to make sense: that is so to conceptualize them that logical thinking through of issues becomes possible; even more, flows naturally.

This points to some sort of case study, but decidedly not the kinds of case study that are currently the norm. The main difficulty of most of the current case studies is that they are *selectively* selected and *selectively* reported to 'prove' or justify a theoretical approach or analysis already accepted. As a result, these cases cannot really serve as adequate raw data for independent investigators to see what can be learnt from them; most cases to be found in the contemporary psychological literature are truly biased. There are, of course, notable exceptions, a striking case coming to my mind is the work of Piaget. Piaget reports the actual behaviour of his subjects with great fidelity so that other investigators can study it independently and reach independent conclusions. An even more striking case of behavioural, raw data are the behaviour records, both published and unpublished amassed by Roger G. Barker and his co-workers.* Were anyone to reduce any of these behaviour records to a coherent conceptual order where each event follows sensibly and necessarily from each preceding event, a major breakthrough in scientific pyschology would have taken place.

Those familiar with the writings of Kurt Goldstein will easily see that the approach reached above is harmonious with Goldstein's basic methodological postulates as presented in *The Organism* [10, pp. 21–7]. Goldstein, who was investigating the effects of brain damage upon patient performance, argues that a patient's behaviour, in test situations and otherwise, should be studied in depth and in context until understanding of what is going on is reached. With the achievement of understanding, prediction of the patient's behaviour in other situations follows as a matter of course. He summarizes, in italics:

> *One single extensive analysis of this sort is much more valuable than many examinations involving many patients, but yielding only imperfect conclusions* [10, p. 26].

The quest for sense and understanding need not be restricted solely to case studies; it can be applied to experimental studies as well. What is called for is a not so novel way of analysing experimental data. Piaget has already been mentioned as a model; almost

* For example see the relevant discussions in Barker, R. G., and Wright, H. F., *Midwest and its Children* [8], and their earlier book: *One Boy's Day* [9].

all his research is, strictly speaking, experimental. What seems to be precluded in the recommended analysis of experimental results is the almost complete dependence we have manœuvred ourselves into upon statistical analysis. All statistics can yield is the identification of broad, central tendencies that are but slightly dissimilar to the unorganized, unordered chaos that we call chance; to the extent that these central tendencies are obviously dissimilar to chance, statistical analysis is not needed since it will only belabour the obvious. Understanding and knowledge cannot be obtained from such slight and nebulous dissimilarities. At best statistical analysis is but a first step in research in that it can identify areas which are promising and which should be submitted to further, finer research. In almost all cases of importance, however, we already know that and can afford to bypass the initial statistical exploration; what we have to do is to develop finer experimental techniques and meaningful ways of analysing and studying the experimental results.*

To summarize the immediately preceding discussion: The main task of scientific psychology at present would seem to be the very careful observation of specific behaviour or actions of persons. These observations may be of actual behaviour in real-life situations, of test results, or of behaviour in experimentally contrived situations. The observations should then be studied and/or enriched until some conceptual sense is yielded; conceptual sense which bears the hallmark of truth – truth, when all is said and done, is phenomenally given, just as the colour red is, and cannot be reduced to an objective external criterion, despite the best efforts of epistemologists. With the achievement of conceptual sense, consequences will also appear which can then be checked. The conceptualization will redeem itself to the extent that the consequences can be checked out. To the extent that we amass more and more instances of behaviour with an agreed conceptualization among students of behaviour, psychology will begin its progress towards really becoming a science.

What about hypothesis formulation and theory building? Nothing has been said about *them*, and aren't they essential to science? I don't know about the essentiality, but they are certainly very desirable to attain. Unfortunately the words 'hypothesis' and 'theory' have been so misused and abused in the contemporary scientific psychological literature as to have lost all significant meaning. The

* As an example of an attempt to approach such an analysis see my paper: *On Cognitive Balance* [11].

most trivial and banal hunch is generally glorified by being called an hypothesis; and I have much too often seen statements that are almost equivalent to the following: 'I will therefore propound a theory that man puts on a coat because he is cold'. By their consistent overuse and 'verbal inflation' the value of these words has followed the value of the German mark in the early 1920s. In order to retain some rigorous meaning, in order to be able to make sense, at least to myself, I use these words far more sparingly and, I believe, much more rigorously.

Consistent with the above analysis we consider the first step in scientific endeavour to be the conceptualization of events which, when successful, yields the objective, logical connectivity within events (structure) and/or the objective, logical connectivity between events (dynamics). But this conceptualization and its logical consequences are not hypotheses. It is only when, after serious thinking is 'invested' in studying the found connections – no human progress can occur unless serious thinking is 'invested' – one gets the feeling that a connection, or perhaps preferably several connections, are but *concrete manifestations of some more general statement or formula* that it becomes proper to talk about a hypothesis. That which is *felt* to be the case is *the hypothesis*. Scientists are then motivated to check for the correctness of their feelings. Three possible outcomes of this checking can occur:

(1) as the checking proceeds, the feeling is changed into a perception or cognition and the hypothesis ceases to be a hypothesis but turns into a true statement (this is what takes place when we prove a hypothesis);

(2) as the checking proceeds, we lose the feeling and the hypothesis disappears as such to be remembered as a case where we were mistaken (this takes place when we disprove a hypothesis); and

(3) nothing happens – the feeling remains as it was (we generally do not talk about this outcome very much but I have a feeling that it is far more prevalent than the preceding two outcomes).

We can permit ourselves to speak of a theory only when we can logically demonstrate that at least some (one or more) of our hypotheses or true statements concerning the events under study are derived from a relatively small set of conceptual primitives and explicit or implicit axioms.

Given this stringent usage of 'hypothesis' and 'theory' it can easily

R

be seen that the science of psychology is in no position to talk about hypotheses, let alone theories. We have yet to do the proper homework in conceptualizing man adequately at the lowest level of scientific endeavour. And when we proceed to ponder over this stringent usage something else can be learned: happy is the scientist who can formulate one or two hypotheses during a lifetime of work; happy is the society of scientists which contains one scientist who formulates a theory. The science of psychology ought to drop its preoccupation with hypotheses and theories and get down to the serious business of trying to understand man. To the extent that it will do that, conscientiously and humbly, the hypotheses and theories will not fail to come.

Well, it looks like this longish peregrination is coming to its end. We have argued that American scientific psychology, especially to the extent that it has adopted behaviourism as its credo, is basically sterile. We have attributed this sterility to a conceptual contradiction between what science, as understood by the behaviourists, presumes a scientific explanation to be and what we factually experience ourselves to be. We then argued that there is room for a discipline of psychology that is not scientific, in the accepted sense, but ameliorative, and that in this respect psychology can already point to some positive achievements. But this was found to be unsatisfying and we were forced to re-conceptualize science in a broader manner, a conceptualization that permitted the behaviouristic definition to remain, but merely as a special, restricted case. With the new conceptualization, we found it possible to show how psychology can, nevertheless, eliminate conceptual contradictions, be true to its subject matter, and be scientific.

What?

If I still have any readers, and if they still remember what was being presented in the opening pages of this chapter, some at least are bound to rise in protest. Nothing of the sort was achieved; the question was being begged. Granted that in the broader re-conceptualization of science prediction as a definitive criterion for science was eliminated and one can now see how non-predictive disciplines can 'legitimately' be included in the family of sciences, the gap which was so troublesome at the outset and the conceptual contradictions which demand resolution are still with us. The re-conceptualization of science hinges on the necessary objective connections within and between events based upon logical analysis, and *logic entails the kind of determination which is at the heart of the conceptual contradiction.*

If anything, what has been demonstrated is that the gap between science and the study of man is truly unbridgeable.

This protest is absolutely correct, as far as it goes. The re-conceptualization of science does not, as it stands, help in overcoming the dilemma posed at the beginning of this chapter. Nevertheless, I believe that it has been helpful. In attempting to clarify this final issue, the chapter will come to its fitting end.

The nub of the difficulty is the determinism inherent in logic. It is true that at present we cannot conceive of any form of logic that will retain its coerciveness (i.e. its mandate for objectivity) and not be deterministic.* So what! It was not too long ago that non-Euclidean space was just as inconceivable. We tend to look down with a tolerant, somewhat superior smile at the confusion and dismay that greeted the discovery of non-Euclidean space; how simple and naïve the scientists and philosophers were in those days. We know better. Do we? May it not be just as simple and naïve to assume that logic, as we know it today, is the last word? May there not be a more general form of logic, which is just as coercive, of which contemporary logic is just a special case, and which at the same time will be able to account, objectively, for man's experience of free will and all that that entails?

Towards the end of his life Erwin Schrödinger shifted from studying inanimate phenomena to studying animate phenomena. In summarizing significant lessons from this shift he writes:

> What I wish to make clear . . . is, in short, that from all we have learnt about the structure of living matter, *we must be prepared to find it working in a manner that cannot be reduced to the ordinary laws of physics.* And that not on the ground that there is any 'new force' or what not, directing the behaviour of the single atoms within a living organism, but because the construction is different from anything we have yet tested in the physical laboratory. To put it crudely, an engineer familiar with heat engines only will, after inspecting the construction of an electric motor, be prepared to find it working along principles he does not yet understand. He finds the copper familiar to him in kettles used here in the form of long, long wires wound in coils; the iron familiar to him in levers and bars and steam cylinders is here filling the interior of those coils of copper wire. He will be convinced that it is the same copper and the same iron, subject to the same laws of Nature, and he is right in that. The difference in construction is enough to prepare him for *an entirely different way of functioning.* He will not suspect that an electric

---

* Let no one introduce probabilistic logic at this point; it is but a special form of determinism.

motor is driven by a ghost because it is set spinning by the turn of a switch, without boiler and steam [6, p. 74, my italics].

May not laws of Nature not reducible to the ordinary laws of physics, may not an entirely new way of functioning, presuppose a radically new logic?

We have argued above that our re-conceptualization of science, though admittedly oversimplified, was essentially correct. It prescribes a beginning step for all scientific endeavour. In our desire to establish a scientific psychology let us begin at the beginning, where it is proper for all beginnings to begin, and strive to avoid the temptation of magical short cuts which though they yield social fame and glory, and remuneration, actually retard and hamper rather than forward the desired end. Let us describe the ordered and queerly ordered psychological phenomena carefully and accurately and then attempt so to conceptualize them as to make intrinsic sense rather than to reach some elusive, actually factually false, prediction. There can be no doubt that as this conceptualization proceeds, some lucky investigator will hit upon a conceptualization which will exhibit the objective coercing properties of logic but which will at the same time remain true to the psychological facts; a lucky investigator then to be recognized by society as being a genius. When such takes place, we will be on the threshhold of formulating the new, required logic explicitly; we will be on the threshhold of a science of psychology which is not involved in conceptual contradictions and which is true to the phenomena it purports to study; a science of psychology which truly can become both creative and ameliorative.

REFERENCES

[1] JAMES, WILLIAM, *Principles of Psychology*. Dover Publications, New York, 1950.

[2] MANNHEIM, KARL, *Ideology and Utopia*. Kegan Paul, Trench, Trubner, London, 1936. (Originally published in German, 1929).

[3] OSGOOD, C. E., The Psychologist in International Affairs. *Amer. Psychologist*, 1964, **19**, 111–18.

[4] MURRAY, HENRY A., The Personality and Career of Satan. *J. soc. Issues*, October 1962, **18**, 36–54.

[5] WHITEHEAD, ALFRED NORTH, *Process and Reality*. Macmillan, New York, 1929.

[6] SCHRÖDINGER, ERWIN, *What is Life*. Cambridge University Press, Cambridge, 1944; Anchor Books, A-88, Garden City, N.Y., 1956.

[7] HEISENBERG, WERNER, *Physics and Philosophy*. Harper Torchbooks, TB 549, New York, 1958.

[8] BARKER, R. G., and WRIGHT, H. F., *Midwest and its Children: The Psychological Ecology of an American Town*. Row Peterson, Evanston, Ill., 1955.

[9] BARKER, R. G., and WRIGHT, H. F., *One Boy's Day*. Harper, New York, 1951.

[10] GOLDSTEIN, KURT, *The Organism*. American Book Company, New York, 1939.

[11] JORDAN, NEHEMIAH, On Cognitive Balance. Institute for Defense Analyses, Arlington, Va., P-178, February 1966.

Index

Index